SLOW URBICIDE

The book presents a new materialist understanding of acts of deliberate destruction of the built environment and, specifically, of the politics of aggressive spatial containment and regularization of urbanity employed within the conflict in Israel/Palestine. Building on recent scholarship on slow violence and urbicidal policies, it discusses the different dimensions of the violence against the urban space, as well as exposes the complex material-semiotic character of the urban territory and of its destruction. By referring to the concepts of "ethno-territoriality" and "the right to the city," the book aims to generate an enhanced understanding of problems situated at the overlap of urban studies and investigations of state-sponsored violence, focusing specifically on issues related to urban warfare.

Adopting a new materialist perspective, the book is a searing examination of political violence in our times. The volume will be of great interest to scholars and researchers of political science, international relations, cultural studies, and urban studies. It will also appeal to NGO professionals and activists across the world.

Dorota Golańska is Associate Professor (Cultural Studies and Religion) at the Department of Cultural Research, University of Lodz, Poland. She has degrees in Cultural Studies, Literary Studies, and International Studies. Her research interests include feminist approaches to political violence and studies of collective memory, especially in relation to traumatic experiences and their representation in culture. She also works on such issues as creative strategies of resistance as well as intersections of memory, art, and activism. In her work she uses philosophical and methodological approaches related to new materialism and posthumanism. Since January 2021 she has served as a Principal Investigator in the project *Political Dimension of Violence Against Cities: Urbicide in Palestine—A Case Study*, funded by the National Science Centre in Poland under grant number UMO-2020/37/B/HS5/00837.

SLOW URBICIDE

A New Materialist Account of Political
Violence in Palestine

Dorota Golańska

LONDON AND NEW YORK

First published 2023
by Routledge
4 Park Square, Milton Park, Abingdon, Oxon OX14 4RN

and by Routledge
605 Third Avenue, New York, NY 10158

Routledge is an imprint of the Taylor & Francis Group, an informa business

© 2023 Dorota Golańska

The right of Dorota Golańska to be identified as author of this work has been asserted in accordance with sections 77 and 78 of the Copyright, Designs and Patents Act 1988.

All rights reserved. No part of this book may be reprinted or reproduced or utilised in any form or by any electronic, mechanical, or other means, now known or hereafter invented, including photocopying and recording, or in any information storage or retrieval system, without permission in writing from the publishers.

The international boundaries, coastlines, denominations, and other information shown in the maps in this work do not necessarily imply any judgement concerning the legal status of any territory or the endorsement or acceptance of such information.

Trademark notice: Product or corporate names may be trademarks or registered trademarks, and are used only for identification and explanation without intent to infringe.

British Library Cataloguing-in-Publication Data
A catalogue record for this book is available from the British Library

Library of Congress Cataloging-in-Publication Data
A catalog record has been requested for this book

ISBN: 978-0-367-69311-4 (hbk)
ISBN: 978-0-367-74413-7 (pbk)
ISBN: 978-1-003-15768-7 (ebk)

DOI: 10.4324/9781003157687

Typeset in Sabon
by Deanta Global Publishing Services, Chennai, India

CONTENTS

Figures   vii
Acknowledgments   viii

Introduction: Politics of Destruction   1

Urbanity Under Siege 1
Slow Violence, Slow Urbicide 5
The Politics of Space 12
  Ethno-territoriality 14
  The Right to the City 16
Design of the Book 19
Notes 23
Bibliography 24

1 **New Materialism and the Study of Political Violence**   31

War as Practice 31
Situating New Materialism 33
Agency Undone 37
Political Violence Through a New Materialist Lens 40
Notes 49
Bibliography 51

2 **Mapping Urbicidal Violence**   58

Urbanity as Target 58
Toward a (New) Materialist Understanding 62
A Topology of Concepts 67
Notes 78
Bibliography 79

CONTENTS

3   Geographical Warfare in Palestine   84
    Lethal Geographies, Slow Violences 84
    Case Study 1. Cartographies of Domination in the West Bank 92
      Violent Cartographies 95
      Environmental Injustice 101
      Parallel Geographies 104
    Case Study 2. Regularization in the Naqab/Negev Desert 107
      Technologies of Drawing 109
      The Violence of Urbanization 111
      Landscape Politics 117
    Notes 122
    Bibliography 126

Conclusions   136
    Bibliography 144

Index   147

FIGURES

3.1 Administrative division of the West Bank (Oslo II Accord) and the Jewish settlements in the area. Compiled based on datasets made available by United Nations Office for the Coordination of Humanitarian Affairs, B'Tselem, and PeaceNow   87

3.2 Precipitation in the Naqab/Negev and location of the Bedouin townships established by the Israeli government. Partly based on data made available by the Israel Meteorological Service   115

ACKNOWLEDGMENTS

This book arises from my longstanding engagement with the political, social, and cultural realities of Israel/Palestine and my regular research trips to the region that have taken place since 2013. Initially motivated by altogether different study interests, over the years, my scholarly work has increasingly focused on the spatial politics in the region, exploring how spatiality has been incorporated as an important dimension of the political project of constructing Israeli territoriality and sovereignty in Palestine. Most of the material covered in this study was gathered during ethnographic fieldwork undertaken in Israel and the West Bank in December 2018, January 2019, and February 2020. It is necessary to underline here that the experience of traveling in Israel, and especially in the Occupied Territories, calls for a carefully situated account of geopolitical developments in the region and how they affect the different populations inhabiting these areas. As a holder of an EU member state passport, while moving through the checkpoints established within the Occupied Territories and at their border with Israel, I was not usually required to go through the extended control procedures, which separated me—much to my discomfort—from other travelers. I could only witness the security routines they had to undergo on an everyday basis while commuting for work, family purposes, or to deal with administrative issues. Due to my specific national belonging, my experience has been substantially different from the experiences of those who are permanently exposed to operations of the Israeli system of surveillance and control. Thus, in the course of my research, my perspective was one of what Bracha Ettinger calls "wit(h)nessing," amounting to emotional, even affective, participation in others' experiences while remaining aware of the unbridgeable differences between our distinct geopolitical positionings. I constantly keep these dissimilarities in mind while conducting my scholarly investigations in Israel/Palestine as well as while drafting written accounts of these experiences.

My work involved examination of the architectural and infrastructural developments in the region, as well as explorations of its topography and

ACKNOWLEDGMENTS

how it has been mobilized for the purpose of asserting Israeli territoriality in Palestine. The fieldwork included visits to urban areas in the West Bank and in the Naqab/Negev Desert and engaging in participant observation or bearing witness to the quotidian violence that geographies of domination systematically generate. Detailed analyses of maps, including investigations undertaken from a historical perspective, substantially added to the final shape of the argumentation, enriching it with explorations of how the cartographical representation of the Occupied Territories and the Israeli mainland have evolved over time since the beginning of the occupation and the inception of the Israeli state, respectively. Comprehensive study of the reports systematically published by such organizations as B'Tselem, the Negev Coexistence Forum for Civil Equality, and PeaceNow has been of invaluable assistance in understanding the scale and the particular characteristics of the researched situation, enabling a better consolidation of the ideas offered in *Slow Urbicide*. These efforts were supplemented by a comprehensive review of the often heartbreaking materials released by various press agencies, NGOs, and activist groups covering incidents of expulsion, land confiscation, dispossession, and house demolition.

Theoretical elaborations and conceptual work on the gathered evidence were predominantly carried out throughout the year 2021, within the scope of the research project Political Dimension of Violence Against Cities: Urbicide in Palestine—A Case Study, generously funded by the National Science Centre in Poland under grant number UMO-2020/37/B/HS5/00837. Spanning a period of over three years (2021-2024), this project is hosted by the Faculty of Philology at the University of Lodz (Poland). One of its objectives is—based on the empirical research and theoretical elaborations—to shed an altogether different light on the dominant understandings of the concept of political violence, looking closely into the shifting temporalities of violence, as well as its invisible daily operations. The study draws both on ethnographic evidence and documentary, historical analysis of urbicidal developments in the region. It has also been greatly informed by engagement with the extensive scholarly literature in the field. All these undertakings have generated material to underpin an elaboration of the concept of "slow urbicide" offered in this book, a term which refers to the form of violence that has been experienced in the studied areas since 1948, or even earlier, gradually contributing to the destruction of their indigenous spatialities and substantially affecting the demography, topography, and natural environment of the region. Even though the notion can well be used in other contexts and in reference to different geopolitical circumstances, it was conceptually crafted to capture specifically the nature of the urbicidal project in Israel/Palestine. Therefore, as is presented in this book, the application of the term "slow urbicide" remains supported by the historical evidence documenting the life of affected communities in this particular area.

ACKNOWLEDGMENTS

In the course of my research, it became strikingly clear to me that what I call the policy of "slow urbicide" draws heavily on more-than-human agencies and forces, manipulatively mobilizing them against the native populations in the region. To do justice to these complex entwinements and assemblages, the book adopts a new materialist philosophical approach, which has significantly informed both the analyses offered in this book and the concepts that it develops. Such a strategy enables a fuller realization of the intricate character of the contemporary tactics of political violence, as well as revealing how different agencies and forces happen to be mobilized for the purpose of the military urbicidal effort. In the context of the ongoing situation of asymmetrical war tackled in this book, it seems necessary to take account of these lethal developments and to document their tacit operations in order to, at least partly, prevent a denial—and thus also a perpetuation—of violence.

It must be acknowledged here, however, that my engagement with new materialism does not come out of nowhere. I have had the privilege of working collaboratively with a broad community of new materialist intellectuals for the last 15 years within diverse transnational institutional circumstances. In this regard, I owe a lot to Iris van der Tuin, a person whom I have known for many years now and who has always been willing to help. In 2014, she invited me to join an outstanding network of researchers gathered within the COST European Cooperation in Science and Technology project on New Materialism: Networking European Scholarship on "How Matter Comes to Matter" (Action IS1307) wherein, for the period of four years, I served as an official representative of Poland. The researchers I met there, as well as the events in which I participated, led to a substantial broadening of my knowledge of new materialism, allowing me to grasp the marvelous diversity of this philosophical ferment. The analysis offered in *Slow Urbicide* benefited a great deal from my participation in this stimulating setting and from the academic interactions with scholars from different geographical and disciplinary contexts that it enabled. It is not possible to name all those who contributed to the exceptional quality of my experience of participating in this network, but—if I am to name just a few of them—I want to express my gratitude to Monika Rogowska-Stangret, Olga Cielemęcka, Katve-Kaisa Kontturi, Felicity Colman, and Anna Hickey-Moody for their friendly support and intellectually invigorating discussions.

Since the work on this book has been conducted over an extended period of time, some ideas, concepts, and cases offered therein have already been presented to selected audiences. A more concise discussion of the urbicidal tactics employed by the Israeli state in the West Bank developed in Chapter 3 was included in my article, "Slow Urbicide: Accounting for the Shifting Temporalities of Political Violence in the West Bank," published in *Geoforum* 132 (2022), pp. 125-134 (Elsevier). More general reflections on the entanglement of human and nonhuman agencies in the

ACKNOWLEDGMENTS

cartography-driven urbicidal project in Palestine were presented within the ad hoc Design Studio New Materialist Articulations at the Technical University of Vienna in April 2021, to which I was invited by the conveners of the event, Iris van der Tuin, Nanna Verhoeff, and Vera Bühlmann. I also presented my elaboration of the concept of "slow violence" as applied to the warfare strategies in Palestine during the conference "(Im)materialities of Violence" at the University of Birmingham in November 2021 within the ERC-funded project entitled Urban Terrorism in Europe (2004-2019): Remembering, Imagining, and Anticipating Violence, where my invited contribution was hosted by Katharina Karcher and Evelien Geerts. I am grateful for these opportunities.

Several people have offered support and understanding in the course of my work on this book. My special thanks go to Marta Woźniak-Bobińska—my hardworking research partner in the project Political Dimension of Violence Against Cities—for her rigor, engagement, and constructive support. I thank the members of my wonderful team at the Department of Cultural Research at the University of Lodz, who continuously offer immense assistance in the everyday running of the department, willingly participating in all its daily tasks and processes (including those that are not exceptionally fascinating). I very much appreciate the editorial work of Alex Ramon and Ginevra House, who proofread the book manuscript, making the text more approachable for readers. I would also like to thank Anna Wosiak for her help in preparing the two maps included in Chapter 3. I am grateful to Aakash Chakrabarty, the editor at Taylor & Francis, for his patience and understanding. Finally, and most importantly, I want to express my voluminous gratitude to my loved ones—my parents, my partner, and my son—for always being with me and giving me a lot of support and encouragement. Working on this book during the time of the COVID-19 pandemic without their continuous assistance would not have been possible.

INTRODUCTION
Politics of Destruction

Urbanity Under Siege

In the post-Cold War era, the deliberate destruction of the built environment, and especially of cities, in inter- and intrastate conflicts has captured the attention of political analysts and scholars. The list of the most notorious cases of this kind of violence includes the widespread destruction of the urban environment during the 1992-1995 Bosnian War (Bogdanovic 1993, 1994; Coward 2006, 2009), the damaging Russian tactics employed within the Chechen campaigns of 1994-1996 and 1999-2000 (Kramer 2005), the ruination of Beirut, and Israeli policies of house demolition in the Occupied Territories, especially the siege of Palestinian cities during the 2002 military operation Defensive Shield (Graham 2004a; Abujidi 2014). Also, as Nurhan Abujidi argues, "the latest developments in the Arab world, in what is controversially called the Arab Spring, is an explicit example of how cities became the very theatre ... of oppression" (2014, loc. 380). Among the most recent instances of enormous destruction of the built environment, we can include the shattering of Aleppo and the demolition of Damascus and Dara between 2013 and 2017 during the war in Syria (Sharp and Panetta 2016), as well as the massive devastations of Iraqi cities (Baghdad, Fallujah, Mosul) in the context of counterinsurgency military strategies employed within the so-called "war on terror" (Graham 2005). The destruction of Mariupol (Ukraine) by the Russian army in March 2022 may serve as the most recent graphic example of urbicidal violence.

Even though, historically, there had been numerous examples of rubblization of cities or villages, what is striking in the above-mentioned cases is the massive, systematic, and deliberate character of violence against the built environment. The attacks on urbanized sites in these instances constitute an important element of war strategy. Noticeably, as Martin Coward underlines, the destruction in many urbicidal cases is considerably "out of proportion to the military aims of the conflict" (2009, 9). The issue is especially worth exploring due to the currently changing patterns of war, which nowadays center on localized struggles over strategic urban territories. Even though cities, or political control over them, have always been considered crucial to intra- and international conflicts, recent times have witnessed an unprecedented scale of deliberate destruction of urban environments, often accompanying ethno-national struggles. Closely interwoven with military technologies, concerns, and strategies, today's cities participate in warfare in significantly reconfigured ways. As Stephen Graham explains, "it is now clear that the intensification of global urbanization, resource shortages, inequalities and population pressures are further deepening the role of urban terrain as the strategic site of military, social and representational struggles" (2002a, n.p.). This substantially affects the ways in which we should understand contemporary instances of political violence, especially if they involve a deliberate assault on urbanity.

The massive scale of attacks on urban environments has recently led to the reconceptualization of the term "urbicide," originally used in the context of important reorganizations of large American cities leading to the destruction of traditional streetscapes by new planning projects, elaborated upon by such critics as Wolf von Eckardt and Marshall Berman. Today the term refers to more extreme forms of conflict and terror connected to urban violence and the unprecedented scale of militarization of urban terrains.[1] The destruction of buildings, or of cultural artifacts, so often accompanying contemporary conflicts, is a multidimensional issue bringing about major consequences. It can be considered, according to Andreas Riedlmayer, a process of killing collective memory (1995)—often embodied in, or associated with, material objects and spaces—and therefore important to the continued existence of political/social/cultural communities. This is exceptionally vital in the context of ethno-national conflicts, especially those involving the production, or serious reconfiguration, of a state's territoriality, perceived as a complex mixture of material, spatial, symbolic, and mental objects and rituals. As Nicholas Adams announces, the survival of architecture and urban life is of crucial importance to the survival of people (1993, 390), which is an issue often omitted, or relegated to the second plan, in analyses of contemporary conflicts. Similarly, Katherine McKittrick notes that even though the term urbicide, through its focus on the destruction of the built environment, "inadvertently abstracts humans from violence against the city" and "depersonalizes acts of violence," it remains very human (2011, 952). Such statement assumes the deep entwinement of human and nonhuman elements within a spatially organized community. For McKittrick, urbicide must be situated in the context of "imperialism, violence, and economic, racial and ethnic terror, while also hinging on specificities: scale, region, economy, place, and how each destructive force is delivered, all matter" (2011, 952). Exploring the politics of destruction in Israel and the Occupied Territories, this book engages with *how* they matter. Thus, in its focus on urbicidal developments, my work aligns with the current debates present, even though still marginally, in the field of cultural studies of conflicts and critical security studies. Recently, however, increased interest in questions of deliberate destruction of urbanity has been expressed by a number of scholars working in a range of other academic fields. When thought of as an important environment co-constituting social and cultural life, urbanity can be approached as a vital element of territorial struggles and ethno-national rivalries. In such a conceptual context, Coward (2006, 2009), for instance, reads urbicide as an attack on the conditions of social heterogeneity that the built environment creates. Accordingly, urbicidal violence should be seen as a chief element of a project of erasing difference (be it racial, ethnic, religious, and so on) from the sociocultural and material landscape of a given community, and—as I aim to demonstrate in this analysis—a crucial component of ethno-territorial politics.

Although the destruction of different kinds of buildings has been widely acknowledged in the literature devoted to the discussion of the dynamics of (ethnic) conflicts, the thorough theorization and conceptualization of this process remain underdeveloped, and the phenomenon has yet to be amply explored. This concerns both the nature of urbicidal violence, the philosophical and cultural groundings of such violence, its scale, as well as how its contemporary forms are situated in the context of the history of urban militarism. Also, neither the unconventional forms of urbicidal tactics nor its shifting temporalities and varying intensities have as yet been sufficiently studied. One of the reasons that the nature of violence against the built environment remains a relatively unexplored issue of political theory is that it has typically been considered just one dimension of other forms of violence (mostly aggression against peoples, ethnic groups, or individuals) and it has therefore been regarded as secondary to, or a side effect of, genocidal projects. This has been rather common and is unsurprising within an anthropocentric philosophical landscape centered primarily on the human dimension of political processes. Thus, while primary attention has traditionally been paid to the systematic killing of people or the destruction of human communities, violence against urban infrastructure, perceived as an accompanying process, has not necessarily been seen as worthy of detailed examination on its own.

Contrary to these assumptions, this book argues that the deliberate destruction of urban areas is a central component of the program of ethno-national and ideological violence, often accompanying colonial projects as much as remaining crucial to the analysis of violence against people. Concerned with the harboring of identity in material objects and places, urbicide serves as an important measure in endeavors to generate specific understandings and experiences of territoriality. Yet, although it usually goes hand-in-hand with strategies of genocide, forced displacement, separation, or the politics of carving out "ethnically pure" enclaves, it should not simply be reduced to them. Rather, it is necessary to acknowledge that it entangles nonhuman and human components with each other; it remains equally vital to pay attention to how it is productive of substantial reconfigurations of more-than-human political realities. Taking into consideration the multifaceted ways in which urbicidal violence is perpetrated, in this book I argue that in order to understand the complex nature of the destruction of urbanity, as well as to figure out what is at stake in urbicide, we need to acknowledge the "material-semiotic" (Haraway 1988) or "material-discursive" (Barad 2003, 2007) character of political violence, by considering the variety of agents and forces involved in it, as well as by recognizing the entangled composition of its effects. The nature of territoriality—a notion which is fundamental to understanding the character of the Israeli colonial project in Palestine—is also material-semiotic (an issue to which I will soon return), and so are the different experiences of (non)belonging that territoriality is capable of producing. However, in order for this to be fully recognized, it is necessary to turn to philosophical and conceptual developments facilitating such relatively novel ways of thinking within the field of political science, international relations theory, and conflict studies.

Feminist new materialism—recognizing the dynamic and constantly shifting co-constitution of matter and meaning, and underlining the important implication of matter in social, political, and cultural processes—seems to offer an adequate "ethico-onto-epistemological" (Barad 2007) tool with which to approach the complex nature of urbicidal politics. I will delineate the conceptual contours of this philosophical perspective in Chapter 1 of this book, but here I would like to briefly indicate that my adherence to new materialism by no means signals a need for taxonomizing another theoretical or epistemological position. Rather, it consists of a partial rereading of the extant conceptualizations while accentuating their different aspects and paying attention to those dimensions of the analyzed phenomenon that have previously been marginalized, or made less visible, in the vast majority of available scholarly considerations. Accordingly, the objective of such a philosophical framing of my analysis is, following Donna Haraway, to make "new patterns from previous disputes" rather than offering an altogether different understanding of the explored processes. As Haraway underlines, new knowledge—theoretical and practical—emerges from such creative recontextualizations (1997, 304–5, n. 32). Thus, new materialism, I argue, offers promising possibilities to look at the ethno-territorial and material-semiotic aspects of Israeli politics toward the Palestinians—a major issue this book explores—from a less conventional analytical perspective. It pays attention to the nuanced operations of urbicidal violence and focuses on the more-than-human forces that it mobilizes in its destructive efforts; it also offers a recalibration of understanding of who (or what) counts as a political agent in the Israeli colonial project in Palestine. As Jason Dittmer evinces, "because power is enacted through assemblage, it must be understood as distributed among the various components of that assemblage, human and non-human" (2014, 388). This analytical lens enables a more thorough engagement with the *how* question of urbicide, exposing those dynamics of social injustice that, "while material in process and effect, are also suffused with representational politics" (Sharp 2021, 991). Bearing this formulation in mind, one of my objectives is to point to the potentially enriching impact that new materialism could have on this field of academic inquiry, shedding light on relatively uncharted aspects of political violence and acknowledging the different speeds at which it unfolds. Subscribing to such ways of thinking and aligning with McKittrick's point of view delineated earlier (2011), this book maintains that the violence against urbanity poses questions as fundamental as those raised by the destruction of human life (Coward 2009). These kinds of damaging tactics serve as one of the crucial elements of exclusionary political forces associated with (ethno)nationalism actively engaged in the processes of territorialization of (ethnic) identity. Such a hypothesis has important implications for a more general understanding of the concept of political violence, which has to be significantly broadened to include instances of targeting, or purposeful erasure of, urban spaces (Coward 2009), taking into consideration its shifting temporalities and silent operations.

Slow Violence, Slow Urbicide

This book sketches a new materialist understanding of acts of deliberate destruction of the built environment and, specifically, of the politics of aggressive spatial containment of urbanity employed within the Israeli colonial project in Palestine.[2] In contrast to the majority of extant analyses of this problem, however, my explorations focus on the different speeds at which violence unfolds, paying attention to the unconventional tools on which its attritional operations rely. Given the convoluted nature of the political tension analyzed in this work, as well as the sinusoidal dynamics and territorial reconfigurations these developments entail, the term urbicide is used here in quite encompassing ways. It refers to a deliberate assault on the material fabric of a city, village, camp, or neighborhood, or, more broadly, a violence against urbanity. As well as its traditional interpretation as an element underlining the politics of destruction, urbicide in Palestine must also be approached as a generative process, capable of producing new—and more desired by the Israeli state—forms of surveilled spatiality. As highlighted in this book, however, the targeting of urban spaces does not always take the form of immediate and spectacular annihilation but can consist—as Eyal Weizman notes—of rearrangement, reconfiguration, closure, or denial of the urban area (2002, 2007). These policies are implemented at different speeds and with varied frequency, leading eventually to the gradual degeneration of particular kinds of urbanity. Such an understanding remains in line with what has been widely practiced by the Israeli governmental circles within the scope of the Israeli ethno-territorial project implemented in Palestine since the proclamation of the State of Israel.

I am, however, far from assuming that such forms of violence should be exclusively correlated with ethno-nationalist tendencies or colonial aspirations, as is the case in Palestine. Rather, it must be acknowledged that acts of violence against the built environment have been common in miscellaneous conflicts and in various geopolitical and ideological contexts. So, even though I limit my explorations to particular case studies, the analysis remains nonetheless exemplary for more general discussions of an array of urbicidal politics. Noticeably, ethno-nationalism and colonialism—both used strategically as vehicles for advancing key political agendas—seem to constitute important driving forces behind many current conflicts and wars. Exploration of selected examples of urbicidal strategies employed in a specific geopolitical context reveals the intricate nature of the problem, its important spatio-temporal dynamics, and its reliance on the entanglement of discursive and material elements. It also uncovers a crucial agency of more-than-human forces, exposing how they have been mobilized, or recruited, for the purpose of accomplishing a political project of territorial expansion.

The question of the Israeli political stance toward the Palestinians has been extensively investigated within the field of political science and international relations theory. These analyses, however, have typically centered on periods of wars and uprisings (intifadas), leaving the phases of what is considered peace beyond the immediate scope of their interests. Contrary to these tendencies, rather than studying conventional Israeli warfare (which obviously includes massive use of urbicidal strategies) during the periods of intensification of conflict, my inquiry centers on the means and phases of what I call "slow urbicidal violence," that is, the kind of violence that seems to be especially efficient in times perceived as interludes between wars, or phases of relative stability—at least as they are experienced by the Israeli citizens, but much less so by the Palestinians. This corresponds to Sari Hanafi's statement about the specific nature of this conflict which is connected to its pretty low intensity, "a spectacle of destruction without/with little death" but in which intentional state-sponsored demolition should be seen not as a "side effect of the war but [as] the main leverage of political pressure" (2012, 192). Given the various peculiarities of this situation, it seems justified to assume that, in the case of Palestine, urbicidal violence has to be understood in more nuanced ways and as operating at various speeds.

To situate my deliberations in an adequate historical context, a brief reconstruction of the employment of urbicidal violence in this geopolitical situation should be offered here. It must be kept in mind that the politics of destruction of the built environment has been systematically used against Palestinian-Arabs since the inception of the Israeli state. Between 1947 and 1948, while the new political entity was being established, hundreds of Palestinian villages and neighborhoods were methodically emptied, blown up, and bulldozed, while the land was confiscated by the Israeli forces (Hassan and Hanafi 2009; Morris 1987; Pappé 2006). This period, called the Nakba (or "catastrophe"), is at the roots of a persistent refugee problem, forcing a huge number of Palestinians to leave their indigenous space and, subsequently, denying their right to return. Similar problems were generated in the aftermath of the Naksa (or "day of the setback," a period after the Six-Day War in 1967), in which a considerable number of Palestinians fled war atrocities or were forcefully relocated. Certain scholars (e.g., Weizman 2004; Graham 2003, 2004a) tend to connect the relatively recent destruction of Palestinian urban communities—especially within the 2002 military operation, Defensive Shield, in which a number of Palestinian towns, villages, and camps situated in the Occupied Territories were massively damaged—with similar actions in 1948 and 1967, as part of the same historical process. They insist on these events being perceived as an intensification of the old policy.

Analogous destructive tactics have been continually implemented in the Israeli heartland since 1948, leading to the gradual erasure of the Arab presence from the Israeli sociocultural and political landscape, a process that was triggered by a systematic degeneration of indigenous urbanity and traditional ways of dwelling associated with this (Jabareen 2015; Leshem 2016). Some of these places were later repopulated by Jewish settlers, while these sites' original names were changed and their vernacular organization altered to reflect the intended Judaization of the region (Leshem 2016, 106). The politics of planting and greenery management also contributed to the reworking of the local scenery (Cohen 1993)[3] and partial erasure of its original character. The demolition of houses has constituted an important dimension of this political project, and it has been a chief part of the policy of reconfiguring the demographic landscape of the then newly established country. As Weizman underlines, along with more subtle means, Israel has typically used the bulldozing of houses as a weapon of collective and individual punishment and intimidation and as a means of shaping the geopolitical configuration of territory (2004, 197). To fully account for the frequency and intensity of urbicidal violence in Palestine, it is nevertheless necessary to acknowledge its convoluted character. It consists of a number of interrelated means, including the material destruction and spatial reconfiguration of Palestinian urbanity, the dissipation of spatiality, the construction of Israeli infrastructures, and extensive invigilating control, which manifests in the constant operation of a state-sponsored apparatus of surveillance, as well as in the application of measures seriously constraining the quotidian functioning of Palestinian communities (Weizman 2007, 2017; Abujidi 2014; Graham 2004a; Hochberg 2015). It should also be emphasized, following

Edward W. Soja, that within such a context urbanity and urbanization have to be understood in quite encompassing ways. As Soja explains, urbanization is "generated primarily in and from dense urban agglomerations, but ... the urban condition has extended its influence to all areas: rural, suburban, metropolitan, exurban, even wilderness, parkland, desert, tundra, and rain forest ... the whole world has been or is being urbanized to some degree" (Soja 2010, 6). Such an understanding of the urban condition, or urbanity, is central to the argumentation that I offer in this book.

The temporalities of urbicidal violence are equally complicated. Except for times of conflict escalation, in which parts of Palestinian urban tissue are intentionally demolished within a period of a couple of days, the politics of destruction operates at a much slower pace, leading to the gradual fragmentation and continuous degeneration of the Palestinian spatiality. Overall, the whole process has a very important material dimension, which obviously combines with its more symbolic, or semiotic, layer. This urges us to approach it through an analytical framework capable of doing justice to this material-semiotic complexity, while keeping in mind its shifting temporalities. As I suggest, the term "slow urbicide"—referring to Rob Nixon's concept of "slow violence" (2009, 2011) rooted in the domain of environmental humanities—could function as a suitable conceptual figuration in order to get to grips with the intricate operations of violence against urbanity implemented by the Israeli government against the Palestinian-Arab population. The notion of "slow urbicide," recently used by Ian Shaw (2019) in the context of urban policies of neglect and abandonment in the UK, has not yet been applied in the analyses of warfare strategies, as the latter are typically associated with more dynamic occurrences. In my opinion, however, not only does the concept of slow urbicide enable acknowledgment of the complex temporalities of urbicidal warfare (recognizing its injurious, indeed vehement, nature), but it also exposes the Israeli state's slow-motion investment in preventing Palestinians' spatially organized self-governance, embodied in the inhabitants' capacity for the ongoing production of urban space.

The genealogy of the term "slow violence" can be traced back to academic concerns with such issues as extensive pollution, contamination of the natural environment, or overexploitation of resources (Nixon 2009, 2011; O'Lear 2016, 2018; Davies 2018, 2019), but also—to a lesser extent—to investigations of house dispossession (Pain 2019; Cahill 2015; Kern 2016), separation of families (De Leeuw 2016), or antimigration policies (Davies and Isakjee 2015). It has important and obvious connections to neoliberal ideologies; however, in the introduction to his book, Nixon (2011) explicitly claims that the inspiration for forging the concept of "slow violence" also comes from his profound engagement with Edward Said's writings on the everyday lives of Palestinians. Acknowledging violence's fluidity and its temporal dimension, the concept, as Thom Davies claims, "uses time as provocation" (2019, 2). For Nixon (2009, 2011), "slow violence" is meant to describe "a violence that occurs gradually and out of sight, a violence of delayed destruction that is dispersed across time and space, an attritional violence that is typically not viewed as violence at all" (2011, 2). Arising from the field of environmental humanities, the concept of "slow violence" can be relevant—as demonstrated by Rachel Pain in her compelling study of chronic urban trauma (2019)—for research on urban politics, tackling the different speeds and delayed effects of miscellaneous reconfigurations of the urban fabric. Similar problems have also been raised by Karen Till's (2011) work on urban dispossession and gentrification projects. As I propose, the increased attention paid to the shifting temporalities of urbicidal strategies could be equally productive, shedding an altogether different light on the investigations of political violence effectuated by scholars working in the fields of political science, conflict studies, and international relations theory.

The project of territorial expansion and demographic reconfiguration of the Occupied Territories progresses in slow motion. The infrastructure-related processes accompanying the Israeli settlement enterprise in Palestine have been well documented in the literature of the field (see Allegra et al. 2017; Alkhalili 2017; Gregory 2004a, 2004b; Hanafi 2009, 2012; Makdisi 2010; Weizman 2002, 2007). Concepts of "verticality" (Graham 2004b, 2016; Graham and Hewitt 2012; Weizman 2002, 2007; Segal and Weizman 2003) and "volume" (Elden 2013, 2021) have been used to capture the context-specific space-centered nature of the Israeli colonial endeavors (especially in the West Bank), mostly from the perspective of what Peter Adey calls "a particular kind of state/technocratic gaze" (2013, 53). However, even though exposing the complexity of the processes mobilized for the construction of Israeli territoriality, these accounts tend to be critiqued for paying scant attention to the inherent dynamics of vertical/volumetric space (Garrett 2016; Campbell 2019) as well as for neglecting its effects on the organization of what Chris Harker calls "intensive relations" within the affected communities (2014; see also Harker 2011). It is also advised that ethnographic explorations of how verticality and volume are experienced and negotiated in embodied ways should be undertaken to better account for the topographical-topological complexity of urban life (Harker 2014; Harris 2015). While not intending to downplay the importance of vertical and volumetric analyses of spatial politics in Israel/Palestine—and appreciating their important contribution to studies on urbicidal developments—I suggest they could benefit from a closer dialogue with scholarship on temporalities of violence, adding another dimension to the examination of the enduring consequences of urbicidal transformations. Thus, the analysis offered in this book aims to partly depart from a purely vertical/volumetric approach to engage with the concept of "slow violence"—exploring how violence operates, to paraphrase Rob Nixon, not only across *space* but also across *time* (2011, 2). Such a shift of perspectives, I argue, enables exposition of how certain destructive tactics, working smoothly and to a great extent unnoticeable to external observers, constitute a systematic and violent assault on Palestinian urbanity, leading to the fragmentation and dissolution of Palestinian space. Hence, urbicide in Palestine must be understood in a very nuanced manner, as operating both through complex entanglement of different means and at different speeds. The notion of slow urbicide, I maintain, may be useful in grasping these interwoven operations, as it invites us to reconsider the weaponization of both *space* and *time* in the Israeli colonial enterprise in Palestine.

Thus, drawing on relatively recent conceptual developments and taking into consideration the tangled operations of urbicidal politics in Palestine, I consider the notion of "slow urbicide" as capable of accounting for the complexity of destructive tactics targeting indigenous urbanity in the region. Such a perspective allows for a transcending of the tendency to ponder urbicidal warfare as limited to instances of intensive open war, instead drawing attention to how political violence could be perpetrated on a more everyday basis, including in periods considered—at least by Israel—as relatively peaceful. Even though slow urbicide seems to operate in subtle and unspectacular ways, its traumatizing effects remain as similarly detrimental as those of fast urbicidal violence. To clarify, with "fast urbicide" I refer to tactics such as the aerial bombing of cities, drone strikes, air raids, and detonation of the built infrastructure, typically associated with military operations performed in periods of open war. Slow urbicide, conversely, signals a chronic condition of emerging harm; it does not, however, stand in direct opposition to fast violence but should be seen as its long shadow. Advancing slowly, it involves gradual destruction of indigenous urbanity through such strategies as physical strangulation, obscure systems of land administration, bureaucratic neglect, pollution, and obliteration of the vernacular landscape, continuously exacerbating the conditions of Palestinian urban areas. Paradoxically, such policies are implemented through means typically associated with urban development rather than destruction and represented in the dominant discourse—quite commonly among colonial enterprises (Mbembe 2001; Mignolo 2011; Quijano 2007)—as "innocent" signs of progress and modernization. Such a strategy tends to conceal these policies' delayed urbicidal effects. Since slow violence, as Nixon argues (2011), is typically unspectacular, it remains difficult to mediatize. It progresses slowly, gradually reaping its deadly harvests, somewhat "out of sight" (Nixon 2011, 2) of the general public. As such, its silent operations could easily be ignored, remaining visible and meaningful only to those who are directly affected by them. This seems to be the most conspicuous peril that slow urbicide generates, as its invisibility can tacitly contribute to the denial of violence, obfuscating its state-sponsored character. It is therefore of crucial importance in the examination of enduring conflicts to focus on how fast violence silently morphs into slow violence (and vice versa), without establishing any kind of straightforward binarism between the two. Refraining from positioning slow against fast violence, it is nevertheless necessary to consider political violence as a process happening at various speeds and with different frequencies. The attentive focus on the unspectacular tactics and invisible workings of "slow urbicide" in Palestine enables such a thorough (re)conceptualization.

As explored in this book, slow urbicidal violence in Palestine refers to the systematic premeditated containment of Palestinian areas, intense Judaization of the region, and deployment of military forces as much as to a whole variety of strategies of spatial manipulation which operate in concealed ways before, after, and beyond the moment of immediate warfare. Thus, examination of slow urbicide helps us to make sense of the empirical realities at hand in Palestine, revealing the necessity of examining not only the conflict as it displays itself in remarkable moments of intense war but also how destructive tactics work in silence, accumulating their catastrophic damage over a significant period of time. A new materialist perspective, I argue, allows for a more complete understanding of these processes, especially of their environmental and material dimensions. As I will explain in Chapter 3, in order to grasp the dynamics and entangled nature of urbicidal politics in Palestine, it is useful to resort to the analysis of "geographical warfare" (Lacoste 1976) in which the forces of the landscape and its physical features are recruited for the purpose of advancing the ideologically motivated political agenda. As such, in my analysis I am more interested in what happens in between the moments of escalation of violence and subsequent peace negotiations. My aim is to pay attention to the mundane, everyday means with which the suppression of Palestinian culture and its important urban dimension have regularly been carried out in both Israel proper and in the Occupied Territories and how these have involved human and more-than-human resources and potentialities. Such an investigative strategy offers an insight into the present nature of the colonization/occupation, rather than delving into its history or projecting possible future politically oriented solutions. This would mostly deal with the already well-researched trajectory of the conflict, often narrowed to the moments of "fast" violence. Conversely, the analytical focus on the periods between wars aids understanding of the situations which regularly lead to outbursts of violence (Ophir et al. 2009) including the earlier Israeli-Arab wars, the Palestinian uprisings, and retaliatory violence, as well as regular individualized episodes of mutual aggression that have been troubling the region for decades. Even though generally "out of sight" of the international community and, perhaps, also of the Israeli citizens supporting the political goals of their governments, slow urbicidal violence remains very visible to those who regularly fall victim to it, while its harmful effects are in fact viscerally and bodily felt on an everyday basis. As Davies explains, "As a spatial concept, slow violence invites us to include the gradual deaths, destructions, and layered deposits of uneven social brutalities within the geographic here-and-now" (2019, 2). This has to be taken into consideration if we want to thoroughly understand how political violence works, as well as to account for its complex multilayered consequences.

The Politics of Space

Even though slow urbicide seems to be primarily defined through its temporal dimensions, it equally has to be understood in spatial terms. In his thorough conceptualization of space, Henri Lefebvre (1991) contends that space should be thought of as a politicized object—a political instrument, a set of ideological superstructures, and a mechanism of social regulation (see also Butler 2012, 42). This applies to its both micropolitical and macropolitical understandings. Space is infused with ideology and politics and plays a strategic role in the definition and maintenance of a state. A state's sovereignty has an important spatial facet which manifests in both the state's control of its borders and in the assertion of sovereignty itself. Sovereignty over space, Lefebvre underlines, is "established and constituted by violence," while "state power endures only by virtue of violence directed towards a space," so that the "hallmarks of the state" are the "founding violence, and continuous creation by violence" (1991, 280). Accordingly, state power is violently imposed—as Chris Butler explains—"in the form of coercive strategies and sanctions, technologies of administrative governance and the abstractions of legal formalism" (2012, 58). In the context of colonialism, the founding principle of violence gets additional meaning—as Achille Mbembe remarks, violence (of conquest) contributes to the creation of a space over which authority (derived directly and exclusively from the fact of conquest) was subsequently exercised (2001, 25). The concept of territory, one of the central state attributes, relies on such a politicized understanding of space—a mixture of the empirical world and mental projections, which makes for its "entirely ideational" (Soja 1996, 79) existence. But it also serves as a physical anchorage for the state, turning the latter into a somewhat inevitable, or natural, being with historically (that is, temporarily) and geographically (that is, spatially) shaped boundaries and "content." Today it is not possible to think of a state as abstracted from its territory (Gottmann 1951) or proceed without acknowledging the state's production of a politicized space over which the state's authority (often violently) spreads. In Lefebvre's account, the state produces a physical space (the national territory), the social space (an edifice of institutions, laws, and conventions built upon a system of values spread via language), and mental space (a system of representations of the state, both formalized and popular) (2003, 94). Spatial relations consist of an entanglement of practices, representations, and the imaginary. Hence, space is neither an inert background or container of social relations; nor is it a product of a purely discursive field. Rather, it actively co-constitutes, and is co-constituted by, social relations (Lefebvre 1991). Such an account signals a complex, multidimensional, or indeed "material-semiotic" (Haraway 1988) understanding of space as both a product of and a condition for the production of social relations, and encourages a conceptualization of space as a cogent, active, and formative element of human geography.

When approached from the perspective of political objectives, space—or territory, understood as a certain organization, or instantiation, of space—is often thought of as a material property (also, through the etymological affinity of Latin *terra* [land] and "territory"; see Elden 2010) as much as a symbolic source of identity of an ethnic group (i.e., as a homeland), which tends to define itself in reference to its spatio-temporal, or geographical and historical, embeddedness. The latter aspect of territory gained another significance with the growth of nineteenth-century nationalism and the emergence of the notion of the nation-state, with its exclusionary politics corresponding well to the idea of the state as premised on processes of (territorial) inclusions and exclusions. So, even though historically territories evolved, as Jordan Branch notes, from being seen as land properties used for the extraction of resources and for generating strategic benefits to be subsequently tied to the "imagined communities" of nationhood (2017, 141; see also Anderson 1983), they remain quintessentially material-semiotic entities. Examining the processes of the material inscription of immaterial (or affective) social relationships, Andrea Brighenti concludes that territories "exist at the point of convergence, prolongation and tension between the material and the immaterial, between spaces and relationships, between extensions (movements) and intensions (affection and passions)" (2010, 223). Thus, territories emerge as complex conglomerates of physical aspects of space and its cultural, or psychic, understandings, as well as constructs brought to life through a range of measuring technologies, historical reconfigurations, political-economic handling of land, and ideological meaning-making practices. All these are infused with constantly shifting power relations. In that sense, a territory, as much as its various resources and features, typically gets subordinated to political ends in the project of producing specific forms of spatially understood territoriality.

As Stuart Elden notes, "territoriality" is typically understood in two ways, as "the condition or status of territory" or as "a mode of operating toward that territory" (2010, 801), imposing a certain form on land (see also Lefebvre 1991). Saskia Sassen understands territoriality "as a legal construct that marks the state's exclusive authority over its territory" (2013, 24), while Robert Sack's formulation connects the territory, power, and people within the concept of territoriality understood in terms of a geopolitical strategy. Sack conceives territoriality as "a primary geographical expression of social power" and "a powerful geographic strategy to control people by controlling area" (1986, 5). This characteristic of territoriality is also alluded to by Richard Ford, when he claims that territoriality—understood as territorial jurisdiction—developed as a result of modern cartographical techniques and rational thinking as much as it is an upshot of the discourse encouraging people to see themselves as "organically connected to other people and to territory in a way that requires jurisdictional autonomy" (1999, 899). In a somewhat different manner, partly inspired by Lefebvre, Elden proposes that it is territory, rather than territoriality, that should be understood as technology, or "a distinctive mode of social/spatial organization, one which is historically and geographically limited and dependent" (2010, 810). These differences in theorizations notwithstanding, states are quintessentially territorial and territorializing entities and are usually imagined as bound to a certain space. The space is often territorialized through acts of violence (of various kinds) which operate at different speeds.

With the aim of deepening the analysis of "slow urbicidal violence" in Palestine, in this book I situate it in the context of two meaningful—and to a certain extent contradictory—concepts, namely "ethno-territoriality" and "the right to the city." They are crucial for understanding the processes related to the production and maintenance of particular forms of territoriality in Palestine, both being principally preoccupied with the notion of space and how the distribution of space is related to issues of social justice or spatial citizenship (Dikeç 2001, 2009; Philippopoulos-Mihalopoulos 2010, 2011, 2015; Soja 2010). Recognition of their, to a certain extent, conflicting nature, connected to the juxtaposition of nationalism's inclination toward ethnic separation and the right to the city's reliance on generative affirmation of difference, exposes the vital importance of these two notions for understanding the material-semiotic character of acts of (slow) violence against urbanity taking place in the context of ethno-national conflicts.

Ethno-territoriality

The Israeli policy in Palestine has been greatly concerned with the issue of physical space as fused with the Zionist principles of Jewish belonging in this region and the idea of the nation's return to the "promised land." This political (in fact, purely colonial) project relies heavily on ethno-territorial assumptions. Unsurprisingly, in the context of nationalism's revival at the twilight of the twentieth century, the concept of ethno-territoriality has recently captured the attention of scholars dealing with questions of ethnic conflict and nationalism in their diverse aspects and dimensions.[4] Given the particular mechanisms in place in the process of constructing Israeli territoriality—first, on the territory incorporated into the newly established state and, second, in the Occupied Territories militarily controlled by Israel since 1967—I find the recourse to the discussion of ethno-territoriality pertinent in approaching the theme that this book tackles.

The production of territoriality seems to be one of the most fundamental objectives of ethno-nationalist politics. It was a chief element of the Zionist colonial project in Palestine, an aspiration to produce a persuasive idea and compelling experience of Jewish territorial belonging in the mythic land. As Adam Moore explains, ethno-territoriality "involves the fusion of territoriality with ethnic or national claims" (2016, 95). The aim of this "social and political project" is "to establish an explicitly spatial basis for claims involving ethnic identity, cultural rights, and political authority by identifying and constructing certain places or territories as belonging to or appropriate for certain ethno-national categories of people and practice, and by extension displacing other categories" (2016, 95). As Moore elaborates, the politics of displacement and relocation accompanying ethno-territorial aspirations can take various forms, "ranging from ethnic cleansing and genocide, to forced removal of an ethnic community from a state's borderlands to urban planning decisions restricting the use and settlement of land by a targeted category, to demands that specific cultural practices be allowed or restricted in certain neighborhoods or villages" (2016, 95). This is aimed at creating an ethnically "pure" environment, where symbols and associations related with the "undesired" ethnic group have to be eradicated or substituted with new artifacts evoking the symbolic and material belonging of the "desired" ethnic group or underlining its "natural" right to the specific land. A consideration of some of these measures seems to be exceptionally relevant for the analysis of the systematic assault on Palestinian urbanity advanced by the Israeli government, both within Israel proper and in the occupied West Bank. Such strategies, however, usually operate in combined, nuanced ways, entangling different policies and acting upon different aspects of the territory, including its spatial and demographical configurations. Acknowledging the complex nature of ethno-territorial aspirations, Moore refers to four general, usually overlapping, dimensions of ethno-territoriality. In his formulation, ethno-territoriality can be enacted discursively (through symbolic mapping and marking of spaces via meaning-making representational strategies), bodily (through physical daily participation in public performances), materially (through urbicidal tactics or specific design of infrastructure and the built environment), and institutionally (through adjustment of political structures and institutions to the ethno-territorial principles) (2016, 95). It must be kept in mind that the delineation of these four dimensions is only provisional and meant to serve certain analytical purposes. In practice, they tend to overlap and merge, translating into complex tactics and ways of thinking that structure the life of a given community.

One of the founding myths of the Zionist expansion in Palestine is embodied in the oft-quoted slogan "a land without a people for a people without a land," questioning the presence of an indigenous population in Palestine prior to the proclamation of the Israeli state. A representation of mythical Palestine as an empty land has typically served as a means of legitimizing Jewish settlement in this region or a need for a homeland understood as "a national space of one's own" (Smith 2009, 163), which is never given but has to be collectively constructed and maintained. The colonial expansion has been habitually justified by a number of such cultural contractions or fabrications, casting doubt on the Palestinian right to the contested land (Pappé 2017). The strategy of invisibilizing—in fact negating—the existence of the Arab population in Palestine has been mobilized in an effort to build what Oren Yiftachel calls "ethnocracy" (2006), a state organized around a principle of a collective "project of exerting ethno-national control over a territory perceived as the nation's (exclusive) homeland" (Yiftachel and Ghanem 2004, 651). Such projects are often embedded in the idea of an imagined homeland, a territory to which a given ethnic group has an unquestionable "natural" right. Territories, however, are generated from space in the process of its "territorialization" (Raffestin 1980), while space itself remains a scarce resource. Hence, ethno-territorial projects strive to naturalize the link between territories and peoples through the (often violent) production and maintenance of territoriality. As mentioned earlier, this occasionally requires "purification" of the territory from "others," both materially and symbolically. Therefore, since the establishment of the State of Israel, its (still contested) territory has been systematically Judaized (also through de-Arabization). This has been performed via the forced relocation of populations and the confiscation of property, as much as through a strategy of renaming geographical areas, towns, and villages, and the reinvention of the region's history, including, as Ilan Pappé mentions (2006), the strategy of memoricide. The latter process consisted of constructing imagined narrative bridges across otherwise discontinuous events from the past and incorporating such mnemonic practices into the nationalist imaginary circulated via the dominant ideology.[5] This contributed to the further politicization of space and the construction of particular forms of territoriality rooted in the principle of "natural" belonging. In Lefebvrean terms, together with a systematic production of physical space (through careful politics of planning and design; see Weizman 2007) and a highly institutionalized social space (based on discriminatory differentiation between Jewish and non-Jewish inhabitants of this space; see Ophir et al. 2009], a mental image of the state as an heir of the rich history and culture of the region has been created with the aim of supporting the project of colonization of Palestine. This has been implemented via—inter alia—a systematic eradication of indigenous cultures and their routine forms of inhabitance.

The Right to the City

The notion of inhabitance is central to Lefebvre's concept of the "right to the city" (1996, 1968). It stands for the demand for access to urban life in all its diversified richness and refers to a multiplicity of political, social, cultural, and material processes. Every right, for Lefebvre, is a manifestation, or the end result, of collective claims made by mobilized citizens/inhabitants. Because they result from struggle, they are always subject to renewed political agitation. Rights, therefore, are entangled with politics, and the right to the city—as elaborated upon by the philosopher—refers to a deeply spatial understanding of politics that tends to place urban space at the very center of its vision. This is due to the close links between urbanization and industrialization, yet the city cannot be reduced merely to the spatial product of the latter. Lefebvre's concept calls for the reintegration of the urban space into the web of social connections, which stands for the appropriation of the space in the city by its inhabitants (regardless of their national, ethnic, class, or religious belonging). The urban space is where the sociality of those inhabiting it is rooted and enacted; it is meant to be constantly remade, as an always-becoming "work," or oeuvre, of its citizens. Such space should be approached as a zone of encounter, with respect to differences, but also mobilizing collective effort to counter the dominance of the state as far as production of spatiality is concerned. Putting inhabitance at the center of spatial politics openly undermines the assumption that everyday dwelling should be regulated by the functional characteristics of habitats advanced by bureaucratic planning and architectural developments. "The right to the city" highlights instead the entitlement to physically occupy space which pertains to the inhabitants (Lefebvre 1996, 158). But inhabitance is not limited to this; it also extends to inhabitants' capacity to participate in collective decision-making about the space. This entails the ability to use the space in daily routines and practices as well as participation in the processes of deciding over the production of urban space (Lefebvre 1996, 179).

Because of its salience—as much as its reference to issues of cultural, or spatial, citizenship—the concept of "the right to the city" has recently been pronounced by many politicians and activists as part of a broader agenda for human rights. The idea has also drawn the attention of a growing number of academics.[6] As rearticulated by many scholars, today the concept often evokes the right to shape the city according to inhabitants' needs and in connection to citizenship's rights. Such an approach stresses the inclusivity of urban space while addressing a whole range of inequalities implicated in current urban processes. This is especially vital in the context of multi-ethnic (urban) societies. As Butler explains, "The *right to the city* legitimates the refusal to allow oneself to be removed from urban reality by a discriminatory and segregative organization" (2012, 144; original emphasis). Lefebvre's proposal, however, remains a radical one, so it would be a betrayal of his original ideas to reduce "the right to the city" to a positivist understanding of it in terms of a legal asset. Rather, it must be seen as a creative means of producing a social space, somewhat away from the functionalist state intervention, and adjusting it to inhabitants' diverse needs and ideas, yet avoiding legal individualism, the latter potentially entrenching segregation, discrimination, or intolerance (see Purcell 2008). Such attitudes and practices, however, are often the case, while the fact of preventing certain groups from participating in the collective act of producing space must be perceived in terms of a denial of "the right to the city."

In an ethnocratic state, where one ethnic group dominates over, and dictates the spatial conditions for, another, the limitations of "the right to the city" pertaining to a specific ethnic group translate into a system of spatial disadvantage, where basic needs to shape the space of inhabitance are not attended to. As Adi Ophir et al. explain, in the Occupied Territories, where the right of the Palestinians to produce space and spatially co-constituted social relations is seriously constrained, the suppression of indigenous forms of dwelling is mainly generated through "the unique logic of withheld or suspended violence, in which the means of violence are on display rather than in actual use, and by the systematic production of uncertainty that strips the subject of rational mastery of her future and destiny" (2009, 22). This uncertainty applies to the future of urban spaces as much as to inhabitants' capacities to decide about them. By sustaining a discriminatory legal system which gives priority to the citizens of Israel over the inhabitants of territories under the Israeli occupation—or, in the case of the Israeli mainland, by privileging the citizens of Jewish identity over others—the rights of a huge segment of the population are being systematically denied. The legal system works differently on Israel's mainland and in the Occupied Territories, as well as generating realities which are experienced dramatically differently by Jewish citizens and non-Jewish residents of the same geographical area. The situation of Palestinian-Arabs is further aggravated by the unequal provision of vital public services (such as transportation, construction permits, maintenance of infrastructure, access to drinkable water, and siting of toxic facilities). This system translates into, to refer to Soja (2010), a "geography of (in)justice," where "spatial justice" is understood as "an integral and formative component of justice itself, a vital part of how justice and injustice are socially constructed and evolve over time" (2010, 1; see also Dikeç 2001, 2009; Philippopoulos-Mihalopoulos 2010, 2011). Such a model of thinking is based on the assumption that there exists a "formative relation between the social and the spatial dimensions of human life" (Soja 2010, 4), meaning that spatiality actively shapes and configures social relations while social processes co-constitute and give meaning to spatialities in which humans and objects are situated.

The politics of space is actively involved in the process of slowly producing the geographies of discrimination, the phenomenon that I call here "slow urbicide." This links the struggles over space to the ideas connected to the concept of "the right to the city," packed, as Soja underlines, "with powerful ideas about the consequential geography of urban life" (2010, 6). Hence, exertion of "the right to the city" is tantamount to the struggle for spatial justice, even though such endeavors in many contexts—including the Palestinian one—often fail. As a result, Palestinians are usually not able to maximize what Mark Purcell understands as the use value of the space (2002, 103). Rather than enjoying the right to the collective production of an urban spatiality that would attend to the needs of its inhabitants, they remain subordinated to violent and unequal geographies. Slow urbicide extensively contributes to the advancement of these discriminatory processes, gradually deepening spatial injustices.

Design of the Book

Slow Urbicide consists of three chapters and recapitulative conclusions, with Chapter 1 exploring the theoretical approach adopted in these investigations, Chapter 2 focusing on the history and meaning of urbicidal violence, and Chapter 3 discussing two case studies of slow urbicide in Palestine. While this introduction can be seen as a robust presentation of concepts that structure the argumentation offered in the book, the chapters that follow should be read in sequence. The organization of the book serves its twofold objective, defined in terms of the investigation of currently used tactics of slow violence against urbanity and the expansion of the new "ethico-onto-epistemological" (Barad 2007) perspective to study political violence and its aftermath. Even though the theoretical and empirical explorations are woven together within the book, a clear division between the delineation of the conceptual approach (Chapters 1 and 2) and its more practical operationalization in further deliberations (Chapter 3) is clearly discernible. Such a construction facilitates the fulfillment of the two complementary goals set up in the book, namely methodological innovation and the analytical study of violence against urbanity in Palestine.

In Chapter 1, entitled "New Materialism and the Study of Political Violence," starting with a discussion of war as practice, I offer a detailed introduction to new materialist ways of thinking, focusing on how this tendency is situated vis-à-vis its immediate predecessors, such as social constructivism and discourse theory. My aim here is to elaborate on the potential advantages that new materialism offers to the study of political violence as well as to a more general analysis of international relations, and especially *how* (slow) political violence is enacted and experienced. It is important to bear in mind that new materialist thinking should be seen as a substantial correction to what Robert Keohane termed "reflectivism" (see Booth et al. 1996) in international relations theory, rather than being positioned in antagonistic relation to it. New materialism's distinctive characteristic is that it pays unprecedented attention to issues of matter and materiality, understanding them as important agents contributing extensively to the production of knowledge and experience. This entails acknowledgment of the material-semiotic nature of all processes, as well as the spatio-temporal contexts in which they are situated. This, I argue, is especially vital in the

INTRODUCTION

context of urban space being a dynamic conglomerate of material arrangements and cultural meaning-making practices. Such a formulation seems to correspond well to Lefebvre's conceptualizations of socialized lived space, which extends beyond the narrow understandings and delineations of urban areas. Space is an organization of physical and spatial forms which materially and mentally entangle with socialized lived time, creating "our biographies and geo-histories" (Soja 2010, 8), and which are connected to broader geographically and historically shaped situations and circuits. In that sense, new materialism helps us to realize that space is not a dead background or inert stage for human activities; rather it should be conceived of as a collection of material and imagined forces, actively shaping and co-constituting social events and experiences, individual and collective. This substantially reconfigures the dominant thinking in terms of temporal metamorphoses of situated social processes, adding an important spatial (that is, also material) dimension to it. As Soja underlines, "the new spatial consciousness" stimulates awareness "that geographies in which we live can intensify and sustain our exploitation as workers, support oppressive forms of cultural and political domination based on race, gender, and nationality, and aggravate all forms of discrimination and injustice" (2010, 19). Analysis of the role that urbanity as well as the forces and rights associated with it play in ethno-national conflicts reveals the complex material-semiotic nature of both urban practices and political violence. To do justice to this complexity, part of Chapter 1 focuses on the concept of agency. Agency—which is absolutely crucial for the domain of international relations theory—is problematized by new materialism in ways that transcend matter's both positivist and constructionist renditions. Thus, this chapter points to the investigative richness that the innovative nature of a new materialist approach could potentially contribute to the field of widely defined political science or cultural studies of politics, broadening the spectrum of political agents which count in the political processes, locally and globally.

Entitled "Mapping Urbicidal Violence," Chapter 2 familiarizes readers with historical understandings of the concept of urbicide, drawing parallels between current and historical instances of violence against the built environment but also focusing on the significant differences between today's uses of urbicidal tactics and their historical equivalents. It offers—following Coward (2009)—a critical overview of the dominant ways of conceptualizing urbicidal violence and critically assesses these tendencies. This part of the book also more thoroughly engages with Coward's materialist claims, fostering an even more complex new materialist understanding of urban destruction. Differently from Coward, I propose to approach urbicidal violence as entangled with—rather than separate from—other manifestations of political violence, placing emphasis on the need to acknowledge its material-semiotic character and the consequences of this. While mapping the various formulations of urbicidal violence, I pay attention to how it contributes to the creation of "placelessness," or to killing "the sense of the place" (McKittrick 2011) of a particular community, substantially reconfiguring the politics of belonging and mutual codependence of spatial and social structures. Thus, in order to understand what is at stake in urbicide, in Chapter 2 I also discuss the concept of "home" and how it is situated vis-à-vis its natural, physical, social, and cultural contexts, as well as how its destruction *matters*. Adopting a cartographic approach, grounded in new materialist ways of thinking, this part of the book offers a *topology of concepts* used for referring to violence against urbanity, highlighting the material dimensions of home and community as much as of their destruction. As I want to underline, the demolition of urban spaces—understood inclusively as spreading far beyond urban areas—amounts to the annihilation, or denial, of "the right to the city" conceived of not only as the right to shape the urban according to inhabitants' needs but, crucially, as the right to active resistance against state policies, manifested, among other ways, in aspirations for self-governance. If the pursuit of "the right to the city" is perceived as a continuous effort at reappropriation of the space, countering the centralized state's endeavors (so meaningful in the context of the Israeli spatial politics in Palestine), then the criminalization and subsequent eradication of Palestinian urbanity as an important context of collective resistance must be seen as a process that may lead to the construction of such forms of violence-based territorial dominance that would be difficult, or even impossible, to contest or resist. In the context of ethno-territorial rivalries, this seems to be of fundamental importance for the efficient production of territoriality in a project of violent colonial expansion. An assault on urbanity could be understood, in such a situation, as a necessary element of the political state-sponsored organization of space, involving representational strategies and material rearrangements. This policy results in the creation of oppressive geographies and spatial injustices based on ideologically shaped ethnic divisions and intentionally impaired participation in decision-making processes by the marginalized groups.

The violent geographies and geographical warfare in Palestine are further explored in Chapter 3 with reference to particular case studies. This part of the book tackles cartography as a powerful instrument in producing spatial injustice through a material-semiotic process of organizing political and physical geographies. The chapter explores spatial strategies of occupation, dispossession, exploitation, and domination as implemented in both the Occupied Territories and Israel proper and how they have been effectively used in the process of production of Israeli territoriality (including in occupied areas). "Geographical Warfare in Palestine" focuses specifically on those spatial manipulations that contribute to the process of material, social, cultural, and symbolic boundary making. The two case studies offered in Chapter 3 seek to reveal the convoluted ways in which urbicidal violence operates at subtle levels and at a relatively slow pace, as well as how it relies on political framing of the colonial project in terms of development and modernization. First, exploring the geographies of occupation generated in the West Bank, my analysis focuses on the state-sponsored measures used as tools in the production of the desired forms of spatiality, facilitating the construction of Israeli territoriality on the occupied areas. Politicization of such agents as, for instance, road infrastructure, plants, or waste remains a significant means for advancing slow urbicidal violence in the region. Second, the analysis of forced urbanization processes in the Naqab/Negev,[7] and how the Israeli state recruits the natural forces active in the region for its colonial enterprise, exposes tacit operations of slow urbicidal violence in the Israeli mainland, revealing the diversity of colonization techniques employed in the various areas remaining under its jurisdiction.

The studies included in this part of the book are by no means meant to be exhaustive. Rather, my intention is to draw attention to the situated material-semiotic, natural-cultural, and human-nonhuman processes of advancing destruction and deracination of indigenous populations through a systematic assault on the traditional organization of urban communities. Policies drawing on similar logic have been undertaken in other areas and against other urban communities in Israel proper (e.g., Galilean cities with substantial Arab populations) and in the Occupied Territories (e.g., the Gaza Strip). Thus, the two case studies discussed in this book serve merely as an illustration of a more general politics of slow-motion destruction, and the list of possible examples could easily be extended. My objective, however, is to point out that the strategy of "slowness" employed by the Israeli state may serve as an effective means of obfuscating the state-sponsored character of such violent spatial developments, gradually leading to the production of forms of territorial authority that are desired by the colonizer. As the book underlines, without spatial awareness, or awareness of the shifting temporalities of urbicidal violence, the production and maintenance of unfair geographies and spatial injustices are likely to remain unchallenged. The unspectacular nature of such forms of urbicidal violence, or its "slowness," successfully invisibilizes its detrimental effects, leaving them often unaccounted for. It is therefore necessary to pay attention to the indirect, sophisticated operations of a whole array of multilayered techniques, as well as to the injustices that they produce in their effort to construct a spatially organized system of control and discrimination.

In the concluding part of *Slow Urbicide* my intention is to provide an answer to the question of what is at stake in urbicide, as much as in documenting violence against urbanity. Informed by findings presented in earlier chapters, this part of the book offers a reflection on the specificity of current warfare and how—or why—it uniquely affects urban communities. The idea is to explore why violence against urbanity has been an increasingly popular strategy and to reveal the rationale behind such policies. A new materialist approach, as must be once more underlined, may be very helpful in demonstrating these points. At the same time, on a more general level, the final part of the book intends to encourage a consideration, informed by the earlier-presented investigations, of the ways in which, as Diana Coole reminds us, humans "encounter, are affected by, respond to, destroy, rely upon and are generally imbricated with matter, and to assume a critical stance by exploring the dangerous ways matter is being reconfigured and distributed" (2013, 468). It is therefore necessary to document and reflect on the current warfare strategies and—especially—their slow, silent, almost invisible operations.

Notes

1 See, for example, Graham (2002b, 2002c, 2004a, 2004b, 2005, 2010), Campbell et al. (2007), Cowen (2007), Shaw (2004), Ramadan (2009), Fregonese (2009), and Weizman (2007).
2 In this book, I use the term "Palestine" to denote the territory of the former British Mandate, whose significant parts were effectively colonized by the Jewish settlers (and soldiers) before and after the official proclamation of the State of Israel in May 1948. These territories are now either considered as belonging to the Israeli state (although the political borders of this organism are still not fully recognized) or remaining under its occupation. The term "Occupied Territories" is used to refer specifically to the lands of the West Bank and the Gaza Strip, which came under the Israeli occupation in 1967, after the Six-Day War. In the aftermath of this war, Israel, as the victorious side of the conflict, managed to spread its military control over the West Bank in the east and reached the eastern band of the Suez Canal in the west. After later negotiations, Israel returned Sinai to Egypt (1973) but remained as an occupying force in the West Bank and Gaza. In 2005 Israel officially withdrew from Gaza, but it continues to block the area from each side, hampering its urban expansion and economic development.
3 For exploration of the politics of biosphere and greenery management in the context of the Israeli presence in Palestine, see also Cohen and Gordon (2018) and Weizman (2017).
4 For the intersection of nationalism and territorial politics, see, for instance, works by O'Loughlin and Ó Tuathail (2009) or Moore (2016); for exploration of the entanglement of nationalism and ethno-territoriality with understanding of human bodies and necropolitics, see Verdery (2000) and Leshem (2015).
5 The reinvention of the Jewish nation and its history as embedded in territorial practices or natural belonging has been discussed, among others, by Hochberg (2015), Zerubavel (2020), Morris (2007), or Sand (2009).
6 Detailed scholarly discussions of the concept of "the right to the city" can be found in Purcell (2002), Mitchell (2003), Dikeç (2007), Leavitt et al. (2009), Marcuse (2009), Harvey (2008), Attoh (2011), Soja (2010), Fernandes (2006, 2007), Dikeç and Gilbert (2002), and Gilbert and Dikeç (2008).
7 I am using the double name of the region throughout the book. The desert is called "Naqab" by the Palestinian-Arab population but it is referred as "Negev" by the Jewish population. I use the two names with a slash to represent the colonial reality of this area.

Bibliography

Abujidi, Nurham. 2014. *Urbicide in Palestine. Space of Oppression and Resilience.* Kindle edition. New York and London: Routledge.

Adams, Nicholas. 1993. "Architecture as the Target." *Journal of the Society of Architectural Historians* 52, no. 4: 389–339.

Adey, Peter. 2013. "Securing the Volume/Volumen: Comments on Stuart Elden's Plenary Paper 'Secure the Volume.'" *Political Geography* 34: 52–54. https://doi.org/10.1016/j.polgeo.2013.01.003.

Alkhalili, Noura. 2017. "Enclosures from Below: The *Mushaa'* in Contemporary Palestine." *Antipode* 49, no. 5: 1103–1124. https://doi.org/10.1111/anti.12322.

Allegra, Marco, Ariel Handel, and Erez Maggor. 2017. *Normalizing Occupation. The Politics of Everyday Life in the West Bank Settlements.* Bloomington: University of Indiana Press.

Anderson, Benedict. 1983. *Imagined Communities: Reflections on the Origin and Spread of Nationalism.* London: Verso.

Attoh, Kafui A. 2011. "What Kind of Right is the Right to the City?" *Progress in Human Geography* 35: 669–685. https://doi.org/10.1177/0309132510394706.

Barad, Karen. 2003. "Posthumanist Performativity: Toward an Understanding of How Matter Comes to Matter." *Signs: Journal of Women in Culture and Society* 28, no. 3: 801–831. https://doi.org/10.1086/345321.

———. 2007. *Meeting the Universe Halfway: Quantum Physics and the Entanglement of Matter and Meaning.* Durham: Duke University Press.

Bogdanovic, Bogdan. 1993. "Murder of the City." *The New York Review of Books* 40: 10.

———. 1994. "The City and Death." In *Strom 6: Out of Yugoslavia*, edited by Joanna Labon, 37–74. London: Storm/Carcanet.

Booth, Ken, Steve Smith, and Marysia Zalewski, eds. 1996. *International Theory: Positivism and Beyond.* Cambridge: Cambridge University Press.

Branch, Jordan. 2017. "Territory as an Institution: Spatial Ideas, Practices and Technologies." *Territory, Politics, Governance* 5, no. 2: 131–144. https://doi.org/10.1080/21622671.2016.1265464.

Brighenti, Andrea M. 2010. "Lines, Barred Lines. Movement, Territory and the Law." *International Journal of Law in Context* 6, no. 3: 217–227. https://doi.org/10.1017/S1744552310000121.

Butler, Chris. 2012. *Henri Lefebvre. Spatial Politics, Everyday Life and the Right to the City.* New York: Routledge.

Cahill, Caitlin. 2015. "A Blade of Grass: Young People, Slow Violence, and the Struggle over Social Reproduction." The Gender, Place, and Culture Jan Monk Distinguished Feminist Geography Annual Lecture. Chicago: Annual Association of American Geographers.

Campbell, David, Stephen Graham, and Daniel B. Monk. 2007. "Introduction to Urbicide: The Killing of Cities?" *Theory & Event* 10, no. 2: n.p. https://doi.rog/10.1353/tae.2007.0055.

Campbell, Elaine. 2019. "Three-dimensional Security: Layers, Spheres, Volumes, Milieus." *Political Geography* 69: 10–21. https://doi.org/10.1016/j.polgeo.2018.11.010.

Cohen, Shaul Ephraim. 1993. *The Politics of Planting.* Chicago: The University of Chicago Press.

Cohen, Yinon, and Neve Gordon. 2018. "Israel's Biospatial Politics: Territory, Demography, and Effective Control." *Public Culture* 30: 199–220. https://doi.org/10.1215/08992363-4310888.

Coole, Diana. 2013. "Agentic Capacities and Capacious Historical Materialism: Thinking with New Materialisms in the Political Science." *Millennium: Journal of International Studies* 41, no. 3: 451–469. https://doi.org/10.1177/0305829813481006.

Coward, Martin. 2006. "Against Anthropocentrism: The Destruction of the Built Environment as a Distinct Form of Political Violence." *Review of International Studies* 32, no. 3: 419–437. https://doi.org/10.1017/S0260210506007091.

———. 2009. *Urbicide. The Politics of Urban Destruction.* New York and London: Routledge.

Cowen, Deborah. 2007. "National Soldiers and the War on Cities." *Theory & Event* 10, no. 2: n.p. https://doi.org/10.1353/tae.2007.0057.

Davies, Thom. 2018. "Toxic Space and Time: Slow Violence, Necropolitics, and Petrochemical Pollution." *Annals of the American Association of Geographers* 108, no. 6: 1537–1553. https://doi.org/10.1080/24694452.2018.1470924.

———. 2019. "Slow Violence and Toxic Geographies: 'Out of Sight' to Whom?" *EPC: Politics and Space. Theme Issue: Spatial Politics of Slow Violence and Resistance* (online first): 1–19. https://doi.org/10.1177/2399654419841063.

Davies, Thom, and Arshad Isakjee. 2015. "Geography, Migration and Abandonment in the Calais Refugee Camp." *Political Geography* 49: 93–95. https://doi.org/10.1016/j.polgeo.2015.08.003.

De Leeuw, Sarah. 2016. "Tender Grounds: Intimate Visceral Violence and British Columbia's Colonial Geographies." *Political Geography* 52: 14–23. https://doi.org/10.1016/j.polgeo.2015.11.010.

Dikeç, Mustafa. 2001. "Justice and the Spatial Imagination." *Environment and Planning A: Economy and Space* 33, no. 10: 1785–1805. https://doi.org/10.1068/a3467.

———. 2007. *Badlands of the Republic: Space, Politics, and Urban Policy.* Malden: Blackwell.

———. 2009. "Space, Politics and (In)justice." *Justice Spatiale/Spatial Justice* 1. Available at: http://www.jssj.org/article/lespace-le-politique-et-linjustice/. Accessed 17 July 2021.

Dikeç, Mustafa, and Liette Gilbert. 2002. "Right to the City: Homage or a New Societal Ethics." *Capitalism Nature Socialism* 13, no. 2: 58–74. https://doi.org/10.1080/10455750208565479.

Dittmer, Jason. 2014. "Geopolitical Assemblages and Complexity." *Progress in Human Geography* 38, no. 3: 385–401. https://doi.org/10.1177/0309132513501405.

Elden, Stuart. 2010. "Land, Terrain, Territory." *Progress in Human Geography* 34, no. 6: 799–817. https://doi.org/10.1177/0309132510362603.

———. 2013. "Secure the Volume: Vertical Geopolitics and the Depth of Power." *Political Geography* 34: 35–51. https://doi.org/10.1016/j.polgeo.2012.12.009.

———. 2021. "Terrain, Politics, History." *Dialogues in Human Geography* 11, no. 2: 170–189. https://doi.org/10.1177/2043820620951353.

Fernandes, Edésio. 2006. "Updating the Declaration of the Rights of Citizens in Latin America: Constructing the 'Right to the City' in Brazil." In *Urban Policies and the Right to the City*, edited by Alison Brown and Annali Kristiansen, 40–52. Paris: UNESCO.

———. 2007. "Constructing the 'Right to the City' in Brazil." *Social and Legal Studies* 16, no. 2: 201–219. https://doi.org/10.1177/0964663907076529.
Ford, Richard T. 1999. "Law's Territory (A History of Jurisdiction)." *Michigan Law Review* 97, no. 4: 843–930. https://doi.org/10.2307/1290376.
Fragonese, Sara. 2009. "The Urbicide in Beirut? Geopolitics and the Built Environment in the Lebanese Civil War (1975-1976)." *Political Geography* 28: 309–318. https://doi.org/10.1016/j.polgeo.2009.07.005.
Garrett, Bradley. 2016. "Picturing Urban Subterranean: Embodied Aesthetics of London's Sewers." *Environment and Planning A: Economy and Space* 48, no. 10: 1948–1966. https://doi.org/10.1177/0308518X16652396.
Gilbert, Linette, and Mustafa Dikeç. 2008. "Right to the City: Politics of Citizenship." In *Space, Difference, Everyday Life: Reading Henri Lefebvre*, edited by Kanishka Goonewardena, Stean Kipfer, Richard Milgrom, and Christian Schmid, 250–263. New York: Routledge.
Gottmann, Jean. 1951. *La politique des états et leur géographie*. Paris: Armand Colin.
Graham, Stephen. 2002a. "Bulldozers and Bombs: The Latest Palestinian-Israeli Conflict and Asymmetric Urbicide." *Antipode* 34, no. 4: 642–649. https://doi.org/10.1111/1467-8330.00259.
———. 2002b. "Clean Territory: Urbicide in the West Bank." *Open Democracy*. Available at: https://www.opendemocracy.net/en/article_241jsp/. Accessed 27 March 2022.
———. 2002c. "Urbanizing War—Militarizing Cities. The City as Strategic Site." *Archis* 3: n.p. Available at: https://archis.org/volume/urbanizing-war-militarizing-cities-the-city-as-strategic-site/. Accessed 20 October 2021.
———. 2003. "Lessons in Urbicide." *New Left Review* 19: 63–77.
———. 2004a. *Cities, Wars and Terrorism: Towards an Urban Geopolitics*. Malden: Blackwell Publishing.
———. 2004b. "Postmortem City: Towards an Urban Geopolitics." *City* 8, no. 2: 165–196. https://doi.org/10.1080/1360481042000242148.
———. 2005. "Remember Fallujah: Demonising Place, Constructing Atrocity." *Environment and Planning D: Society and Space* 23, no. 1: 1–10. https://doi.org/10.1068/d2301ed.
———. 2010. *Cities Under Siege: The New Military Urbanism*. New York: Verso.
———. 2016. *Vertical: The City from Satellites to Bunkers*. London: Verso.
Graham, Stephen, and Lucy Hewitt. 2012. "Getting Off the Ground: On the Politics of Urban Verticality." *Progress in Human Geography* 37, no. 1: 72–92. https://doi.org/10.1177/0309132512443147.
Gregory, Derek. 2004a. *The Colonial Present*. Oxford: Blackwell.
———. 2004b. "Palestine Under Siege." *Antipode* 36: 601–606. https://doi.org/10.1111/j.1467-8330.2004.00438.x.
Hanafi, Sari. 2009. "Spacio-cide: Colonial Politics, Invisibility and Rezoning in Palestinian Territory." *Contemporary Arab Affairs* 2, no. 1: 106–121. https://doi.org/10.1080/17550910802622645.
———. 2012. "Explaining Spacio-cide in the Palestinian Territory: Colonization, Separation, and State of Exception." *Current Sociology* 61, no. 2: 190–205. https://doi.org/10.1177/0011392112456505.
Haraway, Donna. 1988. "Situated Knowledges. The Science Question in Feminism and the Privilege of Partial Perspective." *Feminist Studies* 14, no. 3: 575–599. https://doi.org/10.2307/3178066.

———. 1997. *Modest_Witness@Second_Millennium.FemaleMan©_Meets_ OncoMouse™ Feminism and Technoscience*. New York: Routledge.

Harker, Chris. 2011. "The Only Way is Up? Ordinary Topologies of Ramallah." *International Journal of Urban and Regional Research* 38: 318–335. https://doi.org/10.1111/1468-2427.12094.

———. 2014. "Geopolitics and Family in Palestine." *Geoforum* 42: 306–315. https://doi.org/10.1016/j.geoforum.2010.06.007.

Harris, Andrew. 2015. "Vertical Urbanisms: Opening Up Geographies of the Three-dimensional City." *Progress in Human Geography* 39, no. 5: 601–620. https://doi.org/10.1177/0309132514554323.

Harvey, David. 2008. "The Right to the City." *New Left Review* 53: 23–40.

Hassan, Sheik I., and Sari Hanafi. 2009. "(In)security and Reconstruction in Post Conflict Nahr-al Barid Refugee Camp." *Journal of Palestine Studies* XL, no. 1: 27–48. https://doi.org/10.1525/jps.2010.xl.1.027.

Hochberg, Gil Z. 2015. *Visual Occupations. Violence and Visibility in a Conflict Zone*. Durham: Duke University Press.

Jabareen, Yosef. 2015. "Territoriality of Negation: Co-production of 'Creative Destruction' in Israel." *Geoforum* 66: 11–25. https://doi.org/10.1016/j.geoforum.2015.09.003.

Kern, Leslie. 2016. "Rhythms of Gentrification: Eventfulness and Slow Violence in a Happening Neighbourhood." *Cultural Geographies* 23, no. 3: 441–457. https://doi.org/10.1177/1474474015591489.

Kramer, Mark. 2005. "Guerrilla Warfare, Counterinsurgency and Terrorism in the North Caucasus: The Military Dimensions of the Russian-Chechen Conflict." *Europe-Asia Studies* 57, no. 2: 209–290. https://doi.org/10.1080/09668130500051833.

Lacoste, Yves. 1976. *La géographie, ça sert, d'abord, à faire la guerre*. Paris: Maspero.

Leavitt, Jackie, Tony R. Samara, and Marnie Brady. 2009. "The Right to the City Alliance: Time to Democratize Urban Governance." *Progressive City Magazine* (Fall). Available at: https://www.plannersnetwork.org/2009/10/the-right-to-the-city-alliance-time-to-democratize-urban-governance/. Accessed 17 July 2021.

Lefebvre, Henri. 1968. *Le droit à la ville*. Paris: Anthropos.

———. 1991. *The Production of Space*, translated by Donald Nicholson-Smith. Cambridge, MA: Blackwell.

———. 1996. *Writings on Cities*, edited by Eleonore Kofman and Elizabeth Lebas. Oxford: Blackwell.

———. 2003. "Space and the State." In *State/Space: A Reader*, edited by Neil Brenner, Bob Jessop, Martin Jones, and Gordon MacLeod, 84–100. Oxford: Blackwell.

Leshem, Noam. 2015. "'Over Our Dead Bodies': Placing Necropolitical Activism." *Political Geography* 45: 34–44. https://doi.org/10.1016/j.polgeo.2014.09.003.

———. 2016. *Life after Ruin*. Cambridge: Cambridge University Press.

Makdisi, Saree. 2010. *Palestine Inside Out*. London and New York: W.W. Norton & Company.

Marcuse, Peter. 2009. "From Critical Urban Theory to the Right to the City." *City* 13: 185–197. https://doi.org/10.1080/13604810902982177.

Mbembe, Achille. 2001. *On the Postcolony*. Berkeley: University of California Press.

McKittrick, Katherine. 2011. "On Plantations, Prisons, and a Black Sense of Place." *Social & Cultural Geography* 12, no. 8: 947–963. https://doi.org/10.1080/14649365.2011.624280.

Mignolo, Walter. 2011. *The Darker Side of Western Modernity. Global Futures, Decolonial Options*. Durham: Duke University Press.

Mitchell, Don. 2003. *The Right to the City: Social Justice and the Fight for Public Space*. New York: Guilford.

Moore, Adam. 2016. "Ethno-territoriality and Ethnic Conflict." *Geographical Review* 106, no. 1: 92–108. https://doi.org/10.1111/j.1931-0846.2015.12132.x.

Morris, Benny, ed. 1987. *The Birth of the Palestinian Refugee Problem 1947–1949*. Cambridge: Cambridge University Press.

———. 2007. *Making Israel*. Ann Arbor: Michigan University Press.

Nixon, Rob. 2009. "Neoliberalism, Slow Violence, and the Environmental Picaresque." *MFS Modern Fiction Studies* 55, no. 3: 443–467. https://doi.org/10.1353/mfs.0.1631.

———. 2011. *Slow Violence and the Environmentalism of the Poor*. Cambridge, MA: Harvard University Press.

O'Lear, Shannon. 2016. "Climate Science and Slow Violence: A View From Political Geography and STS on Mobilizing Technoscientific Ontologies of Climate Change." *Political Geography* 52: 4–13. https://doi.org/10.1016/j.polgeo.2015.01.004.

———. 2018. *Environmental Geopolitics*. Lanham: Rowman & Littlefield.

O'Loughlin, John, and Geraóid Ó Tuathail. 2009. "Accounting for Separatist Sentiment in Bosnia-Herzegovina and the North Caucasus of Russia: A Comparative Analysis of Survey Responses." *Ethnic and Racial Studies* 32, no. 4: 591–615. https://doi.org/10.1080/01419870701819087.

Ophir, Adi, Michal Givoni, and Sari Hanafi. 2009. "Introduction." In *The Power of Inclusive Exclusion. Anatomy of Israeli Rule in the Occupied Palestinian Territories*, edited by Adi Ophir, Michal Givoni, and Sari Hanafi, 15–30. New York: Zone Books.

Pain, Rachel. 2019. "Chronic Urban Trauma: The Slow Violence of Housing Dispossession." *Urban Studies* 56, no. 2: 385–400. https://doi.org/10.1177/0042098018795796.

Pappé, Ilan. 2006. *The Ethnic Cleansing of Palestine*. Oxford: Oneworld Publications.

———. 2017. *Ten Myths About Israel*. London: Verso.

Philippopoulos-Mihalopoulos, Andreas. 2010. "Spatial Justice: Law and the Geography of Withdrawal." *International Journal of Law in Context* 6, no. 3: 201–216. https://doi.org/10.1017/S174455231000011X.

———. 2011. "Law's Spatial Turn: Geography, Justice and a Certain Fear of Space." *Law, Culture and the Humanities* 7, no. 2: 187–202. https://doi.org/10.1177/1743872109355578.

———. 2015. *Spatial Justice. Body, Landscape, Atmosphere*. New York: Routledge.

Purcell, Mark. 2002. "Excavating Lefebvre: The Right to the City and Its Urban Politics of the Inhabitant." *Geo-Journal* 58, no. 2&3: 99–108. https://doi.org/10.1023/B:GEJO.0000010829.62237.8F.

———. 2008. *Recapturing Democracy: Neoliberalization and the Struggle for Alternative Urban Futures*. New York: Routledge.

Quijano, Aníbal. 2007. "Coloniality as Modernity/Rationality." *Cultural Studies* 21: 168–178. https://doi.org/10.1080/09502380601164353.

Raffestin, Claude. 1980. *Pour une géographie du pouvoir*. Paris: LITEC.

Ramadan, Adam. 2009. "Destroying Nahr el-Bared: Sovereignty and Urbicide in the Space of Exception." *Political Geography* 28: 153–163. https://doi.org/10.1016/j.polgeo.2009.02.004.

Riedlmayer, Andreas. 1995. "Killing Memory: The Targeting of Bosnia's Cultural Heritage." Testimony Presented at a Hearing of the Commission on Security and Cooperation in Europe, U.S. Congress. 4 April 1995, Community of Bosnia Foundation. Available at: http://www.haverford.edu/relg/sells/killing.html. Accessed 12 February 2021.

Sack, Robert D. 1986. *Human Territoriality: Its History and Theory*. Cambridge: Cambridge University Press.

Sand, Shlomo. 2009. *The Invention of the Jewish People*. London and New York: Verso.

Sassen, Saskia. 2013. "When Territory Deborders Territoriality." *Territory, Politics, Governance* 1, no. 1: 21–45. https://doi.org/10.1080/21622671.2013.769895.

Segal, Rafi, and Eyal Weizman. 2003. *Civilian Occupation*. London: Verso.

Sharp, Deen, and Claire Panetta, eds. 2016. *Beyond the Square. Urbanism and the Arab Uprisings*. London: URpub.

Sharp, Jo. 2021. "Materials, Forensics and Feminist Geopolitics." *Progress in Human Geography* 45, no. 5: 990–1002. https://doi.org/10.1177/0309132520905653.

Shaw, Ian Graham Ronald. 2019. "Worlding Austerity: The Spatial Violence of Poverty." *Environment and Planning D: Society and Space* 37, no. 6: 971–989. https://doi.org/10.1177/0263775819857102.

Smith, Anthony D. 2009. *Ethno-Symbolism and Nationalism: A Cultural Approach*. New York: Routledge.

Soja, Edward W. 1996. *Thirdspace*. Malden: Blackwell.

———. 2010. *Seeking Spatial Justice*. Minneapolis: Minnesota University Press.

Till, Karen E. 2011. "Resilient Politics and Memory-work in Wounded Cities: Rethinking the City Through the District Six in Cape Town, South Africa." In *Collaborative Resilience*, edited by Bruce E. Goldstein, 283–307. Cambridge, MA: MIT Press.

Verdery, Katherine. 2000. *The Political Lives of Dead Bodies: Reburial and Postsocialist Change*. New York: Columbia University Press.

Weizman, Eyal. 2002. "Introduction to The Politics of Verticality." *Open Democracy*. Available at: https://www.opendemocracy.net/ecology-politicsverticality/article_801.jsp. Accessed 17 March 2018.

———. 2004. "Strategic Points, Flexible Lines, Tense Surfaces and Political Volumes: Ariel Sharon and the Geometry of Occupation." In *Cities, War and Terrorism: Towards an Urban Geopolitics*, edited by Stephen Graham, 172–191. Oxford: Blackwell Publishing.

———. 2007. *Hollow Land: Israel's Architecture of Occupation*. New York: Verso.

———. 2017. *Forensic Architecture. Violence at the Threshold of Detectability*. New York: Zone Books.

Yiftachel, Oren. 2006. *Ethnocracy: Land and Identity Politics in Israel/Palestine*. Philadelphia: University of Pennsylvania Press.

Yiftachel, Oren, and As'ad Ghanem. 2004. "Understanding 'Ethnocratic Regimes': The Politics of Seizing Contested Territories." *Political Geography* 23, no. 6: 647–676. https://doi.org/10.1016/j.polgeo.2004.04.003.

Zerubavel, Yael. 2020. "Boundaries, Bridges, Analogies and Bubbles: Structuring the Past in Israeli Mnemonic Culture." *Journal of Israeli History* 38, no. 1: 5–23. https://doi.org/10.1080/13531042.2020.1815982.

1
NEW MATERIALISM AND THE STUDY OF POLITICAL VIOLENCE

War as Practice

In his seminal work, *The New Western Way of War* (2005), Martin Shaw argues that "the defect of most social theory of war and militarism is ... that it has not considered war as practice, i.e., what people actually *do* in war" (2005, 40; original emphasis). The prevailing academic ignorance of this immediately practical dimension of war has produced a situation in which, in line with the causal logic pervading Western scientific efforts, war is predominantly theorized in instrumental terms and in reference to such conceptual abstractions as states, structures, conditions of anarchy, balances, systems, or power. Infused with ideas borrowed from Newtonian physics,[1] political theory conceives of these actors as atomic autonomous entities, preexisting any relations in which they enter, and whose interactions within a closed system result from objective laws and regularities and are thus to a large extent predictable. Figuring merely as a consequence of other forces and events, war remains epiphenomenal. Such a theoretical rendition pays attention to its political goals and effects, remaining in line with Carl von Clausewitz's influential understanding of war as a rational continuation of (interstate) politics with the addition of other means, whose possible uncertain effects, nevertheless, must always be kept in mind (1976). At the same time, the question of what war actually *is* remains, to a considerable extent, an underexplored trope of scholarly investigations, as the vast majority of scholars working in the field of political science and international relations theory do not address in detail the key elements of war, that is, its "empirical content" and the "how" of war.[2] As Hew Strachan notes in reference to the international legal frameworks, one of "the central challenges confronting international relations today is that we do not really know what is a war and what is not" (2007, 2). Even though the definitions and legal regulations are already at hand, the empirical dimension of war cannot be easily subordinated to the extant theoretical and analytical categories. The strategy of bracketing off war's immediately practice-related aspects does not offer critical insight into its real content, even though, as Shane Brighton

DOI: 10.4324/9781003157687-2

claims, "war presents a surfeit of being over knowing" (2011, 102). This means that the focus on the *practices* of war could shed an entirely different light on the understanding of its complex ontology. The problem is somewhat broader, as historically, war—Tarak Barkawi and Shane Brighton suggest—has not typically been perceived as an object of critical inquiry per se; "attention has been fixed on particular wars rather than war as a general force" (2011b, 129). Studied within various disciplines and in divergent scholarly contexts, the trope of war has operated as a "decentered" and "fragmented" theme of academic studies (Barkawi and Brighton 2011b, 129). The result is, in Barkawi and Brighton's words, that "the most basic questions regarding the ontology and epistemology of war have hardly been asked, much less have they issued in a substantial body of theory" (2011b, 127; see also Barkawi and Brighton 2011a).

Recently, however, a growing body of academic scholarship situated within the field of "critical security studies" and "critical war studies" has started to focus on different aspects of the *experience* of war, where war, as a "generative" force (Barkawi and Brighton 2011b, 126; see also Brighton 2011), is conceived of in reference to the embodied practices it entails along with an exploration of what it is capable of doing—both in the short and in the long run, both on the micro- and macroscale. In their framing of the ontology of war, Barkawi and Brighton opt to conceptualize war in terms of an "excess," understood as the capacity of organized violence to exceed the "kinetic exchange" (that is, fighting) and to work as a constitutive "event for politics and society" (2011b, 136). Thus, war should be understood as a multiplicity of practices, objects, and forces that directly affect human bodies as much as they translate into the generative reconfiguration, or disruptive decomposition, of social, cultural, economic, and political systems. Even though partly continuing the legacy of Western anthropocentric philosophy, such lines of criticism—exposing the immediately bodily character of the use of political violence—advocate for a more encompassing (and empirical) understanding of war, which would include, for instance, the bodily experience of injury and pain (Scarry 2005; Sylvester 2011, 2012a, 2012b),[3] or insist on approaching war in terms of an "embodied social practice" (McSorley 2012, 236). Starting from different methodological paradigms (such as feminism, social constructivism, or phenomenology), several recent works quite explicitly challenge the prevailing tendencies of "war studies" to focus on abstract categories and generalizations, instead postulating explorations of human involvement in, and experience of, war,[4] thus shedding light on its inevitably human character.

An understanding of war as practice, however, should not be limited to the study of the experience of the human bodies involved in it. Instead, such a grounding of these critical investigations enables a conceptualization of war as an event compounding a variety of agential forces and processes. War recruits and combines such complex natural-cultural[5] entities as states, nations, ethnic groups, objects, forces, technologies, strategies, infrastructures, (sexed and raced) human bodies, buildings, (in)securities, acts of violence, ideologies, economies, households, animals, international organizations, NGOs, families, microorganisms, representations, memories, resentments, affects, emotions, and other agents within its deadly assemblages. These dynamic entanglements produce important effects. Thus, keeping this richness in mind, in this book I argue that examination of the sole experience of the human body as involved in, and affected by, political violence of different kinds—even though of tremendous importance for contemporary understandings of the *practice* of war beyond a purely functional approach to political violence—is not enough to fully comprehend the ontologies of war and political violence. Rather, it is necessary to take into account the whole range of more-than-human[6] agents involved in these complex "material-semiotic" (Haraway 1988, 595) events. War is relational, and this is what primarily makes it what it is. Therefore, contemporary political violence has to be thought of as a compound human-nonhuman, as much as an actual-virtual, assemblage. Approaching the current war strategies—as well as their goals and effects—in terms of intricate and dynamic entanglements of material and nonmaterial bodies[7] and forces is what translates into a different perspective of thinking ethically and politically about current instances of state-sponsored violence. This is relevant especially in the context of the emergence of what Mary Kaldor calls "new wars," whose characteristics include "the politics of identity, the decentralization of violence, [and] the globalized war economy" (1999, 138). In such circumstances, war emerges as an amalgam of processes which, on the one hand, remains narrated into a form of knowledge about it, but which, on the other hand, profoundly shapes and sustains this narration as much as it is shaped by it in return. The multifarious and dynamic entanglement of the discursive and the material in the ontology of war is generative, hence likely to produce meaningful, although often unexpected, effects. In its performative ontology, as a material-discursive ensemble produced within a number of agential *apparatuses* and *assemblages*, working through different modalities of agencies and compositions of power, war generates (or annihilates, which is an equally "productive" move) histories, states of affairs, and future im/possibilities. Approaching war in such ethico-onto-epistemological[8] ways fits well within the new materialist philosophical strand, within which—as already signaled in the Introduction—the argumentation offered in this book is positioned.

Situating New Materialism

In the last couple of decades, beginning in the late 1990s, a turn to matter (or a material turn) has been gaining momentum within the social and natural sciences, as well as in the humanities. Neither a violent rupture with the constructivist approaches associated with poststructuralism and discourse theory (its direct "chronological" predecessors in cultural criticism) nor a straightforward return to previous forms of materialism (Coole 2005, 451), this new philosophical tendency nevertheless constitutes a meaningful shift in conceptualizing the relationship between the material and the discursive in the "practices of knowing in being" (Barad 2003, 829). In its attempt at transcending, at least to a certain extent, the thinking linked to the paradigm of the "linguistic turn," new materialism (or neo-materialism), initially inspired mostly by the works of Manuel DeLanda (1996, 2006) and Rosi Braidotti (2000, 2002, 2006), calls for a detailed examination of matter as lively, generative, and processual. This applies to the materiality of human bodies, although it is not limited thereto. Even though this philosophical strand, in Braidotti's words, aims at "[r]ethinking the embodied structure of human subjectivity after Foucault" (2000, 158), new materialist approaches do not restrict the scope of their interests to the exploration of the bodily dimension of humanity, instead encompassing also other material entities, both animate and inanimate. Critical toward the constructivist tendency to privilege language, values, and culture in analyzing broadly understood politics, new materialism nevertheless acknowledges that constructivist insights have made obvious the inability to return to questions of materiality and matter in purely representational or naturalistic ways. In other words, constructivist legacies thrive within the new materialist endeavors devoted to revealing the compound, entangled nature of our world.

In her influential contribution to these ways of thinking, Donna Haraway points to the complex mutual co-constitution of the material and the semiotic, rendering obsolete any thinking in terms of straightforward binary oppositions (1988, 2003). In a similar way, Karen Barad's "agential realism" acknowledges that matter is as active as our interpretative frameworks, arguing that matter and meaning co-form each other (Barad 2003, 2007; more on this will follow). As it can be inferred from the brief references above, new materialism draws heavily on the achievements of social constructivism and often tends to reread many of the seminal poststructuralist *oeuvres*. At the same time, however, it constitutes a challenge to those predominant tendencies of cultural studies, which limit cultural critique to an analysis of the ideological structures of power and meaning. Instead, it prefers to pay more attention to the notion of "matter," typically elided from the dominant Western philosophies, pointing to its metamorphous nature and underlining its agential faculties. Nonconfrontational and monistic in its construction, the new materialist ferment renounces thinking in terms of the dualisms persistent in the humanist tradition, which is manifest in its paying special attention to material processes, making meaning, or *mattering*, possible. Preoccupied with the inherent dynamism of matter and sensitive to the complexity of the phenomena troubling our world at the turn of the millennium, new materialist analyses combine detailed studies of microlevel situations while locating them within the broader macrolevel processes and spaces, looking into the various ways these two are entangled and co-form each other. They also focus on how materializations are inevitably saturated with power relations and how power sustains itself, also through material processes. As DeLanda clarifies,

> to give a complete explanation of a social process taking place at a given scale, we need to elucidate not only the micro-macro mechanisms, those behind the emergence of the whole, but also the macro-micro mechanisms through which the whole provides its component parts with *constraints* and *resources*, placing limitations on what they can do while enabling novel performance.
> (2006, 34; original emphasis)

Pointing to the extensive networks of different actors—including political, material, social, cultural, and discursive entities and forces which are always already entangled—new materialism seems to offer an illuminating perspective from which to approach compound processes populating contemporary politics and cultures.

What makes new materialism potentially attractive for political science is, as Diana Coole (2013) suggests, its nuanced maneuvering between the opposite poles of empirical realism (prevailing in this field of academic inquiry since the end of the Second World War) and the sophisticated criticism of constitutive powers offered by poststructuralism, emerging as part of the turn to what Robert O. Keohane calls "reflectivism" in international relations theory (1988). The clash of these two strands was effectuated as part of the so-called "third debate" running through this field of studies, which mostly focused on the radical epistemological and methodological differences between positivism and a then recently emerged group of approaches that challenged the underlying assumptions of realism, offering instead research strategies embedded in discourse analysis.[9] By no means have these discussions been limited to the academic field of political science or international relations theory; they have permeated the entire branch of the social sciences.

Working from within the domain of critical science and technology studies and inspired by complexity theory and quantum physics, Karen Barad explains that these two paradigms—realism on the one hand and social constructivism on the other—provide us with quite different ways of thinking, both of which are, nonetheless, equally anthropocentric in their respective orientations. The former is centered on the idea of rationality pertaining to the human (autonomous) subject producing knowledge about things that objectively exist in the world and that can be empirically accessed, rationally known, and accurately represented.[10] The latter assumes that the matter of bodies (both human and nonhuman) is an effect of the productive social and cultural field, that is, a result of human activity, ultimately derived from the agency of language (Barad 2007). Accordingly, for social constructivism, matter as such does not matter; what matters instead are the meanings that it conveys. As John Smith and Chris Jenks rightly note, constructivist accounts, in their preoccupation with the cultural, tend to overestimate the effect of human authorship, which often results in recentering, rather than decentering, the human subject as the locus of agency (2005, 147). Unsatisfied with the extant approaches, Barad, subscribing to new materialism's postanthropocentric spirit,[11] calls for "a robust account of the materialization of *all* bodies—'human' and 'nonhuman'—including the agential contributions of all material forces (both 'social' and 'natural')" (2007, 66; original emphasis). She postulates a "nonrepresentational form of realism that is based on an ontology that does not take for granted the existence of 'words' and 'things' and an epistemology that does not subscribe to a notion of truth based on their correct correspondence" (2007, 56). As Barad asserts, *"experimenting and theorizing are dynamic practices that play constitutive role in the production of objects and subjects and matter and meaning"* (2007, 56; original emphasis). This attention to practices, or inquiry into the different relationalities of matter and meaning, is what lets us more comprehensively study their effects and how they are constitutive of the natural-cultural entities. Herein resides the significant potential of new materialist ways of thinking for such academic disciplines as political science or international relations theory, that is, scholarly fields which have traditionally been rather unwilling to accept approaches undermining realist paradigms (and positivist methodologies related to them), but which have become increasingly vulnerable to constructivist critique. In Coole's words, in such a context, new materialism offers an interesting alterative, taking

> an empirical interest in emergent materialisations without being simply empiricist; it does not call for the abandonment of constructivist investigations and critiques of power relations but seeks to contextualise them more broadly; it is not a crude representationalism or uncritical return to some putative immediacy. Rather, it recognises the way concepts and experience, meaning and matter, emerge historically and reciprocally as embodied actors immerse themselves in and engage with/within material and social environments. ... It reopens the real to social scientific inquiry, but without renouncing the critical reflexivity that constructivism insists upon.
> (2013, 455)

Thus, new materialism is a significant correction of (rather than a violent rupture with) social constructivism, constituting a meaningful attempt to transcend the anthropocentric thinking prevalent in Western philosophy from its very inception.[12] In the study of various aspects of politics, typically considered a human domain, it can serve as a tool to shed light on how the human is implicated in, impinged upon, and conditioned by matter. It reveals how bodies, territories, lands, spaces, industries, plants, infrastructures, minerals, animals, microorganisms, technologies, affects, emotions, interpretations, and so on all actively shape and participate in political life and are in turn co-constituted by it. New materialist theorizing explores how the renowned interest in, and detailed account of, materiality and processes of spatio-temporal materializations can reformulate the dominant understandings of what counts as political. It urges us to investigate the *how* question of politics: by what kind of processes politics is effectuated; what kind of effects it generates; what bodies it mobilizes and reshapes; how it engenders the global; and how local practices and experiences are formed, constrained, or produced by macrolevel processes and phenomena; or vice versa—how the local sustains and materializes them. At the same time, it investigates how human encounters with material things produce affects[13] and how these affects move (within) the more-than-human collectives; it reveals the overlaps of different bodies and forces and how they are immersed in material-semiotic contexts, and so on. As a result, as Bruce Braun and Sarah Whatmore rightly assert in their discussion of the content of contemporary politics, it is "no longer possible to imagine either the human as a living being or the collectivities in which we live apart from the more-than-human company that is now so self-evidently integral to what it means to be human and from which collectivities are made" (2010, xvii). Such reformulation of how politics is understood leads to the situation in which, as Diana Coole and Samantha Frost point out, "the sheer materiality and mass of bodies—their numbers, their needs, their fecundity, their productivity, their sustainability and so on—is becoming a key dimension of political analysis and intervention" (2011, 24). No longer is it possible to approach the political actuality according to the logic of either-or. For the proponents of new materialist thinking, society is—and always has been—both materially real and culturally mediated, which makes it possible, in Coole and Frost's words, "to accept social constructionist arguments while also insisting that the material realm is irreducible to culture or discourse and that cultural artifacts are not arbitrary vis-à-vis nature" (2011, 27). Such thinking offers new avenues of scholarly enquiry into the materiality and agency of inclusively understood "things" in politics without resorting to purely realistic onto-epistemological and ethical assumptions.

Agency Undone

What makes new materialism an especially interesting approach in the study of the shifting spatialities and temporalities of political violence and war is its unprecedented focus on the issue of agency, a concept that has for long been located at the core of political science and international relations theory. In both its voluntaristic and fatalistic accounts, in the study of politics, agency is thought of as pertaining to individual subjects (or states). Such thinking is based on the assumption that only rational entities can act in agential ways and assumes that agency has to be understood as intentional (cf. Latour 2005). Even though this conceptualization has, since the second half of the twentieth century, been experiencing a profound crisis as a result of extensive criticism from thinkers associated with postmodernism, feminism, deconstructionism, and constructivism,[14] it has remained central to the traditional renditions of both domestic and international politics. The danger of this critical situation generated by the "third debate" within the international relations theory, as Coole diagnoses, is that it could potentially lead to a radical reappraisal of the concept of agency in the form of either "individualistic and voluntaristic," or its metamorphosis into an "eviscerated" notion rendering politics "trivial" and "lacking transformative means" (2005, 127). A novel notion of agency is therefore necessary to sustain the politically motivated belief in the transformative qualities of politics. Such thinking remains in line with new materialist formulations and this philosophical approach's necessarily political character. As Felicity Colman cogently explains, even though there is no single definition of the notion of "agency" within the diverse ways of new materialist thinking, a common-sense understanding of it transpires. Agency emerges as referring to "the relationality of the political cultural position that and by which matter and things are defined, distributed, and organized—by their relationality to other matter and things; and which do not have a pre-existing ontology" (Colman 2018, n.p.). Overall, new materialism seeks to reposition the human among other actants, although the propositions of the theorists and philosophers associated with this strand greatly differ from each other. In the remainder of this section, I offer a brief overview of those conceptualizations that have stirred a great deal of discussion and inspired interesting applications.

In a rather moderate spirit, Coole proposes to replace the traditional notion of agency in political science and international relations theory with that of "agentic capacities" and urges us to recognize their "irremediably embodied," as much as singular and situated, nature (2005, 2013). In such an account, "agentic properties emerge and interact across the agentic spectrum" (Coole 2005, 128) and endure within a corporeal experience rather than pertaining to the transcendental subject. Agency remains in the process as an effect of constant, intensive, perceptual, and culturally mediated relations and entanglements with the world. It emerges as "provisional concentrations of agentic capacities that acquire more or less coherence and duration, depending upon their context," which "can only be grasped as moments within the whole spectrum of agentic properties" (Coole 2005, 135). Bound to located corporeal and collective practice, agency "is a capacity immanent in the social field" (Coole 2005, 138) or the intersubjective.

Coole's initial account—heavily influenced by the phenomenological philosophy of Maurice Merleau-Ponty—focuses on the agentic capacities distributed across animate (or rather human) entities. In her later work (2013), however, she pays increasingly more attention to inhuman agents and forces and how they generatively assemble with the human, even though she decides to retain most of her earlier formulations.

In a far more radical way than Coole, Jane Bennett talks about the agential materiality of "thing-power," signaling the possibility that "attentiveness to (nonhuman) things and their powers can have a laudable effect on humans" (2004, 348). Nevertheless, as Bennett underlines in Spinozist fashion, "a thing has power by virtue of its operating *in conjunction* with other things," meaning that "thing-power, as a kind of agency, *is the property of an assemblage*" (2004, 354; original emphasis); thus its ontology resides in its relational character. In *Vibrant Matter* (2010), Bennett's preoccupation with things (but not disinterest in humans!) leads her to argue that nonhuman matter is imbued with a liveliness exhibiting distributed agency which can no longer be understood as an effect of intentionality. Similarly, insisting on agency's more-than-human character, Barad underlines that it cannot be understood as "something that someone or something has" (2007, 235) but as "enactment" (2007, 214). Starting from the philosophy of science, Barad openly contests the human-centered concept of agency and explains that material-discursive entanglements (or "intra-actions," as she prefers) entail complex coproductions of more-than-human matter, time, and spaces, as well as their various context-specific significations. This is far removed from traditional conceptualizations according to which the human acts on matter. Instead, all entities are thought of as agential actors/actants in the world as they continuously (materially-discursively, spatially-temporarily) come into being (Barad 2007). Physical matter and social reality are co-constitutive since—rather than being seen as ontologically different from each other—each plays an agentic role in the other's constant becoming. In Serpil Oppermann's words, such an approach transforms "the language of otherness to that of differential co-emergence" (2013, 67), as nothing seems to be ontologically autonomous. As Sofie Sauzet explains, this theoretical move enables thinking that agency is manifest in different forms "as relations, movements, repetitions, silences, distances, architecture, structures, feelings, things, us/them/it, words" (2018, n.p.). Employing the more-than-human notion of agency, Bennett's and Barad's respective theories nevertheless reveal that new materialist accounts of the actual should not be read as a lack of interest in the human. Rather, new materialism reformulates the ontological assumptions linked to humanism, pointing to the extensive relationalities and assemblages extending far beyond the human.

New materialist philosophy radically displaces anthropocentrism and humanism, two traditional planes on which the concept of agency developed and from where—especially in the context of political science and international relations theory—it was then projected onto other entities, such as classes or states, serving as invented avatars of human cognitive faculties, rationality, and self-consciousness.[15] Thus, it is necessary to reorganize these taken-for-granted trajectories of thinking. As Coole lucidly elaborates, "it is not that agency has conventionally been defined as a property unique to humans; inversely, the characteristics that have traditionally been held to define humans and to render them a distinctive and privileged species have been used to define the characteristics of agency" (2013, 457). The brute, inert, and non-reflexive material sphere, lacking agency and power, has served as a meaningful "other," or foil, to the figure of the rational subject, against which he could come into its transcendental being. Disavowing such human-centric framing of agency and replacing it with a language of "agentic capacities" distributed across a whole diversity of material bodies is what, Coole explains, allows us to "decouple agency from humans while raising questions about the nature of life and of the place or status of the human within it" (2013, 457). Such a conceptualization urges us to think about the capacity for agency as contingent on particular configurations of material-discursive forces, which are nevertheless dynamic and changeable. So even though new materialist analyses might well result in the identification of capacious agents similar to those offered by conventional accounts, as Coole notes, "their emergence has to be traced and not presumed, which will likely result in their capabilities for agency being recognised as more partial, contextual and provisional" (2013, 458).

While Coole insists that it is necessary to keep reflexivity (and, perhaps, also responsibility[16]) as a defining attribute of agentic capacities for ensuring that such a theoretical project will remain capable of inspiring political change, many other new materialist thinkers (such as Bruno Latour, Karen Barad, Donna Haraway, or Jane Bennett) propose, as mentioned earlier, to further flatten these ontologies and consider agency as pertaining to the relationality of animate and inanimate, or reflexive and non-reflexive, bodies. What has to be kept in mind is that—regardless of its various theoretical renditions—within new materialism, agency is always posited as political, that is, as Colman reminds us, "not just as a methodological critical tool that acknowledges its own self-telling or performing, but as an ethical modality by and with which practitioners can be attendant to the political generated by the entanglement of matter" (2018, n.p.). This turns agency into a concept that is vital not only for studying the complex, relational ontologies of the contemporary political world, but also a tool of meaningful intervention in the struggle for broadly defined equality and justice.

Political Violence Through a New Materialist Lens

The "material turn" within political science and international relations theory, as explained earlier, has been part and parcel of the broader critique of anthropocentrism across the humanities and the social sciences. Within the area of the study of politics (understood both domestically and internationally), the various theoretical endeavors of the proponents of new materialist thinking have aimed at unmasking the inability (and reluctance) of the existing epistemic frameworks to fully account for the more-than-human forms of agency and their various contributions to the making of *the political*. In line with the dominant approaches in political science, political violence—a recurring theme of this book—is usually defined in instrumental terms as a deliberate use of force to achieve political goals. It refers to state-sponsored violence against other states, non-state actors (guerillas, activist groups, and organizations), and its populations and citizens. The concept can also be employed in reference to the means used by the non-state actors against the state. Acts of political violence comprise physical and psychosocial measures of intimidating, or injuring, the targeted populations with an aim to coerce them into a desired behavior. The range of strategies used for this purpose is wide and encompasses such violent means as bombardments, shellings, shootings, arrests, torture, detention, dispossession, and demolition of property, as much as the denial of human rights and basic needs; restriction (or denial) of access to food, education, healthcare, and sanitation; or limitation of the freedom of speech. Perhaps, given the anthropocentric bias of the disciplines within which *the political* has been primarily conceptually located, it should come as no surprise that the study of politics in general, and of political violence in particular, has typically been—at least declaratively—humancentric. Traditionally, the domain of politics has been perceived as embracing human interactions, a milieu in which human institutions operate, and a field preoccupied with the fate of human collectivities (nations, states, the international community, etc.). The turn to matter, however, explicitly addresses the urgent need to resituate the debates on *the political* within the broader processes of materialization, encouraging interest in, and recognition of, the embeddedness of politics in networks of more-than-human relations and forces. It urges us to acknowledge that broadly understood things, or bodies, play an equally agential role in the processes of *becoming* of politics as cultural and social discourses do and that these meaningful contributions have to be taken into consideration if we want to truly account for the complexities of contemporary political processes, including the unfolding of political violence. New materialist thinking can prove to be helpful in approaching these dynamic enactments.[17]

Politically oriented, new materialism critically engages with the *how* question of political violence (and the *how* question of war), positioning it as a complex relationality of material-discursive *practices* which generate meaningful and situated effects. This may be understood in reference to Michel Foucault's notion of a *dispositif* (interpreted through new materialist critique), that is, an apparatus defined in terms of a thoroughly heterogeneous ensemble consisting of discourses, institutions, architectural forms, regulatory decisions, laws, administrative measures, scientific statements, philosophical, moral and philanthropic propositions—in short, the said as much as the unsaid. Such are the elements of the apparatus. The apparatus itself is the system of relations that can be established between these elements.

(1980, 94)

As Mirko Nicolić notes, Barad turns the Foucauldian notion of apparatus into the group of performative material-semiotic processes of inclusions and exclusions (2018, n.p.), situating them as "boundary-drawing practices" (Barad 2007, 140) or "the material conditions of possibility and impossibility of mattering; they enact what matters and what is excluded from mattering" (Barad 2007, 148). In the study of political violence, not only does such an approach center on what means are employed, where, and against whom, or how efficient they are (these pertain to the domain of strategic studies); it also explores the complex networks of more-than-human agents and forces which constitute the experiential *content* of political violence, investigating how decisions to use political violence come into being in specific material-semiotic and spatio-temporal contexts, how violence operates with and on particular bodies, which natural-cultural agents it mobilizes, and what kind of effects it generates in particular parts of the world. Such a perspective acknowledges the inevitable entanglement of knowing in being and acting, testifying to the "ethico-onto-epistemological" character of violence as well as—in Barad's idiom—its "spacetimemattering" (Barad 2007, 2011, 2014), that is, the complex becoming of the ensemble of space, time, and matter which is productive of meaningful reconfigurations of the world. The performative, relational ontology of political violence—in contradistinction to linguistic understandings of performativity—incorporates the material and discursive, social and scientific, natural and cultural, animate and inanimate, human and nonhuman factors and forces, where agency emerges as a quality of the assemblage rather than pertaining to the entities preexisting the relations. It is, in Kathrin Thiele's account, an ontological proposition "in which individualized things and objects are no longer presupposed as simply 'there,' in which even the world itself is not simply 'given' and 'out there,' but in which everything is accounted for as an enactment of the *entangled* nature of nature" (2016, n.p.; original emphasis). Thus, from such a philosophical perspective, it is necessary to consider the multiscale and multitemporal character of violence in order to truly account for its complex and multidimensional *becoming*. In the following I offer a limited, but hopefully informative, sample of such thinking and how relevant and generative it can turn out to be in the context of analysis of war and violence.

New materialist investigations interrogate how political violence emerges as a dynamic assemblage of different agents and forces operating at diverse scales and how it generates meaningful material reconfigurations of the world, locally and globally. In such an account, things and discourses alike actively condition acts of violence; for instance, they participate in the complex processes of materializing the targets of political intervention through the use of rhetorical means as much as the agential involvement of things, such as surveillance- and combat-enabled population-centered unmanned systems, operated remotely from the allegedly safe space of military bases located in sites geographically distant from those inhabited by the targeted populations.[18] The target (hence, an object) becomes "knowable" because of the complex visualizing and mapping technology that contributes to its materialization as something with provisional boundaries as much as a "thing" locatable in space.[19] The material operation of the technology employed for this purpose is not given but rather constituted by a series of other practices: legal, scientific, technological, educational, spatial, military, architectural, political, ideological, and so on. Hence, materialization (and often—subsequent criminalization) of the target takes place at the intersection of different forms of knowledges and practices, which reconfigures the world by drawing boundaries between what matters (and how) and what does not. This is intimately entwined with power relations. For instance, the use of such a system is certainly conditioned by the speech acts contributing to the construction of the potential "national threat," or definitions of "threatening behaviors" as much as "dangerous objects," mobilizing affects (such as fear) and stimulating actions (such as a willingness to become bodily involved in combat). Such emotional (that is, connected to affects already qualified in language[20]) associations are often related to the fact, or feeling, of belonging to a certain ethnic community and possibly translate into loyal affiliations being at the roots of a readiness to participate in violent, often deadly, interactions with "threatening others."

The discursive construction of a threat, however, is premised on the material "evidence," coproduced by advanced surveillance systems which actively sustain the boundary-making discourses and legitimize political intervention (or brutal aggression), enabling, for instance, the conducting of what is called a "shadow war."[21] These technologies—combining, for instance, the hardware of the drone with the software enabling its remote operation, with a number of other material devices supporting the processing of data (producing, for example, detailed digital visualizations) and immersive interaction with the persuasive screened material[22]—actively contribute to the materialization of targeted violence and effectuate the spatial materialization of "the target" in the first place. This is heavily shaped by political and ideological moves, such as—for example—transnational discourses on terrorism (especially, but not exclusively, in the aftermath of 9/11, or in the context of the persistent Israeli military involvement in Palestine and the politics of resistance practiced by the Palestinians), identified "threats" to "national security," and the justification of the "necessity" of undertaking counterinsurgency actions[23] to "prevent" the escalation of aggression. Such framing facilitates the turning of an act of political violence into a right and legitimate action, often carried out on behalf of the "nation." The targeted killing or targeted destruction (both extremely material), in such an account, emerges as a securitization move and materializes as a necessary policy which might, nevertheless, produce certain troubling side effects (or "collateral damage," if you will). Thus, this complex material-semiotic process, taking place simultaneously at different scales and mobilizing diverse technologies and forces, adds to the criminalization of specific bodies, communities, or spatial areas, serving as a justification for state-sponsored actions undertaken against them, thus gradually contributing to the materialization of new forms of territorially organized power.

The critical mass of spatially located material acts of political violence steadily reshapes the demography of the region (this reconfiguration can be seen in terms of ethnic cleansing or genocide, or—in the case of the Israeli politics in Palestine—in terms of Judaization or de-Arabization of the particular geographical areas). It reconfigures the targeted infrastructure, sometimes resulting in an almost complete erasure of the functional built environment, substantially affecting the material conditions of the living (and dying) of the affected communities or forcing their relocation. It may also disrupt the inherent spatio-temporal morphology of a community, understood as a group of people, which—together with a bulk of more-than-human bodies—share a common materially-socially, or historically-geographically, constructed space. Whereas, in cases of politically motivated targeted killing or targeted destruction, the spatially-removed operator of the drone might suffer from posttraumatic stress disorder triggered by visceral participation in combat enabled by advanced visualization technologies,[24] and the targeted individuals are annihilated, seriously injured, or captured, the aerial systems of surveillance and destruction (together with other technologies of war) are subsequently commodified (and marketized as "tested in combat") within the global capitalist system, and materialize as products facilitating securitization of critical infrastructures of Western cities and their well-off inhabitants.[25] At the same time, the forcibly relocated (or expelled) people, displaced and traumatized by the experience of injury, personal loss, and dispossession, while moving through the space, suddenly materialize as a challenge, or another "threat," for the host space (of another state) in which they arrive when fleeing violence and destruction, often engaging with different practices of resistance and survival (battling with natural-cultural forces), which are not always successful. What kind of traces do these difficult journeys leave on the bodily-intellectual archives of memory, and how do these different material-semiotic experiences translate into national-scale political agendas or grassroots activism?

New materialism is interested in the role natural forces play in these struggles and in how their agencies are often mobilized for political projects. How do the spatial performances of the migrants affect, and how are they in return affected by, the cultural representations of otherness related to raced, sexed, classed, and so on bodies present in particular geopolitical and sociocultural contexts, or territories, and what kind of effects do these entanglements generate for both these particular spaces and these particular bodies? In this way, by paying attention to the processes of spatio-temporal materialization, new materialism does not discount social constructions of gender and their intersections with class and race. It is vitally interested in considering how material bodies, spaces, and conditions contribute to the formation of subjectivity and its various situated performances.

Physical bodies and how they move through the world inform the experiences of these bodies (and others) as much as they feed the ideological structures of language and culture, or the whole representational realm, equally constitutive of bodies and their experiences. In its non-essentializing approach to "matter" of the body, new materialism assumes that identities and differences are products of complex interactions between matter inside and outside bodies, and between the social, environmental, and spatial conditions in which bodies (are forced to) exist, also as an effect of political violence. What kind of boundaries do such material-semiotic ensembles produce? And how do they affect understandings of national security as frequently premised on the bodily insecurity of the irregular migrants or *sans papiers*? How does the move toward securitization transform into the insecuritization of those who are perceived as a "threat"?[26] How does the vulnerable status of the latter translate into official legal regulations and interventional territorializing policies (such as, for instance, the demolition of camps,[27] ghettoization, or the walling-off of areas inhabited by members of particular groups)? What kind of memory politics do such bodily performances mobilize and enact? The absences that political violence generates—the ruined buildings and infrastructures, devastated environments, massacred people, eradicated traditions—become equally agential. These absences generate effects by shaping the interpretations of the existing material remains, as well as of the violent contexts which have produced them. This mobilizes other affects and intensities with a potential to be translated into political action, although of a different kind. What kind of challenges do the attempts at documenting political violence create? What does, in this context, high-resolution satellite picturing enable (and how)? And whose interests might it serve? And what does it obscure by, for instance, functioning within the legal regulations of particular states regarding the resolution of satellite imagining available to potential buyers,[28] functioning within a (highly militarized and politicized) capitalist market? Such questions could obviously be multiplied, exposing the complex entanglements of different geographical, economic, social, and cultural contexts co-constituted by, and co-constitutive of, the particular event of political violence and its meaningful effects.

By no means is this narrative meant to be exhaustive. Its purpose is to point to the deep connectedness of different processes and forces, the intense, multiscale, entangled circulations of things and significations, which produce meaningful materializations, or "spacetimematterings," within *the political*. Even though it seems to be only remotely related to the specific geopolitically located issues explored in this book, it nevertheless exposes the ways in which human bodies—especially those affected by political violence—are entangled with both the material landscapes in which they are placed and the far more reaching discourses and knowledges, as well as technological instruments and understandings, generated within or through them. It also reveals the complex, multiscale character of political violence and how it is embedded in a number of accompanying material-semiotic practices and apparatuses rather than being an isolated force operating in its own right (more on this will follow in Chapter 2). Such an encompassing and tangled understanding of the eventful nature of politics, which new materialist ways of thinking enable, sparks new ways of "understanding political matters and the matter of politics" (Braun and Whatmore 2010, xii). It also encourages a constant rescaling of the analysis, from the localized perspective of selected communities or individuals to global processes and transnational circuits or environmental transformations, while paying attention to the complex interweaving of the natural and the cultural, or the material and the semiotic, in the always situated processes of consolidation of political realities.

Not only does such an account of political violence go beyond the traditional "flat discourse" (Weizman 2002) of geopolitics, but it also infuses with vitality the extant approaches to the politization of space, exposing the knotted nature of spatial processes. Obviously, interest in these issues is not a new occurrence in the scholarship exploring contemporary forms of warfare and political control, and several theoretical perspectives have already gained currency in the field. Based on the analysis of the spatio-political developments in Israel/Palestine, Weizman (2002, 2007) and Graham (2004a, 2010, 2016) pioneer in offering elaborations of "verticality" as a crucial dimension for understanding the current forms of militarism. Detailed examinations of what is placed above and below the "territory" may, according to verticality discourse, serve the purpose of explaining the geographies of injustice produced *on the surface*. Broadening these investigations, Stuart Elden proposes to focus on "volume," which for him is a shift showcasing "a new level of vulnerability ... of a protected territory, the body of the state" (2009, xxii). So, while the vertical approach (Weizman 2002, 2007; Graham 2004a, 2004b, 2010, 2016; Graham and Hewitt 2013) tends to look at the territory from a predominantly aerial perspective, the interest in its volumetric qualities (Crampton 2010; Elden 2009,

2010, 2013, 2017, 2021; Billé 2018, 2019, 2020; Hawkins 2019) enables a more thorough, and perhaps also a more encompassing, analysis of what happens within the (imagined) body of a state. Such a reconfiguration of thinking also implies a transition from conceptualizing the state's territory in terms of a bounded space controlled by a certain authority to thinking in terms of the state's three-dimensional material terrain with specific metric qualities. As Elden explains, such a reorientation allows for examination of "the political materiality of the territory, and its complexities" (2021, 170), paying attention to how space motivates, aggravates, or is mobilized as a tool of political violence.

As already signaled in the Introduction to this book, vertical and volumetric accounts are typically critiqued for adopting a rather "technical gaze" (Adey 2013) or a disinterested "god-trick" (Haraway 1988) perspective, while avoiding a more situated engagement with the virtues and potentials of the examined space and how it shapes, and is impinged upon, the political processes. Neither do they attempt at theorizing the agential faculties of the vertical/volumetric space, paying minimal attention to its inherent dynamics and ignoring the natural forces co-constituting its constant becoming. As I aim to demonstrate in this book, new materialist ways of thinking, in such a context, can substantially contribute to invigorating the otherwise static and disengaged perspectives offered by vertical and volumetric accounts of political violence (or securitization strategies), opening new conceptual paths for a more nuanced and situated analysis of political processes. While keeping within the bound of interrogating "the relation between the geophysical and the geopolitical" (Elden 2017, 207), new materialism's preoccupation with the agential nature of more-than-human assemblages allows for a conceptualization of the violent developments enabled by tangled, conjunctive operations of geophysical agents (the natural forces present on site, the climate, the resources, the local ecosystems, the topography, etc.) and the human-induced phenomena (pollution, urbanization, toxicity, excavation activities, agriculture and planting, etc.). Given the fact that most of these processes unfold at a rather slow pace, they may well remain unnoticed (and untheorized) in the prevailing analyses of political violence, seemingly operating at the margins of more spectacular events and attention-drawing occurrences. In such circumstances, they may also be deliberately "objectified" in the discourse of both domestic and international politics as happening to a large extent beyond the immediate agency of the state (or international community). Such framing contributes to obfuscating the intentional, indeed state-induced, character of many destructive developments recruited for the purpose of sustaining specific forms of territoriality. Thus, in order to fully understand the tacit operations of certain types of political violence, it is necessary, as Lorraine Dowler and Jo Sharp argue, to ground the "geopolitical discourse in practice (and in place)—to link international representation to the geographies of everyday life" (2001, 171), and to remain attentive, in a truly new materialist spirit, "to the ways in which the material is both shaped and placed by the representational, while at the same time shaping and placing it" (Sharp 2021, 991). New materialist thinking seems to offer adequate conceptual tools for such a nuanced analysis.

Pluralization of the notion of agency beyond its traditional humancentric renditions and exploration of how agency is distributed across and enacted through an assemblage (Dittmer 2014, 388) draw attention to how space conditions "things" and "processes" that happen within it and how it itself constantly reemerges from these complex agential constellations. New materialism urges us to transcend thinking of space as a passive container for politics, encouraging its conceptual interpretation in dynamic, relational ways. This philosophical position invites attentive interrogation of the materialities and geophysicalities of the space (Steinberg and Peters 2015), exposing, as Elaine Campbell explains, its "processual rather than formed" and "hybridized" character, which is "contingently constituted and constitutive of bodies, texts, practices, affects, discourses, and materialities" (2019, 19). Space, when understood as metamorphous and agential, becomes "a relational emergent configuration of different elements which is always-already-in-the-making" (Campbell 2019, 18), while its transformations are enabled by "the contingent, creative, dynamic and unpredictable interplay of multiple trajectories of power" (Campbell 2019, 19). Such a perspective sheds an altogether different light on the extant vertical and volumetric analyses of space's participation in political processes, thus broadening the understanding of the ways in which different "things" and their agencies participate in, or are intentionally brought into, *the political*.

Along with the ideas of the thinkers presented earlier in this chapter, in this book I aim to demonstrate that a new materialist study of political violence in general, and slow urbicide in particular, can serve as an illuminating trope to reveal the quintessentially material-semiotic character of *the political*. It also intends to dislocate the predominant instrumental understandings of violence as solely embedded in the causal logic of atomic realism. Rather, it postulates focusing on the manifold material-semiotic *practices* of violence, and on all the entangled processes which co-constitute violence, temporarily and spatially, paying attention to the kind of effects they generate in the world in its differing scales and contexts. The case of Palestinian spatiality discussed in this book is exceptionally telling in this regard, as—for the purpose of implementation of its colonial policy—the Israeli state seems not only to master the topographical knowledge of the region and its inherent volumes and agencies, recruiting them for the achievement of political goals; it also succeeds in constructing a representational logic which effectively occludes the violent developments that the state deliberately orchestrates. The realization of a slow-motion colonial strategy, partly relying on the development of specific infrastructure on the one hand and mobilization of context-specific agencies on the other, generates important—albeit delayed—effects for the Palestinians inhabiting the targeted regions, gradually exacerbating their living conditions and steadily estranging the indigenous population from its land. Interrogation of the *how* question of the political violence in Palestine, as much as accounting for its shifting temporalities, can thus be interpreted as an informed effort at countering the intentional politics of occlusion, revealing the systematic state-sponsored investment in the meaningful reconfigurations of Palestinian spatiality.

Concluding this chapter, it is worth underlining that, in its insightful investigations of the complex circulations and entanglements of bodies and meanings stemming from committed feminist theorizing, new materialism's orientation remains openly political. In Coole's words, it is meant to constitute a "political-ethical intervention" (2013, 452) and aims to produce and operationalize a politically engaged social theory, focusing on the actual conditions of existence, positioning them in complex material-semiotic and spatio-temporal contexts, and revealing their inherent injustices and inequalities. As Thiele notes, the ethics of mattering expressed in Barad's engaged conceptualization, which is explicitly inspired by feminist theories and politics, has to be seen as *"an ethics that aims at disrupting indifference"* (2016, n.p.; original emphasis). No longer, in such an account, can political theory ignore the bodies/things/forces and how they are situated within, and co-constituted by, the material-semiotic spaces which they share with other bodies/things/forces. And no longer is it possible to disregard how they are immersed in and formed by, as well as how they participate in sustaining, socioeconomic and political structures. These broader contexts often shape their needs and prescribe how (or whether) these needs can be attended to or their desires satisfied; they also structure the ways in which the resources facilitating participation in political life, or resistance thereto, can be obtained and effectively used. As such, within these ways of thinking, increased attention is paid to the concept of agency, as it also refers us—in Barad's words—to the "possibilities of worldly re-configurings" (2012, 55).

Notes

1 For discussion of the domination of the Newtonian paradigm within international relations theory, see Kavalski (2012, 2015).
2 This last question is, at least to a limited extent, debated by strategic studies but only inasmuch the employed actions and resources can effectively contribute to the accomplishment of the defined goals. The *how* here refers to the practical aspects of war, that is, how it is empirically fought and how it mobilizes resources and forces.
3 For the issue of bodily experience in/of war, see Brighton (2011).
4 An elaborate discussion of the bodily experience of war can be found in Fierke (2004), Shapiro (2011), Monaghan (2012), and Skjelsbaek (2012).

5 This expression derives from the concept of "natureculture" coined by Haraway (2003).
6 The concept of "more-than-human" implies excess rather than any kind of hierarchy.
7 This understanding of the notion of the body relies on Gilles Deleuze's definition, according to which "a body can be anything; it can be an animal, a body of sounds, a mind, or idea; it can be a linguistic corpus, a social body, a collectivity" (1988, 127). They all have some sort of material existence. As such, the body is defined in dynamic terms, through its potentials, so—again—in reference to what it *can do* or what it can *become* rather than, statically, to what it *is*. This approach does not privilege any specific bodies (e.g., human). Instead, it argues that all bodies evince certain capacities and agencies to enter into affective relations with others.
8 The term "ethico-onto-epistemological," as proposed by Barad (2007), is meant to signal the recognition of the intricate relations between and contingence of ethics, ontologies, and epistemologies, which cannot be thought of in isolation from each other.
9 The term "discourse analysis" in political science and international relations theory is far from unambiguous, as it encompasses a number of approaches and research strategies. A comprehensive overview of this broad strand of theorizing, although limited to the understanding of discourse in rather narrow linguistic terms (i.e., not including visuals, for instance), is offered in Milliken (1999). A more inclusive notion of discourse, as constituted not only by text but also visual materials, is offered by, for instance, Campbell (2003) and Hansen (2011a, 2011b).
10 For a realist operationalization of such onto-epistemological assumptions, see Mearsheimer (1995).
11 It is worth noting here that even though Barad's works have been exceptionally influential for the theorists and philosophers working within the strand of new materialism, she never uses the label of "new materialism" in reference to her own work.
12 For an interesting discussion on the establishing of the divide between the human and the nonhuman in ancient philosophy, see Basnett (2018).
13 See, for instance, Bennet (2004).
14 This criticism focused on the deconstruction of individual subjectivity, offering instead antiessentialist theories of identity, undermining the inherent autonomy of the subject of power (or knowledge), popularizing understandings of subjectification as tantamount to subjection (as demonstrated by Foucault [1975]), pointing to the nature of subjectivity as a constant, reiterative performance of ideological constructions (as explained by Butler [2011]), or challenging the teleological character of history.
15 It is worth noting that these characteristics, as exposed by feminist philosophers, have in Western culture been typically used to define the concept of "masculinity."
16 I am not discussing this aspect of Coole's new materialist thinking in this book as, in her conceptualization, it mostly refers to the environmental crisis and humans' complicity in it. Even though this is the issue currently hotly debated upon within the field of political science and international relations theory, I leave it unexplored here, as it falls beyond the scope of the argumentation offered in this book.
17 For some elaboration of new materialist ways of thinking in international relations theory, see Aradau (2010), Barry (2013), Cudworth and Hobden (2013), Lundborg and Vaughan-Williams (2015), Vaughan-Williams (2015a, 2015b), and Marlin-Bennett (2013).

18 For analysis of the "drone-wars" and a "networked" organization of war, see, for instance, Duffield (2002), MacGinty (2010), Singer (2009), Turse (2012), Arquilla and Ronfeldt (2001), and Plaw and Fricker (2012).
19 Compelling analyses of the visualization in contemporary warfare was offered by Gregory (2010), Niva (2013), Bousquet (2009), and Denes (2010).
20 For the discussion of the "workings" of affects and emotions, see the insightful analysis offered by Massumi (2002).
21 These instruments, as Holmqvist (2013) suggests, include targeted killings of individuals in secret operations as well as the use of population-centered combat-enabled unmanned aerial weapon systems (drones). Holmqvist offers a phenomenological, thus materialist, analysis of the use of drones in contemporary warfare, arguing that this kind of reading should take into consideration aspects such as the immersive capacities of the screen used by the remote drone operators and the vehicle's ability to capture surveillance images of "objects of war," as well as its capacity for dropping bombs. On the other hand, Holmqvist writes about human-material assemblages, which I consider as contradicting, to a certain extent, (new) materialist thinking, especially as regards her understanding of human as opposite to material. In this book I approach both the human and the inhuman as complex "material-discursive" (Barad 2003, 2007) entities.
22 See, for instance, Holmqvist (2013).
23 For elaboration of contemporary counterinsurgency, see, for example, Ucko (2009).
24 The discussion of traumatic experiences of the remote drone operators is offered by Shaw and Akhter (2011).
25 For discussion of the marketization of warfare systems, see Graham (2003).
26 The issue of the highly vulnerable status of refugees has been elaborated upon by Freedman (2018a, 2018b) and Huysmans (2006). The politics of "managing" migration are discussed by, among others, Long (2013), Lutterbeck (2006), Neal (2009), and Vaughan-Williams (2015a, 2015b).
27 One such vaughan is the French-British policy toward the so-called "Calais Jungle." Detailed analyses of the life and death of the camp have been produced by Ibrahim and Howarth (2018) and Djigo (2016).
28 An interesting discussion of the intersection of technologies of satellite imagining, geopolitics, neoliberal, and legal discourses is offered by Weizman (2017).

Bibliography

Adey, Peter. 2013. "Securing the Volume/Volumen: Comments on Stuart Elden's Plenary Paper 'Secure the Volume.'" *Political Geography* 34: 52–54. https://doi.org/0.1016/j.polgeo.2013.01.003.

Aradau, Claudia. 2010. "Security That Matters: Critical Infrastructure and Objects of Protection." *Security Dialogue* 41, no. 5: 491–514. https://doi.org/10.1177/0967010610382687.

Arquilla, John, and David Ronfeldt. 2001. *Networks and Netwars: The Future of Terror, Crime and Militancy*. Santa Monica: RAND.

Barad, Karen. 2003. "Posthumanist Performativity: Toward an Understanding of How Matter Comes to Matter." *Signs: Journal of Women in Culture and Society* 28, no. 3: 801–831. https://doi.org/10.1086/345321.

———. 2007. *Meeting the Universe Halfway: Quantum Physics and the Entanglement of Matter and Meaning*. Durham: Duke University Press.

———. 2011. "Nature's Queer Performativity." *Qui Parle: Critical Humanities and Social Sciences* 19, no. 2: 121–158. https://doi.org/10.5250/quiparle.19.2.0121.

———. 2012. "Interview with Karen Barad." In *New Materialism: Interviews & Cartographies*, edited by Iris van der Tuin and Rick Dolphijn, 48–70. Ann Arbor: Open Humanities Press.

———. 2014. "Diffracting Diffraction: Cutting Together-Apart." *Parallax* 20, no. 3: 168–187. https://doi.org/10.1080/13534645.2014.927623.

Barkawi, Tarak, and Shane Brighton. 2011a. "Absent War Studies: War, Knowledge and Critique." In *The Changing Character of War*, edited by Hew Strachan and Sibylle Scheipers, 524–541. Oxford: Oxford University Press.

———. 2011b. "Powers of War: Fighting, Knowledge, and Critique." *International Political Sociology* 5: 126–143. https://doi.org/10.1111/j.1749-5687.2011.00125.x.

Barry, Andrew. 2013. "The Translation Zone: Between Actor-Network Theory and International Relations." *Millennium: Journal of International Studies* 41, no. 3: 413–429. https://doi.org/10.1177/0305829813481007.

Basnett, Caleb J. 2018. "Animals and Human Constitution: Greek Lessons, Posthuman Possibilities." In *Posthuman Dialogues in International Relations*, edited by Erika Cudworth, Stephen Hobden, and Emilian Kavalski, 15–30. London and New York: Routledge.

Bennet, Jane. 2004. "The Force of Things: Steps Towards an Ecology of Matter." *Political Theory* 32, no. 3: 347–372.

———. 2010. *Vibrant Matter: A Political Ecology of Things*. Durham and London: Duke University Press. https://doi.org/10.1177/0090591703260853.

Billé, Franck, ed. 2018. "Speaking Volumes. Cultural Anthropology." Available at: https://culanth.org/fieldsights/series/speaking-volumes. Accessed 7 March 2022.

———, ed. 2019. "Volumetric Sovereignty. Society and Space." Available at: http://societyandspace.org/2019/03/04/volumetric-sovereignty-part-1-cartography-vsvolumes/. Accessed 7 March 2022.

———, ed. 2020. *Voluminous States: Sovereignty, Materiality, and the Territorial Imagination*. Durham: Duke University Press.

Bousquet, Antoine J. 2009. *The Scientific Way of Warfare: Order and Chaos on the Battlefields of Modernity*. New York: Columbia University Press.

Braidotti, Rosi. 2000. "Teratologies." In *Deleuze and Feminist Theory*, edited by Ian Buchanan and Claire Colebrook, 156–172. Edinburgh: Edinburgh University Press.

———. 2002. *Metamorphoses: Towards a Materialist Theory of Becoming*. Cambridge: Polity Press.

———. 2006. *Transpositions: On Nomadic Ethics*. Cambridge: Polity Press.

Braun, Bruce, and Sarah Whatmore. 2010. "The Stuff of Politics: An Introduction." In *Political Matter: Technoscience, Democracy, and Public Life*, edited by Bruce Braun and Sarah Whatmore, ix–xl. Minneapolis and London: University of Minnesota Press.

Brighton, Shane. 2011. "Three Propositions on the Phenomenology of War." *International Political Sociology* 5, no. 1: 101–105. https://doi.org/10.1111/j.1749-5687.2011.00122_6.x.

Butler, Judith. 2011. *Bodies That Matter: On the Discursive Limits of Sex*. London and New York: Routledge.

Campbell, David. 2003. "Cultural Governance and Pictorial Resistance: Reflections on the Imaging of War." *Review of International Studies* 29, no. 1: 57–73. https://doi.org/10.1017/S0260210503005977.

Campbell, Elaine. 2019. "Three-dimensional Security: Layers, Spheres, Volumes, Milieus." *Political Geography* 69: 10–21. https://doi.org/10.1016/j.polgeo.2018.11.010.

Clausewitz, Carl von. 1976. *On War*. Princeton: Princeton University Press.

Colman, Felicity. 2018. "Agency." In *New Materialism Almanac*, edited by David Gauthier and Sam Skinner. Available at: https://newmaterialism.eu/almanac/a/agency.html. Accessed 17 June 2021.

Coole, Diana. 2005. "Rethinking Agency: A Phenomenological Approach to Embodiment and Agentic Capacities." *Political Studies* 53: 124–142. https://doi.org/10.1111/j.1467-9248.2005.00520.x.

———. 2013. "Agentic Capacities and Capacious Historical Materialism: Thinking with New Materialisms in the Political Science." *Millennium: Journal of International Studies* 41, no. 3: 451–469. https://doi.org/10.1177/0305829813481006.

Coole, Diana, and Samantha Frost. 2010. "Introducing New Materialism." In *New Materialisms: Ontology, Agency, Politics*, edited by Diana Coole and Samantha Frost, 1–43. Durham: Duke University Press.

Crampton, Jeremy W. 2010. "Cartographic Calculations of Territory." *Progress in Human Geography* 35, no. 1: 92–103. https://doi.org/10.1177/0309132509358474.

Cudworth, Erika, and Stephen Hobden. 2013. "Of Parts and Wholes: International Relations Beyond the Human." *Millennium: Journal of International Studies* 41, no. 3: 430–450. https://doi.org/10.1177/0305829813485875.

DeLanda, Manuel. 1996. "The Geology of Morals: A Neo-Materialist Interpretation." Available at: http://www.t0.or.at/delanda/geology.htm. Accessed 20 September 2021.

———. 2006. *A New Philosophy of Society: Assemblage Theory and Social Complexity*. London and New York: Continuum.

Deleuze, Gilles. 1988. *Foucault*, translated by Séan Hand. Minneapolis: University of Minnesota Press.

Denes, Nick. 2010. "From Tanks to Wheelchairs: Unmanned Aerial Vehicles, Zionist Battlefield Experiments, and the Transparence of the Civilian." In *Surveillance and Control in Israel/Palestine: Population, Territory and Power*, edited by Elia Zureik, David Lyon, and Yasmeen Abu-Laban, 171–195. New York: Routledge.

Dittmer, Jason. 2014. "Geopolitical Assemblages and Complexity." *Progress in Human Geography* 38, no. 3: 385–401. https://doi.org/10.1177/0309132513501405.

Djigo, Sophie. 2016. *Les migrants de Calais: Enquête sur la vie en transit*. Marseille: Agone.

Dowler, Lorraine, and Jo Sharp. 2001. "A Feminist Geopolitics?" *Space and Polity* 5, no. 3: 165–176. https://doi.org/10.1080/13562570120104382.

Duffield, Mark. 2002. "War as a Network Enterprise: The New Security Terrain and Its Implications." *Cultural Values* 6, no. 1&2: 153–165. https://doi.org/10.1080/1362517022019793.

Elden, Stuart. 2009. *Terror and Territory: The Spatial Extent of Sovereignty*. Minneapolis: University of Minnesota Press.

———. 2010. "Land, Terrain, Territory." *Progress in Human Geography* 34, no. 6: 799–817. https://doi.org/10.1177/0309132510362603.

———. 2013. "Secure the Volume: Vertical Geopolitics and the Depth of Power." *Political Geography* 34: 35–51. https://doi.org/10.1016/j.polgeo.2012.12.009.

———. 2017. "Legal Terrain: The Political Materiality of Territory." *London Review of International Law* 5, no. 2: 199–224. https://doi.org/10.1093/lril/lrx008.

———. 2021. "Terrain, Politics, History." *Dialogues in Human Geography* 11, no. 2: 170–189. https://doi.org/10.1177/2043820620951353.

Fierke, Karin. 2004. "Whereof We Can Speak, Thereof We Must Not Be Silent: Trauma, Political Solipsism and War." *Review of International Studies* 30: 471–491. https://doi.org/10.1017/S0260210504006187.

Foucault, Michel. 1975. *Surveiller et punir: Naissance de la prison*. Paris: Gallimard.

———. 1980. *Power/Knowledge: Selected Interviews and Other Writings 1972–1977*, edited by Colin Gordon. New York: Pantheon Books.

Freedman, Jane. 2018a. "'After Calais': Creating and Managing (In)security for Refugees in Europe." *French Politics* 16: 400–418. https://doi.org/10.1057/s41253-018-0071-z.

———. 2018b. "Violences de genre et 'crise' des réfugiés en Europe." *Mouvements* 93, no. 1: 60–65. https://doi.org/10.3917/mouv.093.0060.

Graham, Stephen. 2003. "Lessons in Urbicide." *New Left Review* 19: 63–77.

———. 2004a. *Cities, Wars and Terrorism: Towards an Urban Geopolitics*. Malden: Blackwell Publishing.

———. 2004b. "Postmortem City: Towards an Urban Geopolitics." *City* 8, no. 2: 165–196. https://doi.org/10.1080/1360481042000242148.

———. 2010. *Cities Under Siege: The New Military Urbanism*. New York: Verso.

———. 2016. *Vertical: The City from Satellites to Bunkers*. London: Verso.

Graham, Stephen, and Lucy Hewitt. 2013. "Getting Off the Ground: On the Politics of Urban Verticality." *Progress in Human Geography* 37, no. 1: 72–92. https://doi.org/10.1177/0309132512443147.

Gregory, Derek. 2010. "Seeing Red: Baghdad and the Eventful City." *Political Geography* 29: 266–279. https://doi.org/10.1016/j.polgeo.2010.04.003.

Hansen, Lene. 2011a. "The Politics of Securitization and the Muhammed Cartoon Crisis: A Post-structuralist Perspective." *Security Dialogue* 42, no. 4&5: 357–369. https://doi.org/10.1177/0967010611418999.

———. 2011b. "Theorizing the Image for Security Studies: Visual Securitization and the Muhammad Cartoon Crisis." *European Journal of International Relations* 17, no. 1: 51–74. https://doi.org/10.1177/0967010615588725.

Haraway, Donna. 1988. "Situated Knowledges. The Science Question in Feminism and the Privilege of Partial Perspective." *Feminist Studies* 14, no. 3: 575–599. https://doi.org/10.2307/3178066.

———. 2003. *The Companion Species Manifesto*. Chicago: Prickly Paradigm Press.

Hawkins, Harriet. 2019. "(W)holes—Volume, Horizon, Surface—Three Intimate Geologies." *Emotion, Space and Society* 32: 1–9. https://doi.org/10.1016/j.emospa.2019.100583.

Holmqvist, Caroline. 2013. "Undoing War: War Ontologies and the Materiality of Drone Warfare." *Millennium: Journal of International Studies* 41, no. 3: 535–352. https://doi.org/10.1177/0305829813483350.

Huysmans, Jef. 2006. *The Politics of Insecurity: Fear, Migration and Asylum in the EU*. London: Routledge.

Ibrahim, Yasmin, and Anita Howarth. 2018. *Calais and its Border Politics. From Control to Demolition*. London and New York: Routledge.

Kaldor, Mary. 1999. *New & Old Wars: Organized Violence in a Global Era*. Cambridge: Cambridge University Press.

Kavalski, Emilian. 2012. "Waking IR Up From Its 'Deep Newtonian Slumber.'" *Millennium: Journal of International Studies* 41, no. 1: 137–150. https://doi.org/10.1177/0305829812451717.

———. 2015. "Complexifying IR: Disturbing the 'Deep Newtonian Slumber' of the Mainstream." In *World Politics at the Edge of Chaos: Reflections on Complexity and Global Life*, edited by Emilian Kavalski, 253–271. Albany: SUNY Press.

Keohane, Robert O. 1988. "International Institutions: Two Approaches." *International Studies Quarterly* 44, no. 1: 83–105.

Latour, Bruno. 2005. *Reassembling the Social: An Introduction to Actor-Network-Theory*. Oxford: Oxford University Press.

Long, Katy. 2013. "When Refugees Stopped Being Migrants: Movement, Labour and Humanitarian Protection." *Migration Studies* 1, no. 1: 4–26. https://doi.org/10.1093/migration/mns001.

Lundborg, Tom, and Nick Vaughan-Williams. 2015. "New Materialisms, Discourse Analysis, and International Relations: A Radical Intertextual Approach." *Review of International Studies* 41: 3–25. https://doi.org/10.1017/S0260210514000163.

Lutterbeck, Derek. 2006. "Policing Migration in the Mediterranean." *Mediterranean Politics* 11, no. 1: 59–82. https://doi.org/10.1080/13629390500490411.

Mac Ginty, Roger. 2010. "Social Network Analysis and Counterinsurgency: A Counterproductive Strategy?" *Critical Studies on Terrorism* 3, no. 2: 209–226. https://doi.org/10.1080/17539153.2010.491319.

Marlin-Bennett, Renée. 2013. "Embodied Information, Knowing Bodies, and Power." *Millennium: Journal of International Studies* 41, no. 3: 601–622. https://doi.org/10.1177/0305829813486413.

Massumi, Brain. 2002. *Parables for the Virtual*. Durham: Duke University Press.

McSorley, Kevin, ed. 2012. *War and the Body: Militarization, Practice and Experience*. London and New York: Routledge.

Mearsheimer, John J. 1995. "A Realist Reply." *International Security* 20, no. 1: 82–93. https://doi.org/10.2307/2539218.

Milliken, Jennifer. 1999. "The Study of Discourse in International Relations: A Critique of Research and Methods." *European Journal of International Relations* 5, no. 2: 225–254. https://doi.org/10.1177/1354066199005002003.

Monaghan, Tina. 2012. *Gender, Agency and War: The Maternalized Body in US Foreign Policy*. London: Routledge.

Neal, Andrew W. 2009. "Securitization and Risk at the EU Border: The Origins of Frontex." *Journal of Common Market Studies* 47, no. 2: 333–356. https://doi.org/10.1111/j.1468-5965.2009.00807.x.

Nicolić, Mirko. 2018. "Apparatus x Assemblage." In *New Materialism Almanac*, edited by David Gauthier and Sam Skinner. Available at: https://newmaterialism.eu/almanac/a/apparatus-x-assemblage.html. Accessed 12 June 2021.

Niva, Steve. 2013. "Disappearing Violence: JSOC and the Pentagon's New Cartography of Networked Warfare." *Security Dialogue* 44, no. 3: 185–202. https://doi.org/10.1177/0967010613485869.

Oppermann, Serpil. 2013. "Material Ecocriticism and the Creativity of Storied Matter." *Frame: Journal of Literary Studies* 26, no. 2: 55–69.

Plaw, Avery, and Matthew S. Fricker. 2012. "Tracking the Predators: Evaluating the US Drone Campaign in Pakistan." *International Studies Perspectives* 13, no. 4: 344–365. https://doi.org/10.1111/j.1528-3585.2012.00465.x.

Sauzet, Sofie. 2018. "Phenomena—Agential Realism." In *New Materialism Almanac*, edited by David Gauthier and Sam Skinner. Available at: https://newmaterialism.eu/almanac/p/phenomena-agential-realism.html. Accessed 12 February 2021.

Scarry, Elaine. 2005. *The Body in Pain: The Making and Unmaking of the World*. Oxford: Oxford University Press.

Sharp, Jo. 2021. "Materials, Forensics and Feminist Geopolitics." *Progress in Human Geography* 45, no. 5: 990–1002. https://doi.org/10.1177/0309132520905653.

Shapiro, Michael. 2011. "The Presence of War: Here and Elsewhere." *International Political Sociology* 5, no. 2: 109–125. https://doi.org/10.1111/j.1749-5687.2011.00124.x.

Shaw, Ian Graham Ronald, and Majed Akhter. 2011. "The Unbearable Humanness of Drone Warfare in FATA, Pakistan." *Antipode* 44, no. 4: 1–20. https://doi.org/10.1111/j.1467-8330.2011.00940.x.

Shaw, Martin. 2005. *The New Western Way of War*. Cambridge: Polity.

Singer, Peter. 2009. *Wired for War: The Robotics Revolution and Conflict in the Twenty-First Century*. New York: Penguin.

Skjelsbaek, Inger. 2012. *The Political Psychology of Rape: Bosnia and Herzegovina*. London: Routledge.

Smith, John, and Chris Jenks. 2005. "Complexity, Ecology, and the Materiality of Information." *Theory, Culture and Society* 22, no. 5: 141–163. https://doi.org/10.1177/0263276405057048.

Steinberg, Philip, and Kimberley Peters. 2015. "Wet Ontologies, Fluid Spaces: Giving Depth to Volume Through Oceanic Thinking." *Environment and Planning D: Society and Space* 33, no. 2: 247–264. https://doi.org/10.1068/d14148p.

Strachan, Hew. 2007. *Clausewitz's On War: A Biography*. New York: Grove Press.

Sylvester, Christine, ed. 2011. *Experiencing War*. Abingdon: Routledge.

———. 2012a. *War as Experience*. London: Routledge.

———. 2012b. "War Experiences/War Theory/War Practice." *Millennium: Journal of International Studies* 40, no. 3: 483–503. https://doi.org/10.1177/0305829812442211.

Thiele, Kathrin. 2016. "Quantum Physics and/as Philosophy: Immanence, Diffraction, and the Ethics of Mattering." *Rhizomes: Cultural Studies in Emerging Knowledge* 30. Available at: http://www.rhizomes.net/issue30/thiele.html. Accessed 16 March 2021.

Turse, Nick. 2012. *The Changing Face of Empire: Special Ops, Drones, Spires, Proxy Fighters, Secret Bases and Cyberwar*. New York: Haymarket Books.

Ucko, David. 2009. *The New Counterinsurgency Era: Transforming the U.S. Military for Modern Wars.* Washington, DC: Georgetown University Press.

Vaughan-Williams, Nick. 2015a. *Europe's Border Crisis: Biopolitical Security and Beyond.* Oxford: Oxford University Press.

———. 2015b. "'We Are Not Animals!' Humanitarian Border Security and Zoopolitical Spaces in Europe." *Political Geography* 45: 1–10. https://doi.org/10.1016/j.polgeo.2014.09.009.

Weizman, Eyal. 2002. "Introduction to The Politics of Verticality." *Open Democracy.* Available at: https://www.opendemocracy.net/ecology-politicsverticality/article_801.jsp. Accessed 17 March 2018.

———. 2007. *Hollow Land: Israel's Architecture of Occupation.* New York: Verso.

———. 2017. *Forensic Architecture. Violence at the Threshold of Detectability.* New York: Zone Books.

2
MAPPING URBICIDAL VIOLENCE

Urbanity as Target

As signaled in the previous chapter, the practices of war should be understood as involving simultaneous operations of diverse human and nonhuman forces, unfolding at different scales and on different planes. The multidimensional impact of war's ravages is often difficult to grasp and impossible to estimate in accurate ways. Acts of warfare significantly affect people, the material contexts in which they dwell, political systems, and economic circuits; they also shape, and are shaped by, ideological discourses mediating understandings of everyday life. If aimed at, often indirectly, eradicating the identities of communities perceived as "dangerous," "threatening," or "meaningless," war strategies tend to target the icons of cultural heritage, serving as evocative symbols of belonging to, and emotional affiliation with, an ethnic or religious group. They also cause massive dispossessions, forced relocations, or the protracted displacement of members of the affected communities. This complexity of after-effects of war's depredations has to be recognized in the process of conducting any study tackling operations of political violence. The assemblage-like nature of the *practices* and *apparatuses* of war has to be kept in mind, especially in cases when particular academic explorations focus only on specific dimensions of the examined atrocities and their aftermath.

Accordingly, the narrative offered in this book aspires to remain sensitive to the diversity of entanglements involved in the *experiences* and *practices* of war, even though it specifically centers on the issues related to the deliberate destruction of the built environment, or—even more precisely—the strategy of slow urbicide, in the context of the ethno-national and ethno-territorial Israeli policies implemented in Palestine. My purpose is not only to reveal this complexity, but also to point out that the deliberations on the character, measures, and circumstances of (slow) urbicidal violence cannot refer exclusively to abstract concepts or delineations; rather, they need to be always carefully positioned within the political, sociocultural, and material contexts in which they happen and by which they are actively co-formed.

Violence against urbanity must continually be seen as connected to, and entwined with, a multiplicity of other interlocking processes. These processes are also complexly consequential. Their outcomes can only be analytically seized if adequately situated within thick material-semiotic realities of war co-constituted by, among other things, ideological narratives, geopolitical interactions, technological developments, and historical and geographical circumstances.

The demolition of a city/village/neighborhood/camp is a substantially material event, a radical reconfiguration of a geographical setting, and often a deliberate "man-made blank on the map" (Hewitt 1983, 259). As a result of the networked practices of political violence, the materiality of the spatially organized and historically layered built environment is sometimes suddenly turned into equally material piles of rubble—a meaningful remnant of the former presence of the tangled life of urban community—often endowed with a huge mnemonic potential. The act of shattering the urban tissue violently disrupts the material-semiotic morphology of an inhabited physical/social space and disorders, at least temporarily, the communal life encompassing both human and nonhuman bodies and forces. Such military policy inevitably concerns itself with urban spaces perceived as centers of power and social capital—as well as, if approached in Lefebvrean (1968) terms, laboratories of potential political resistance—understood in a human, material, industrial, and cultural sense. Violent demolition of the material architecture radically decomposes the multifarious, compound fabric of the spatial system, unleashing further processes of metamorphosis experienced by the affected (communities of) bodies. Effectuated both materially and symbolically, and produced by a collection of politically informed materializations (e.g., of "threats," "dangerous bodies," or "insurgent activities"), the demolition of urban space produces miscellaneous effects, which transform individual human beings, communities, geographies, spaces, landscapes, political agendas, natural environments, movements of people, circulation of goods and services, extensive infrastructures, redevelopment plans, spatially and historically situated biographies, and so on. Urbicidal violence—either fast or slow—heavily upsets the routine functioning of the targeted community, as much as it sparks multidirectional processes unfolding at different scales. This can happen in a variety of spatial circumstances and historical contexts, as evidenced by the evolution of academic thinking about this troubling occurrence.

My analysis relies on those understandings of urban demolition which relate it to the circumstances of war and conflict, including the interludes between wars. Nevertheless, it also acknowledges the weight of other theoretical developments and concepts, which are informative for better grasping the *content* of the discussed phenomenon. Given such an analytical strategy, it is necessary to mention that the first widely discussed use of the term "urbicide" in scholarly investigations should be traced back to the works of Marshall Berman (1987a, 1987b, 1996), who applies it to the rapid and extensive redevelopments of the urban tissue in the city of New York, motivated by its speedy growth and dynamic spatial expansion. Berman speaks about urbicide in terms of violence against urbanity which involves the "destruction of places, sights, sounds, activities, institutions (of building)" (1996, 1), which is aimed at annihilating parts of the physical built environment as well as eliminating certain forms of social existence. He points out that "urbicide" pairs with capitalist reconfigurations of social (or urban) life and has already been incorporated into the process of urban development (1996, 18). Inspirational and illuminating for more general understandings of violence against urbanity, Berman's account—preoccupied with redevelopment enterprises—solely concerns those material-social reconfigurations of cities which are not directly related to any ethno-national conflicts,[1] even though, as already demonstrated by scholars (e.g., Fullilove 2016 [2004]), the processes of urban renewal in the mid-twentieth-century United States negatively affected mostly African-American communities, remaining heavily racist in character. Nevertheless, Berman's reflection is situated away from the dominant contemporary approaches to urbicidal processes, and thus resides—at least to a certain extent—beyond the scope of the analysis offered in this book. Still, referencing his work here seems important, as—in contrast to other ways of theorizing urban destruction—it explicitly deals with the "experience" of spatial damage and what it entails for urban communities,[2] and especially how it negatively impacts upon urban ecosystems. If coupled with investigations of other aspects of particular instances of violence against urbanity, such an approach enables a better understanding of what is at stake in urbicide and how it reconfigures the life of spatial communities.

Historically speaking, examples of the deliberate destruction of cities or settlements have been relatively rare, with war being the most common context in which they have typically been carried out. By targeting sites of communal life, the politics of demolition entirely (and deliberately) blurs the distinction between military and civilian participation in war or conflict. There is a broad repertoire of historical examples of rubblization of urban spaces (the destruction of Carthage in 146 BC by the Romans being the most notorious case), yet the twentieth century offered a substantial increase in the number and scale of demolished urban environments. The destruction of European (e.g., Berlin, Dresden, Coventry, Warsaw) and Japanese (e.g., Tokyo, Hiroshima, Nagasaki) cities through carpet or nuclear bombing during the Second World War is a significant and striking case of enormous devastation of urban communities. The scale of these destructions was unprecedented, as was the lethal nature of the means recruited for that purpose.[3] Similar tactics were used by the United States during the Vietnam War, where the environment of the entire state was deliberately destroyed through bombing and bulldozing, as well as by the dropping of herbicides, terminally affecting the vegetation in the extensive targeted area (see, for example, Thomas 1995). The destruction of housing also extensively impacted Cambodia and Laos at that time. The strategy of ruination was widely used in Afghanistan in the 1980s by the Soviet Union. In 1982, the Syrian city of Hama was completely destroyed on the order of President Hafiz al-Assad (Makiya 1994, 391). Iraqi urban spaces were demolished during Operation Desert Storm in the 1990s, while the same tactics were used by Saddam Hussein against a number of Kurdish villages and in areas inhabited by minoritarian Shi'ite Muslims, Assyrian Christians, and Turkomans. The twilight of the twentieth century witnessed a deliberate demolition of a considerable quantity of cities and villages during the conflict in the territories of the former Yugoslavia and as a part of Russian destructive campaigns in Chechnya.

It seems that at the beginning of the twenty-first century the issue of urbicidal tactics reentered discussions within political science and international relations theory, as violence against the built environment has been turned into the common measure employed during the wars in Afghanistan, Iraq, Syria, and—most recently—Ukraine, leading to the tremendous devastation of strategically important cities and neighborhoods. The spectacular and highly mediatized fatal damage to Damascus, Aleppo, Baghdad, Mosul, and Fallujah has become notorious to the wider public and now stands as an arresting example of urbicidal violence. Mariupol—shattered by the Russian army in March 2022 within the invasion on Ukraine—counts as the most recent example of urbicidal violence. At the same time, quite surprisingly, the process of the systematic and persistent destruction of Palestinian communities (cities, villages, neighborhoods, and camps), as a part of the Israeli policy toward the Palestinians unfolding continually since 1947, even though explored by a number of internationally renowned scholars, remains somewhat less known or accessible to wider audiences. Given its spatial-temporal durability, this permanent tension, regularly transitioning into open war, constitutes a persuasive illustration of the complex and premeditated nature of urbicidal violence. It also clearly exposes the networked character of its convoluted operations and reveals the tangled processuality of its after-effects. The enduring nature of the Israeli colonial project in Palestine allows for the situating of urbicidal tactics within their historical and spatial circumstances, as well as for tracing the continuous metamorphoses of the *content* of the urbicide, which—in the case of Palestine—currently operates at a much slower, yet equally destructive, pace, taking the form of what I propose to call "slow urbicide." By *content* I mean the dynamic entanglements of the *how*, the *why*, the *what*, the *where*, and the *who* of this form of political violence. Attention to the material and spatial aspects of this conflict, as well as how they connect with its other (e.g., cultural/ideological) dimensions to form dynamic material-semiotic assemblages, may offer an enlightening perspective on the complex issues of slow violence or slow urbicide. As I will demonstrate in the following pages, a new materialist approach seems to serve this objective well.

Toward a (New) Materialist Understanding

Perhaps the most widely known contemporary materialist approach to urbicide can be found in the influential conceptualization of Martin Coward (2006, 2007, 2009), who advocates for considering the assault upon the built environment as a form of violence in its own right. Declared as nonanthropocentric, this account has also been an inspiration for my own thinking about urbicidal violence and considerably co-shaped the perspective offered in this analysis. This does not mean, however, that my understanding of violence against urbanity (or urban spaces)—heavily informed by the new materialist ways of thinking laid down in the previous chapter of this book— is identical to that proposed by Coward, even though what the two theorizations undoubtedly share is an increased interest in the material aspects of urbicidal destruction. Our respective approaches to *the material*, and especially to the conceptualization of its agential capacities and operations, as well as to how it participates in the constitution of an urban community, are quite distinct from each other, and subsequently lead us into substantially different understandings of what constitutes the *content* of urbicide.

In an attempt at overcoming the anthropocentric bias pervading the study of political violence, Coward (2006, 2009) offers an approach to urbicidal violence which aims to transcend the dominant understandings of this phenomenon that can be found in the extant literature of the field. He identifies three interpretative themes through which destruction of the built environment is usually approached in the context of war or conflict (2009). The first theme assumes that the destruction of buildings should be approached as so-called "collateral damage" or a nondeliberate result of military action. As A.P.V. Rogers explains, such destruction results from military action and is "incidental" rather than a form of violence in its own right. The shattering of the material environment, in such an account, is proportional to the goals of combat and is considered a military necessity (1996, 15). However, Coward explains, if "the destruction is neither accidental nor attendant to achievement of another aim (i.e., that elements of the built environment were targets in their own right), then it cannot qualify as collateral damage" (see also Riedlmayer 1994, 1995). Even though it is often the case, this understanding of destruction of the built environment currently prevails in political science and often serves as a means of manipulative rhetoric in the hands of the governments responsible for urbicidal destruction. This conceptualization also assumes the potentially legitimate nature of such violence.

The second theme considers the demolition of buildings as part of a strategy of eradicating cultural heritage. This interpretation associates such destruction with genocide or ethnic cleansing, arguing that the damaging of cities or villages forms part of broader projects of exterminating people or ethnic groups. The destruction of material culture, the targeting of buildings qualified as cultural heritage, is in this case seen as an element of ethnic cleansing or of cultural genocide (see, for instance, Shaw 2007; Roberts and Guelff 2000; Orentlicher 1999; Riedlmayer 1994). It is aimed at achieving, in Coward's words, "the objective of ethnic/cultural homogeneity" (2009, 25). Hence, certain buildings must be demolished because they stand for the heterogeneity of the community or its multicultural/multireligious nature. This interpretation focuses on the destruction of buildings that bear certain symbolic meanings. Yet, as Coward underlines, most of the built environment destroyed during ethnic conflicts does not count as cultural heritage, consisting instead of ordinary homes or structures. Thus, "the interpretation of urban destruction as an attack on cultural heritage provides only a partial (though striking) account of the destruction of the built environment" (Coward 2009, 28).

The third theme assumes that the devastation of buildings provides a metaphor for political analysis. Accordingly, ruins and rubble are not approached in themselves, that is, as "a material fabric of culture, but, rather, as signs evocative of ideas and values" (Coward 2009, 28). Understood in semiotic terms as referring to concepts, they frame "the horizons of the political imaginaries of both participants and observers" (Coward 2009, 28), influencing courses of action. Destruction of the built environment, and especially of meaningful and recognizable structures (such as, for instance, the Old Bridge in Mostar in Bosnia), is understood as a symbolic policy, which may serve as a means for mediating the understanding of broader political (military) processes.

As Coward (2009) notes, it seems that none of these interpretations succeeds in capturing the complexity of violence committed against the built environment *in its own right*, while, as he insists, there is a specific logic to urbicide which urges us to consider its distinctiveness. Rather, they acknowledge the demolition of buildings as a phenomenon secondary to other policies by treating it, respectively, as ancillary to military violence, an element of wider (i.e., more meaningful and culturally shaped) patterns of violence, or as a sign referring to deeper concepts (2009, 34). Perspectives associated with social constructivism or discourse theory (conceiving of destruction in symbolic or metaphorical terms) promote the view that the systematic targeting of city architecture is based solely on the cultural value of the buildings or on the fact that they mean something (which refers them to "something more" than their mere material superficiality). Concepts such as warchitecture, cultural cleansing, identicide, or cultural genocide aim to capture these processes (Herscher 2008; Mehrag 1999, 2001). As Coward indicates (2009), although of immense value, these perspectives do not do justice to the character of contemporary violence against the built environment and give a rather limited picture of the knotted reality of urban destruction. Coward, therefore, signals the need to approach the violence against the urban space from a different conceptual perspective which can adequately recognize the material aspects of the built environment and of its intentional destruction. By focusing on urbicidal violence in post-Cold War politics, he proposes thinking about urban space as producing the material "condition of possibility of heterogeneous existence" (2006, 430). Accordingly, urbicide should be defined as "the destruction of heterogeneity *qua* coexistence in and through the shared spaces constituted by the built environment" (2006, 432; original emphasis; see also Coward 2009, 53). Given that the material infrastructure, or what can be considered to belong to the public space of the urban community, at least theoretically facilitates coexistence with others (whose fundamental alterity serves as constitutive of one's identity), the assault upon the material conditions of an urban community comprises "a politics of exclusion aimed at establishing the fiction of a being-without-others" (Coward 2006, 434). This pertains especially to ethno-nationalist political projects.

Remaining within post-humancentric logic, Coward, however, never conceptualizes the agency of more-than-human matter, even though he pays attention to the constitutive role of the built environment for the emergence of shared spatiality as a condition for heterogeneity (2006, 429). He nevertheless applies the latter term mostly in reference to human (ethnic, religious, racial, etc.) diversification, even though he also briefly mentions the radical alterity of nonhuman "things" as formative of one's own identity (2009, 108). As he writes,

> the built environment is thus constitutive of a shared spatiality in which it is not so much that space—understood as a neutral, measured medium—is shared, but that the relations established by buildings which orient experiences of the built environment always already admit of the possibility that there is an other sharing the same building (as landmarks from which relational networks unfold) and, thus, the same spatiality. This sharing thus establishes a general condition of heterogeneity: of coexistence.[4]
>
> (2006, 429)

As such, although constituting a significant attempt to transcend anthropocentric logic, this conceptualization continues to a great extent to be preoccupied with the human (identity) aspects of state-sponsored violence. This does not mean that it is not useful in the context of thinking about more-than-human matter in agential terms. After all, as explained in the previous chapter, post-anthropocentrism does not completely lose its interest in the human, but rather perceives the human as one among many other constitutive elements of the world. What I consider a certain limitation of Coward's theory, however, is his—perhaps intentional—avoidance of explicit recognition, and subsequent conceptualization, of the agential capacities of "things,"[5] as well as his scant interest in the complex dynamics of the urban community comprising more-than-human agents and forces. He also circumvents the acknowledgment of this singular material-semiotic entanglement which constitutes the *content* of the urban environment—as much as the content, or the *how*, of urbicidal violence—and leaves unexplored the question of how the different spatiotemporal materializations of landscape/ cityscape contribute to meaningful reconfigurations of the world. Similar shortcomings can be discerned in many other theorizations of the deliberate destruction of the built environment. This general tendency may testify to the fact, that—as signaled in Chapter 1—the possibility of thinking about nonhuman matter in agential ways has been significantly limited, if not entirely blocked, within the mainstream humanism-infused theorizations[6] populating both the field of political science and related areas of study.

While Coward approaches urbicide as a form of violence *in its own right*, he also admits that it is "never present in a pure, singular form," but rather "coexists with a number of other forms of violence such as genocide or state-sponsored repression" (2006, 427). For him, however, it is not useful to reduce one of them to the other (as proposed by, for example, Shaw 2004[7]). He prefers to think about them as separate logics, simultaneously working within the same context of conflict. Hence, this delineation aims to propose a "useful category of analysis" where "drawing out the conceptual contours of one [form of violence] implies a certain focus and an interest in the entailments of that violence" but "does not necessarily imply the absence of any other forms of violence" (2006, 427). Such a strategy testifies to the more general scientific tendency to offer abstracted definitions of terms which would have the potential of universal applicability in cases similar to each other (or, perhaps, which would be instrumental in "materializing" these cases), offering a typology of processes and phenomena classified as being different from one another. We have to keep in mind that within the logic of taxonomizing the scholarly (or political, artistic, or other) work, such categories and definitions are essentially conflict based— one is not what the other is; one is related to the other, albeit by negation. Premised on such negativist assumptions, any kind of classification may, in a powerful way, serve as a canonizing device and be used as a tool to establish a field of study with its distinctive concepts, definitions, methodologies, and research techniques. This scheme (saturating Western academic environments) can potentially have a limiting effect on what scholars working within this field can do in their studies once the theoretical and epistemic categories are picked up and operationalized in their work (cf. van der Tuin 2015). Classifications, therefore, can have silencing entailments, as anything which does not fit within the established system risks being disregarded and challenged. This offers a rather limited flexibility and is meant to produce understandings that would fit well within the existing grid, by filling in the identified gaps on the extensive map of the already recognized knowledge. I am not convinced that the inclination toward offering analytical delineations of concepts and constraining their possible applications could be productive in explorations of the tangled *practices* and *apparatuses* of war and political violence, and especially of how they are experienced by the targeted communities. Neither am I assured that the strategy of abstracting concepts from their more encompassing contexts (of, for example, other forms of violence) can offer insight into the complex assemblage-like logic of conflict and its eventful character. My proposition, grounded in new materialist assumptions, is rather to consider the *co-constitutive* character of different situated aspects of violence and of different context-specific political projects. Such an approach inquires into *how* urbicidal violence compiles with the politics of genocide, ethnic cleansing, memoricide, reinvention of the past, de-development,[8] nationalism, ethnocentrism, "legalized" forms of exclusion, intentional marginalization, spatial injustice, and many other logics operating within, and depending upon, singular spatial-temporal situations and circumstances, and how, as such, it is a product of particular "spacetimematterings."[9]

Certainly, the fondness toward the delineation of clear concepts and designations should be situated against the wider historical and cultural background of academic endeavors as derivative of the more general construction of the Western scientific project exported worldwide via complex techniques of colonial/patriarchal/capitalist domination and premised on the suppression of other (e.g., indigenous) ways of knowing which have served as meaningful "others" for Western culture.[10] These efforts are embodied in the strategies of offering clear-cut classifications (of bodies, processes, phenomena, etc.), a move that guarantees an illusion of control over the studied material, and falsely promises production of disinterested, detached, objective knowledge. Iris van der Tuin, a feminist new materialist philosopher, captures the nature of this quest for the ordering of worldly reconfigurations and precise documentation of its operations in the term "classifixation,"[11] signaling a Western obsession with control via the generation of accurate "representations" of the world. The term, in her words, is also meant to "demonstrate how a classification is not a neutral mediator but is thoroughly entangled with the work that it does" (2015, 19) or, in fact, the materialization of the depicted phenomena. In her insightful analysis, van der Tuin refers back to Foucault's (1994 [1966]) salient criticism and questioning of the classificatory, or "taxonomical," tendency to organize (not only) academic work in a grid-like order, which points out that "all classifications exist under the spell of an episteme" (van der Tuin 2015, 28). Foucault's genealogical approach enables him to expose how the taxonomy emerges as a conjunctive operation of language and things which co-constitute one another through the complex play of a word (classifier) and a world (classified),[12] which embodies new materialist ways of thinking. Referring to Haraway's influential concept, assuming the materially-semiotically located nature of always partial knowledge, van der Tuin evinces that Foucault's criticism clearly exhibits that "classifications do not provide Truth, but descriptively express situated knowledge" (2015, 28).

This is the kind of thinking through which I intend to approach the extant scholarship on urbicidal violence (this expression is only meant as an umbrella term rather than conveying any personal preference). In my opinion, substantially informed by new materialist philosophy, the abundance of different terms forged in diverse culturo-political, discursive, spatial, and material contexts testifies to the fact that there might be no unitary, or single, understanding of urbicidal violence, as these events are always part and parcel of broader networks of entangled material circumstances, political motivations, representational frameworks, and spatial arrangements. So even though the nature of destruction, approached as an artificially isolated (f)act, may seem to be to a great extent universal or unanimous, in reality its ontology stems from the different material-semiotic relational becomings, or assemblages, of bodies (including "things") and forces. Accordingly, new materialism does not presuppose any single understanding of urbicide as a form of "violence in its own right" [as Coward suggests (2006, 2009)]. By addressing the complex material-discursive and relational ontology of violence, which is generative of meaningful reconfigurations, new materialism underlines its assemblage-like character, its network effect, as much as its eventful nature. By doing so, it is interested in *how* the deliberate violence against the built environment in specific material-semiotic circumstances compiles with other discourses and other material processes (like other acts of political violence) and what kind of material-semiotic effects it produces in the world.

A Topology of Concepts

Adopting a new materialist approach, and making use of its methodological insights, this book argues that (slow) urbicidal violence cannot be perceived as a phenomenon isolated from its extensive material-discursive contexts and effects and must be accounted for as a situated process. Hence, as I mentioned earlier, conceptualization of the deliberate destruction of the built environment as a form of violence in its own right may not be exceptionally productive as far as a thorough understanding of this complex occurrence is concerned, especially if applied to—instead of being inferred from—particular empirical cases. The destruction of cities/villages/camps/neighborhoods is a part of an entanglement of different policies, situated in diverse spatiotemporal circumstances, carried out through various means, and producing highly singular effects. The intention to grasp the "essence" of this complex bundle of processes within a single definition or concept will necessary be, at least to a certain extent, reductive; thus—somewhat contrary to its more general intention—it will never bring results capable of doing justice to the peculiarities of the actual cases of urbicidal destruction, remaining enclosed with a rather technical and disengaged model of producing knowledge. When reviewing the extant literature in the field, it is revealing that in fact the concepts and classifications elaborated by scholars working on separate instances of violence against the built environment tackle quite different aspects of this phenomenon and embody the situated specificities and characteristics of the analyzed events (even though very often this situatedness is not explicitly acknowledged). Drawing on new materialist strategies of thinking, which disavow dualistic logic and renounce either-or reasoning, I approach them as equally informative, even though tailored to singular political developments. In what follows I offer a cursory overview, or a sketchy cartography, of selected concepts developed by academics focusing on the analysis of the deliberate demolition of urban space while taking into consideration the important material aspects of the community and of its intentional destruction. By no means is my discussion meant to be exhaustive. Its purpose is to point to certain continuities and convergences of these formulations, casting light on the importance of the physical dimension of the (urban) community and how it entangles with its cultural and political facets, or how the space and social relations mutually co-form each other. Such a perspective also helps us to realize what is at stake in urbicidal violence as well as how destruction *matters*.

A cartographic approach to understanding urbicidal violence constitutes a qualitative shift and complies with a new materialist research ethics that renounces thinking in terms of dualism (in which one thing is understood as the other of the other). Instead, it invests in mappings of intersections, interferences, and convergences, which can be very informative for the overall understanding of the examined phenomenon. New materialist cartographical thinking is not premised on binarized fixations as much as avoiding linear ordering, the latter being a legacy of Western investment in conceptualizing the transformations of the world in line with ideas of progress and development. Rather than being grounded in the logic of negation (or of one against the other), the cartographical approach provokes transversal and transhistorical dialogue and is interested in genealogical historiographies and archaeologies of knowledge. As van der Tuin suggests, it should be seen in Deleuzian fashion as a "topology" rather than a "typology" (2015, 20; see also Deleuze 1988, 13). As such, for reasons identified in the earlier section of this chapter, by no means is it my intention to elaborate another classification of thinking about urbicidal violence. Instead, in an effort to disavow taxonomical strategies, my objective is to offer a deeper understanding of a selection of extant conceptualizations and the processes they address, indicating how they converge, or are sometimes similar to—rather than radically different from—each other. I also want to indicate that a certain way of thinking about the urban community transpires from these theoretical propositions, and that this understanding clearly acknowledges a community's material and spatial dimension (and what is lost when the latter is demolished), even though it leaves its agency somewhat unrecognized. Hence, in my necessarily partial rereading of these concepts, I follow Haraway's suggestion that "taxonomizing everyone's positions without regard to the contexts of their development" may be problematic for knowledge production processes (Haraway 1997, 304). Thus, my very limited cartography constitutes a modest attempt at reconceptualizing, rather than classifying, extant ways of thinking about urbicidal violence.

It is impossible to understand the horrifying experience of having one's home demolished without realizing what the idea of "home" stands for. The concept of "home" appears to be absolutely crucial for human geography and the centrality of it has been confirmed by scholars working within such academic disciplines as anthropology, architectural and environmental psychology, ethnoarcheology, planning, and urban studies. The fact that it is conceived of as an element of more extensive systems (communities, urban formations, landscape, ethnic cultures, etc.) clearly demonstrates that this microcosm functions within broader contexts and co-constitutes, and is co-constituted by, a number of larger-scale processes and phenomena from which it can never be completely isolated. Thus, the destruction of home is an event that generates consequences at different scales and significantly affects all these previously mentioned broader systems. As Kim Dovey suggests, home has to be seen as a relational entity, "as a principle for establishing a meaningful relationship with the environment" (1978, 27; quoted in Porteous and Smith 2001, 26). Home is situated at the nexus of material conditions and emotional meanings, physical comfort, and mental belonging, a conglomerate of material structures and cultural and social significations and associations. The concept thus encompasses such elements as territoriality (which also ties its physical space to larger systems, such as neighborhood, town, village, even country), affections (signaling belonging, familiarity, comfort), and spatiality (acting as a framework of everyday routines and a system of measurement). Home also functions within the more encompassing imaginary of nation, often operating as a tangible embodiment of cultural phantasms and a residue of myths. It is not possible to understand what home really means if any of these dimensions is elided or ignored, as the "ontology" of home is deeply relational. Demolition of it, therefore, dramatically reconfigures the micro- and the macrocosm of community life. This is also why individual homes—as well as more composite arrangements of the built environment consisting of material structures serving as homes, institutions, symbolic sites, public and recreational places, and various routes connecting them into a singular spatial entity (albeit tied to other similar systems)—have regularly been turned into targets of warfare in which the demolition of homes has been deliberately engineered.

Taking into consideration the varying scales of this occurrence, J. Douglas Porteous and Sandra E. Smith propose the term "domicide," which is understood as *"the deliberate destruction of home by human agency in pursuit of specified goals, which causes suffering to the victims"* (2001, 12; original emphasis), a "murder of home" (2001, 3), caused by human agency and involving "some form of planning," where "the rhetoric of public interest or common good is frequently used by the perpetrators" (2001, 12). Domicide can have an extreme or local scale. The extreme cases of intentional destruction of home, which are more linked to the theme of this book, happen in a number of diverse circumstances, such as war, ethnic cleansing, and strategic resettlement related to different processes, including construction of new infrastructures, colonization, or geopiracy. For the two authors, the significance of domicide is connected to the special status that home enjoys in our lives (2001, 4), so the (willful) destruction of home can leave "one of the deepest wounds to one's identity and self-esteem, for both of these props to sanity reside in part in objects and structures that we cherish" (Porteous and Smith 2001, 5). However, this statement has to be situated politically, as home is not just a place of dwelling, but also stands for one's homeland, which signals a deep attachment to both people and familiar objects or structures, as much as to landscape, environment, or the imaginary representations of the community to which one belongs (Porteous and Smith 2001, 6). This complex positioning of home urges us to consider its destruction on different planes—personal and private, material and cultural, social and political. Thus, domicide constitutes an assault upon the spatial entanglement of the physical, material place and emotionally loaded meanings and attachments, generating consequences across a number of political and conceptual horizons, from personal to communal and from individual to (inter)national.

The way of thinking of home (and of its deliberate destruction) offered by Porteous and Smith clearly signals the constitutive role that material structures (of buildings, cities, landscape, environment) play in the life of a community and how they shape its specific spatiotemporal characteristics and routines. Porteous and Smith draw extensively on other authors, whose conceptualizations underline this formative role of physical places and solid arrangements. As Nora Johnson explicitly states, highlighting the agential role of physical space, "We are all profoundly affected by the places we live, often without realizing it. Their problems and paradoxes become our own, changing us and making us part of them" (1982, 6; quoted in Porteous and Smith 2001, 39). David Lowenthal, in a different way, points to the fact that "Patterns in the landscape make sense to us because we share a history with them" (1975, 5; quoted in Porteous and Smith 2001, 40), binding the people and the environment together in a common spatial-temporal experience in which both are involved and entwined. Similarly, Arien Mack claims that "landscape and people are morphologically akin ... they constitute in some primal cultural sense the nature of each other" (1991, 11; quoted in Porteous and Smith 2001, 44). Indicating the affinity of people and the material structures which they inhabit, Anne Winning states that "to dwell authentically, is to be incorporated into the landscape of home" (1990, 257; quoted in Porteous and Smith 2001, 55). Eventually, Porteous and Smith also underline the material, corporeal dimension of home, comparing it to "a second body" and claiming that it "shapes you and, in turn, is shaped in your image" (2001, 54). This is also evident in the strategy adopted by the authors of coupling domicide with memoricide, which indicates that the erasure of the physical space which sustains and materializes memory (individual and/or collective) undermines the identity of those affected by these tangled processes, threatening their continuity, their ability to mobilize and resist, and also, often, jeopardizing their survival. What therefore transpires from Porteous and Smith's argument is the concept of home as a physical place which is endowed with culturally and socially motivated meanings, but also as a clearly material structure which significantly affects and sustains these significations. Moreover, the home enters into constitutive relations with other buildings and material infrastructures, as much as with the landscape and environment, forming complex dynamic organizations in which all elements affect, and are affected by, one another. And even though nowhere do the two authors unequivocally problematize the agential capacities of the material or the spatial, such an implicit assumption seems to significantly mark their understanding of home (and of the consequences of its destruction).

According to such a formulation, both home and the more extensive organization of spatiality it forms with other buildings and material structures are essentially a lived and living space. Place is a more-than-physical but also definitely more-than-human reality. And while the human dimensions of (urban) communities have been extensively explored, also in the context of violence, the material aspects of these developments have typically appeared as secondary, and interest in them seemed to be superfluous. Breaking—at least partly—with this tendency, the geographer Kenneth Hewitt (1983) focuses more extensively on the nature and consequences of the destruction of material urban tissue. Writing in reference to the massive damage inflicted on German and Japanese cities as a result of the extensive area bombings by the Allies during the Second World War, and taking into account the nuclear politics of the Cold War, Hewitt (1983)[13] offers the concept of "place annihilation," focusing not only on the great number of people killed and injured in these raids, but also—interestingly—on the deliberate rubblization of cities and neighborhoods. For Hewitt, place annihilation is comprised of "the destruction of inhabited settlements, especially dense city core areas, in the continued presence of their longtime inhabitants"; "large, concentrated fatalities and injury among resident civilian populations"; the "predominance of noncombatants among the casualities and, specifically, of children, students, women, the old, and the infirm"; "the destruction of homes of civilians"; the "indiscriminate 'wall-to-wall' devastation of civic life support and culture: shops and markets, hospitals and schools, libraries, banks, theaters, churches, zoos and landmarks" including those of artistic or cultural significance; and "practices that prevent or disrupt emergency measures for devastated areas and for aiding causalities" (Hewitt 1983, 276).[14]

Given the academic discipline that Hewitt represents, his focus is on the destruction of place rather than on other aspects of the phenomenon that he studies. Nevertheless, he pays attention to its complex nature combining the destruction of resident civilians, residential communities, and neighborhoods, which together translates into the annihilation of the urban environment, or of what he calls "civil ecology" (1983, 257). For Hewitt, "place cannot be fully comprehended as merely a set of spatial relations, biophysical habitat, and impersonal socioeconomic functions. Its material attributes are indeed essential ingredients and vital clues to its larger meanings," even though he still perceives these ingredients as "shaped into places by the personal works, exchanges, and intelligent participation of resident communities" (1983, 258). This reliance on the entangled, complex character of place in Hewitt's elaboration is worth noting. The emphasis placed on the physical dimension of the city, somewhat atypical for analysts situated within the field of international relations theory, testifies to Hewitt's disciplinary orientation, although nowhere in his text does he explicitly mention the agential role of these materialities, preferring to think about them in terms of matter shaped exclusively by human agency. The important role of material objects for the formation of a community is nevertheless implicitly acknowledged in Hewitt's analysis, and especially in his focus on reconstruction ventures, testifying to the deep and persistent affiliations with the materiality of (once) inhabited places, since such investment in the material dimension of communal existence serves as a means to resist cultural dissolution. Such a framing of the understanding of urban existence testifies to Hewitt's recognition of the constitutive role of material urban structures in the processes of materialization of a communal life, with all its rights and potentials.

Preoccupied with the constitutive role of land, or territory, for the development and continuity of communities, Sari Hanafi (2009, 2012) offers the concept of "spacio-cide," tailored specifically to understand the exceptional nature of the Israeli colonial project in Palestine. Radically different from genocidal policies, spatiocide, as Hanafi aptly explains, "targets land for the purpose of rendering inevitable the 'voluntary' transfer of the Palestinian population primarily by targeting the space upon which the Palestinian people live" (2012, 191). Spaciocide's target is a place which is to be turned into a land without (indigenous) people to be later resettled by the desired representatives of the colonizing nation. It is meant to transfer "*topos* to *atopia*, turning *territory* into mere *land*" (Hanafi 2012, 192), thus producing uprooted, deracinated, and deterritorialized bodies, that is, subjects who no longer have a tangible relationship to their original territories (Hanafi 2009, 118). Somewhat paradoxically, this strategy of destruction constitutes a premise for the production of new forms of (Israeli) territoriality, based on the principle of "natural" belonging in a given geographical area. The destruction of houses, or whole cities, villages, neighborhoods, and camps, as well as the dispossession of the populations inhabiting these areas, has served since 1947 as a significant means of this policy, co-constituted by discursive strategies as much as (legal) procedures introduced as part of the state of exception—all of which contribute to the materialization of the very specific situation of targeted communities whose continuity is seriously threatened.

Spaciocide has been made possible by state-sponsored processes of land confiscation (leading to the disturbance of the Palestinian social fabric) as well as to the specific division of the Occupied Territories into zones (more on this will follow in Chapter 3). This produces increased fragmentation of both the political authorities and the space, hampering any harmonious spatial development of the targeted communities, and turning them into isolated enclaves, geographically cut off from the longer spatial chains of circulation of goods, services, and people. Such a policy interrupts the processes of spontaneous relational functioning, denaturalizing community life, and producing an array of spatial injustices. Spaciocidal strategy has been made possible through the nuanced operation of "military-judicial-civil apparatuses" (Hanafi 2012, 194) controlled by the Israeli state, which substantially co-constitute the materialization of the colonial project, based on the principle of (spatial) separation and careful management (or naturalization) of the instrumentally used state of exception. Thus, the term proposed by Hanafi points to "both the magnitude of the wrecking and destruction, and the deliberate exterminatory logic of the space livability that underpins the assault on the space, whether it is a built/urban area, landscape or land property" (Hanafi 2012, 193). The uprooting of people from their spatial environment—through, as I suggest, strategies of slow urbicide—gradually leads to the eradication of community life or "to kill[ing] by geography," with the aim to produce "placelessness" and "cultural starvation" (Hewitt 1983, 259). Targeting the material dimension of community life, this policy contributes to the growing spatial discontinuity of Palestinians, dissolving their "togetherness" and unsettling—via the strategy of deracinating—their common affinity and belonging. Quite explicitly, a deliberate assault on space gradually translates into the controlled cultural and political eradication of the indigenous population's practices of dwelling, dissolving its everyday more-than-human topologies, and thus slowly destroying its capacities for space-based organized resistance and self-governance.

"Root shock" is the term that Mindy Fullilove (2016 [2004]) applies to describe what happens to the community when its geography is destroyed.[15] By defining this psychological state, Fullilove pays attention to the enduring powers of a physical place in community life, the overwhelming role of spaces that we share with others for the emotional balance and physical well-being of individuals, indicating that the demolition of these places translates into "the loss of a massive web of connections" (2016, Introduction) and produces the landscape of loss and upheaval. Root shock is experienced by those who have lost the material structure of their community, whose homes have been destroyed and whose neighborhoods have been bulldozed. As a medical term, it describes "the traumatic stress reaction to the destruction of all or part of one's emotional ecosystem" (2016, Chapter 1). This clearly indicates the complex interdependency of the built environment and the people inhabiting it, as well as the constitutive role of the material infrastructure for the emergence of social daily routines and habits which produce the feeling of predictability and comfort, and which testify to the rootedness of people in the material environment. As Fullilove explains, at the level of the individual, root shock

> is a profound emotional upheaval that destroys the working model of the world that had existed in the individual's head. Root shock undermines trust, increases anxiety about letting loved ones out of one's sight, destabilizes relationships, destroys social, emotional, and financial resources, and increases the risk for every kind of stress-related disease.
>
> (2016, Chapter 1)

At the community level, Fullilove continues, root shock

> ruptures bonds, dispersing people to all the directions of the compass. Even if they manage to regroup, they are not sure what to do with one another. ... even if the neighborhood is rebuilt exactly as it was, it won't work. The restored geography is not enough to repair the many injuries to the mazeway.
>
> (2016, Chapter 1)

Such an experience, as Fullilove explains, stays with the affected people for ever; it also affects the following generations, rippling out beyond those who are directly involved in dispossessions or forced relocation. The destruction of the built environment, which co-constitutes the community life and social relations and is meant to survive the individuals who inhabit it, casts a long shadow on the future and the continuity of the affected community, dismantling its inherent ecosystem, heavily traumatizing the whole generations, and influencing their (in)capacity to repair what was lost. Thus, root shock can be inherited through cultural, social, bodily, and place memory. As Karen Till notes, "these forms of violence often work over a period of many years, often decades, and continue to structure current social and spatial relations, and as such also structure expectations of what is considered 'normal'" (2012, 6).

As evidenced by the above deliberations, the community arises from a plethora of relationships, from which a certain type of materially-semiotically understood spatiality emerges. It is filled with memories and activates the ways in which the past is remembered and rehearsed on an everyday basis. If it is understood as constituted by its inhabitants through ongoing acts of making places, then it emerges as the complex nexus of material objects, bodies, social groups, rituals, and collective memory. Human and nonhuman lives engage there with each other through complex temporal and spatial pathways, as well as via symbolic and material places (Till 2012). As Till rightly evinces, "we can understand place as always becoming, as within and beyond us" (2012, 9). Therefore, the material-semiotic urban fabric—when harmed and restructured by acts of physical demolition, displacement, division, and by social trauma resulting from state-perpetrated violence which is often impossible to resist—is difficult to rebuild or reconstruct. In such a context, urbicidal violence must be understood as one that targets the specifically relational nature of urbanity, where the latter—as Coward notes—"refers both to the material conditions that constitute the town or city as such, and the way of life occurring in such material conditions" (2006, 428). This statement becomes valid only if we approach the materiality of buildings and the landscape as co-constitutive of the microcosm of a community, a relational agent which qualitatively affects the relations in which it participates in the process of multidimensional *sym*-poiesis (Haraway 2013, 2015; original emphasis) or making-together. Pointing to the intensity of place-based attachment and the constitutive role of the built environment in the community building processes, Till pays attention to the ecologies of space, which—from my perspective—seem to be material-semiotic in character. As she writes, "*Ecological characteristics* provide structure for individuals and social groups ... The *morphological qualities* of place are the material and social environments that nurture inhabitants and offer support through familiarity, routine, aesthetically comfortable spaces, and a sense of belonging and security" (2012, 10; original emphases). As she further elaborates, "Taken together, these social ecologies of place include everyday routines, social institutions, material landscapes (the fabric, taste, sounds, and scents of places), symbolic systems of meaning and identity, and shared memories" (Till 2012, 10).

The unsettling of thus understood spatial ecology must necessarily be a traumatizing experience. Not only does it dramatically threaten the actual survival of a community, but it also results in an erasure of its collective memory, which cannot be fully sustained without the material structures co-constitutive of mnemonic processes. Such conceptualization aligns with memory studies scholarship, which questions the traditional understandings of sites as abstract locations, focusing instead on the power of place that encourages conversations about contemporary issues, including cultural and social memory.[16] In societies traumatized by violence, as Till underlines, people often return to particular places to revisit difficult feelings of loss, anger, or guilt, because they conceive of those places as having a distinct presence—material, sensual, spiritual, psychic, and social (2012).[17] This importance of the physical or spatial dimension for community life is also evident in the endeavors to rebuild, if possible, the destroyed places to resemble as closely as possible what was demolished or to resettle and recreate the location after the dramatic events that disrupted the physical and psychosocial continuity of the site. Reconstruction projects, or recreations of similar structures in a different place, could be viewed as an attempt to hide this discontinuity, seen as a rupture in the place's "metabolism of functioning" (Hewitt 1983).

While ethno-territorial projects—in their systematic, tacit endeavors to produce specific forms of territoriality—tend to deliberately damage urban spaces and spatially co-constituted social relations, they also lead to an eradication of "the right to the city" of these spaces' inhabitants, impairing their capacities for shaping their surroundings according to their needs and efficiently countering the state's (territorial) authority. Slow-motion warfare strategies seem to be exceptionally treacherous in this regard. In the context of enduring conflicts, gradually leading—through slow forms of urbicidal violence or "slow wounding" (Joronen 2021)—to the erasure of certain organizations of social relations and their replacement with the dominant power's more "desired" equivalents, this loss of rights seems to be the most striking danger. This kind of unspectacular operation of state-sponsored political violence steadily disrupts well-established spatiotemporal routines and produces a whole range of spatial injustices. In order to understand its miscellaneous consequences, however, it is necessary to bear in mind the crucial role of material infrastructures and natural landscapes in community-sustaining processes, drawing attention to the agential role of materialities in producing the urban tissue and urban life, both understood in terms of material-semiotic assemblages.

It remains equally important, however, to explore how violence against the materially-semiotically understood urbanity severely affects human bodies. As McKittrick elucidates,

> While place annihilation certainly differs according to time and place, the devastation, so clearly pointed to in the term urbicide—the deliberate killing of the city—brings into sharp focus how violence functions to render specific human lives, and thus their communities, as waste.[18]

(2011, 952)

This calls for realization that "multitudinous urbicidal acts ... are always inhabited with disposable 'enemies', impoverished dwellers, those 'without'"

(McKittrick 2011, 952). The politics of killing a place, or destruction of a community, should thus be situated in the context of what Mbembe (2003) refers to as "necropolitics," normalizing colonial power and knitting together geographic violence and human life. In the act of urbicidal destruction, as McKittrick describes, "the execution of place and people is bound up in the corpse, the displaced survivors, the perpetually lifeless and disposable" (2011, 952). The more-than-human dimension of urbicidal violence—understood as a form of violence that targets both places and human bodies at the same time—can only be truly realized by bringing into sharp focus "practices that politicize place-life and place-death differently," empirically evidencing "the unsurvival of the weakest" (McKittrick 2011, 954) by destroying their sense of space, hence producing experiences of placelessness and loss. Such a process has long-lasting consequences for the targeted community, whose traditional life routines dissolve, capabilities for place-based organization diminish, and aspirations for self-governance fade away. Importantly, such ways of thinking expose the hidden logic of violence against urbanity, aiming at deracination of the community's spirit and limitation of any forms of resistance against the state's central (colonial) authority. By reconfiguring the urban community and its traditional forms of organization, and by denying its right to produce forms of spatiality fitting within the scope of their situated needs and aspirations, the state aims to gradually produce absolute forms of territoriality with a desired distribution of administrative power spreading over the territory as much as the people inhabiting it. Thus, by disrupting the material-semiotic forms of traditional dwelling, and contributing to the loss of the sense of a place by the members of the targeted communities, the state—through a range of different urbicidal policies—engages in an ongoing process of constructing preferred forms of spatiality, as well as investing in the meaningful reconfiguration of regional demographics. In the case of the indigenous populations whose experiences are discussed in this book, negation of the "right to the city" pertaining to the inhabitants of the Palestinian-Arab urban areas (ranging from neighborhoods, through villages and camps, to cities) should therefore be understood as an inherent part of the broader Israeli colonial project in Palestine. As I will elaborate upon in more detail in the next chapter, this meticulously orchestrated policy is implemented both in the Israeli heartland and the territories remaining under the Israeli occupation. At the same time, the slow-motion strategy works to effectively occlude the state-sponsored colonial efforts, denying the urbicidal violence systematically troubling the concerned regions and severely wounding their populations.

Whereas my intention in this chapter was to look at what is potentially lost when a home is demolished as a part of deliberate policy, or what dissolves when urban communities are intentionally targeted with violence, in the following one I will explore in greater detail the *how* question of slow urbicide in Palestine. My aim will be thus to cast light on how the different materialities and apparatuses are mobilized and how they agentially act in the politically and geographically informed processes of the intentional demolition of indigenous urban communities in the West Bank and in the Naqab/Negev region. Hence, while this chapter centers mostly on the material-semiotic nature of urban living, the following part is mostly concerned with the material-semiotic means employed for the purpose of restricting, or entirely eradicating, these forms of dwelling with an aim of producing the experiences of placelessness and rootlessness among the members of the indigenous populations inhabiting the two analyzed geographical areas.

Notes

1 It is nevertheless connected to intersecting class and ethnic differences.
2 Interestingly, Berman already points to the networked character of urbicidal destruction—"the hopelessly tangled webs that connected landlords, bankers, insurance underwriters, welfare departments, junkies, thieves, real estate speculators, crooked politicians, 'finishers' ... professional arsonists and the dazed, weeping people out on the street" (1987b, n.p.).
3 As Hewitt (1983) observes, even though the strategy of carpet bombing of cities inhabited by civilians was then condemned by many political leaders who postulated that it should be outlawed as a military measure, they often also "tested" the very same means in the villages of their colonial territories, albeit on a scale of bombardment that was significantly smaller. However, in contradistinction to Hewitt's analysis, which considers the scope of these events as "trivial" (1983, 261) in comparison to the similar developments in Europe during the Second World War, I argue that, from the perspective of the affected communities, the question of the scale of such a policy does not appear in any way relevant. As Hewitt indicates, the list of examples of such policies includes British punitive air raids against peoples in Mesopotamia, Sudan, Somaliland, and the Northwest Frontier of India as well as French airstrikes in Morocco. See also Divine (1966) and Gottmann (1943), on whose work Hewitt draws in his study.
4 As Coward himself notes, his focus on urban heterogeneity may be vulnerable to critique of those indicating that cities inhabited by relatively homogenous populations have also historically become targets of deliberate destruction. However, he goes on to indicate that "such a critique fails to separate the historical and empirical fact of homogeneity from the existential principle of publicness that characterises the buildings that compose the built environment," which means that the historical homogeneity of a particular urban space "does not in any way invalidate the notion that buildings are constitutive of a spatiality that is, in principle, public" (Coward 2006, 430).
5 In his later work, Coward (2012) engages with Jean-Luc Nancy's approach to alterity and Jane Bennett's theorizations of the vibrancy of things to expose the assemblage-like nature of globalized urbanity. Although separate from his work on urbicidal violence, he nevertheless acknowledges the constitutive role of material infrastructures for the emergence of the urban political subjectivity. He focuses on questions of relationality as crucial for understanding of community, stating that "between us in the city is neither an empty space nor simply of human bond. Rather between us is a surface of contact, a point of articulation, at which heterogeneous elements are assembled into complex ecologies of sub-

jectivity. Between us is the urban fabric from houses to large technical infrastructures" (Coward 2012, 479).
6 This applies to both liberal political theory, which situates the individual subject in the center of the political world, as much as to dominant (neo)realist conceptualizations of world politics, giving priority to sovereign states as principal actors of international relations.
7 Shaw (2004) proposes considering urbicide an element of genocidal violence.
8 For the concept of de-development, see Roy (1987).
9 It may seem that Coward's (2006, 2009) suggestion to transcend the anthropocentric analyses of violence against the built environment and consider it as a form of violence *in its own right* has been an exception in contemporary political science scholarship and draws attention to the need to take inanimate object seriously. However, his interest in matter, at least on the theoretical level, is in my opinion partly misleading, as it still seems to subscribe to the either-or logic, although prioritizing the element, which has hitherto been typically crossed out from the mainstream theorizations. Thus, differently from Coward's recommendation, my new materialism-informed account of urbicidal violence proposes to consider materiality as co-constitutive of the practices of violence, rather than a distinct form of them.
10 A comprehensive analysis of "epistemicide" embedded in the project of Western science is offered by Santos (2007a, 2007b, 2007c, 2014, 2018). For the discussion of the Western way of producing knowledge—while suppressing other forms of knowing—see also Golańska and Bywalec (2022) and Golańska et al. (2022).
11 Van der Tuin (2015) rehearses this term in the context of the problematic efforts at canonizing feminist scholarship, pointing to the classificatory move in the domain of feminist epistemologies as being a repetition of the positivist tendencies in Western science.
12 For an insightful analysis of the feminist ontology of language, see Kirby (1997, 2006, 2008, 2010, 2011).
13 It is important to mention that Hewitt's analysis remains infused with the Cold War circumstances of nuclear predicament and he explicitly admits that he thinks of massive place annihilation as a possible scenario to be put in practice in the case of a nuclear conflict.
14 See also Rumpf (1962) and Hasting (1979), on whose works Hewitt draws.
15 Fullilove writes in the context of the American project of urban renewal, which in the period between 1940s and 1970s uprooted a great number of African-American communities in a significant number of North American cities.
16 Questions of place-based mnemonic strategies have been explored by Till (2012), Hayden (1995), Lacy (1995), Dorrian and Rose (2003), Kester (2004), and Kwon (2004).
17 See, for instance, Fullilove (2016), Till (2005, 2008, 2011, 2012), Adams et al. (2001), and Kelley (1995).
18 See also Davis (2006), Sundberg (2008), and Sundberg and Kaserman (2007). For interpretation of urbicidal policies in a colonial context, see Goonewardena and Kipfer (2006); for racialized policies of placelessness, see McKittrick and Woods (2007), McKittrick (2006), and Peake and Ray (2001).

Bibliography

Adams, Paul C., Steven Hoelscher, and Karen E. Till. 2001. *Textures of Place*. Minneapolis: University of Minnesota Press.

Berman, Marshall. 1987a. "Among the Ruins." *New Internationalist* 178: n.p.
———. 1987b. "Life in the Shadows: The Underside of New York City." *New Internationalist* 167: n.p.
———. 1996. "Falling Tower. City Life After Urbicide." In *Geography and Identity: Living and Exploring the Geopolitics of Identity*, edited by Dennis Crow, 172–191. Washington, DC: Maisonneuve Press.
Coward, Martin. 2006. "Against Anthropocentrism: The Destruction of the Built Environment as a Distinct Form of Political Violence." *Review of International Studies* 32, no. 3: 419–437. https://doi.org/10.1017/S0260210506007091.
———. 2007. "'Urbicide' Reconsidered." *Theory & Event* 10, no. 2: n.p. https://doi.org/10.1353/tae.2007.0056.
———. 2009. *Urbicide. The Politics of Urban Destruction*. New York and London: Routledge.
———. 2012. "Between Us in the City: Materiality, Subjectivity, and Community in the Era of Global Urbanization." *Environment and Planning D: Society and Space* 30: 468–481. https://doi.org/10.1068/d21010.
Davis, Mike. 2006. *Planet of Slums*. New York: Verso.
Deleuze, Gilles. 1988. *Foucault*, translated by Séan Hand. Minneapolis: University of Minnesota Press.
Divine, David. 1966. *The Broken Wing: A Study of the British Experience of Air Power*. London: Hutchinson.
Dorrian, Mark, and Gillian Rose. 2003. *Deterritorialisations*. London: Black Dog Publishing.
Dovey, Kim. 1978. "Home as an Ordering Principle in Space." *Landscape* 22: 27–30.
Foucault, Michel. 1994 [1966]. *The Order of Things: An Archaeology of Human Sciences*. New York: Vintage Books.
Fullilove, Mindy T. 2016 [2004]. *Root Shock*. New York: New Village Press. EBook.
Golańska, Dorota, and Grzegorz Bywalec. 2022. "The Relationality of Knowing: From Economies of Care to Epistemic Justice." In *Investigating Cultures of Equality*, edited by Dorota Golańska, Aleksandra M. Różalska, and Suzanne Clisby, 22–41. New York and London: Routledge.
Golańska, Dorota, Aleksandra M. Różalska, and Suzanne Clisby. 2022. "Investigating Cultures of Equality: Relationality at Work in Situated Research." In *Investigating Cultures of Equality*, edited by Dorota Golańska, Aleksandra M. Różalska, and Suzanne Clisby, 1–21. New York and London: Routledge.
Goonewardena, Kanishka, and Stefan Kipfer. 2006. "Postcolonial Urbicide: New Imperialism, Global Cities and the Damned of the Earth." *New Frontiers* 59: 23–33.
Gottmann, Jean. 1943. "Bugeaud, Gallieni, Lyautey: The Development of French Colonial Warfare." In *Makers of Modern Strategy: Military Thought from Machiavelli to Hitler*, edited by Edward M. Earle, 234–259. Princeton: Princeton University Press.
Hanafi, Sari. 2009. "Spacio-cide: Colonial Politics, Invisibility and Rezoning in Palestinian Territory." *Contemporary Arab Affairs* 2, no. 1: 106–121. https://doi.org/10.1080/17550910802622645.
———. 2012. "Explaining Spacio-cide in the Palestinian Territory: Colonization, Separation, and State of Exception." *Current Sociology* 61, no. 2: 190–205. https://doi.org/10.1177/0011392112456505.

Haraway, Donna. 1997. *Modest_Witness@Second_Millennium.FemaleMan©_Meets_ OncoMouse™ Feminism and Technoscience*. New York: Routledge.

———. 2013. "Sowing Worlds: A Seed Bag for Terraforming with Earth Others." In *Beyond the Cyborg: Adventures with Donna Haraway*, edited by Margaret Grebowicz and Helen Merrick, 137–146. New York: Columbia University Press.

Haraway, Donna, in conversation with Martha Kenney. 2015. "Anthropocene, Capitalocene, Chthulhocene." In *Art in the Anthropocene: Encounters among Aesthetics, Politics, Environments and Epistemologies*, edited by Heather Davis and Etienne Turpin, 255–270. London: Open Humanities Press.

Hastings, Max. 1979. *Bomber Command*. New York: Dial Press.

Hayden, Dolores. 1995. *The Power of Place*. Cambridge, MA: MIT Press.

Herscher, Andrew. 2008. "Warchitectural Theory." *Journal of Architectural Education* 61, no. 3: 35–43. https://doi.org/10.1111/j.1531-314X.2007.00167.x.

Hewitt, Kenneth. 1983. "Place Annihilation: Area Bombing and the Fate of Urban Places." *Annals of the Association of American Geographers* 73, no. 2: 257–284. https://doi.org/10.1111/j.1467-8306.1983.tb01412.x.

Johnson, Nora. 1982. *You Can Go Home Again: An Intimate Journey*. Garden City: Doubleday.

Joronen, Mikko. 2021. "Unspectacular Spaces of Slow Wounding in Palestine." *Transactions of the Institute of British Geographers* 46, no. 4: 995–1007. https://doi.org/10.1111/tran.12473.

Kelley, Jeff. 1995. "Common Work." In *Mapping the Terrain*, edited by Suzanne Lace, 139–148. Seattle: Bay Press.

Kester, Grant. 2004. *Conversation Pieces*. Berkeley: University of California Press.

Kirby, Vicki. 1997. *Telling Flesh: The Substance of the Corporeal*. New York and London: Routledge.

———. 2006. *Judith Butler: Live Theory*. London and New York: Continuum.

———. 2008. "Natural Convers(at)ions: Or, What if Culture Was Really Nature All Along?" In *Material Feminisms*, edited by Stacy Alaimo and Susan Hekman, 214–236. Bloomington: Indiana University Press.

———. 2010. "Original Science: Nature Deconstructing Itself." *Derrida Today* 3, no. 2: 201–220. https://doi.org/10.3366/drt.2010.0204.

———. 2011. *Quantum Anthropologies: Life at Large*. Durham and London: Duke University Press.

Kwon, Miwon. 2004. *One Place After Another*. Cambridge, MA: MIT Press.

Lacy, Suzanne, ed. 1995. *Mapping the Terrain*. Seattle: Bay Press.

Lefebvre, Henri. 1968. *Le droit à la ville*. Paris: Anthropos.

Lowenthal, David. 1975. "Past Time, Present Place: Landscape and Memory." *The Geographical Review* 65: 1–36. https://doi.org/10.2307/213831.

Mack, Arien, ed. 1991. *Home: A Place in the World*. New York: New School for Social Research.

Makiya, Kanan. 1994. *Cruelty and Silence: War, Tyranny and Uprising in the Arab World*. London: Penguin.

Mbembe, Achille. 2003. *On the Postcolony*. Berkeley: University of California Press.

McKittrick, Katherine. 2006. *Demonic Grounds: Black Women and the Cartographies of Struggle*. Minneapolis: University of Minnesota Press.

———. 2011. "On Plantations, Prisons, and a Black Sense of Place." *Social & Cultural Geography* 12, no. 8: 947–963. https://doi.org/10.1080/14649365.2011.624280.

McKittrick, Katherine, and Clyde Woods, eds. 2007. *Black Geographies and the Politics of Place*. Cambridge: South End Press.

Mehrag, Sarah Jane. 1999. "Making It, Breaking It, and Making It Again: The Importance of Identity in the Destruction and Reconstruction of War-torn Societies." M.A. thesis. University of Exeter.

———. 2001. "Identicide and Cultural Cannibalism: Warfare's Appetite for Symbolic Place." *Peace Research* 33.2: 89–98.

Orentlicher, Diane. 1999. "Genocide." In *Crimes of War: What the Public Should Know*, edited by Roy Guttman and David Rieff, 153–157. London: W.W. Norton.

Peake, Linda, and Brian K. Ray. 2001. "Racializing the Canadian Landscape: Whiteness, Uneven Geographies and Social Justice." *The Canadian Geographer* 45, no. 1: 180–186. https://doi.org/10.1111/j.1541-0064.2001.tb01183.x.

Porteous, J. Douglas, and Sandra E. Smith. 2001. *Domicide. The Global Destruction of Home*. Montreal and Kingston: McGill-Queen's University Press.

Riedlmayer, Andreas. 1994. "The War on People and the War on Culture." *The New Combat* 3 (Autumn): 16–19.

———. 1995. "Killing Memory: The Targeting of Bosnia's Cultural Heritage." Testimony Presented at a Hearing of the Commission on Security and Cooperation in Europe, U.S. Congress. 4 April 1995, Community of Bosnia Foundation. Online. Available at: http://www.haverford.edu/relg/sells/killing.html. Accessed 12 February 2021.

Roberts, Adam, and Richard Guelff, eds. 2000. *Documents on the Laws of War*. Oxford: Oxford University Press.

Rogers, A. P. V. 1996. *Law on the Battlefield*. Manchester: Manchester University Press.

Roy, Sara. 1987. "The Gaza Strip: A Case of Economic De-development." *Journal of Palestine Studies* 17, no. 1: 56–88. https://doi.org/10.2307/2536651.

Rumpf, Hans. 1962. *The Bombing of Germany*, translated by Edward Fitzgerald. New York: Rinehart and Winston.

Santos, Boaventura de Sousa, ed. 2007a. *Another Knowledge Is Possible: Beyond Northern Epistemologies*. London: Verso.

———. 2007b. "Beyond Abyssal Thinking: From Global Lines to Ecologies of Knowledges." *Review* 30, no. 1: 45–89.

———. 2007c. *Cognitive Justice in a Global World: Prudent Knowledge for a Decent Life*. Lanham: Lexington.

———. 2014. *Epistemologies of the South. Justice Against Epistemicide*. London and New York: Routledge.

———. 2018. *The End of Cognitive Empire: The Coming of Age of Epistemologies of the South*. Durham and London: Duke University Press.

Shaw, Martin. 2004. "New Wars of the City: Relationships of 'Urbicide' and 'Genocide.'" In *Cities, War and Terrorism: Towards an Urban Geopolitics*, edited by Stephen Graham, 141–153. Oxford: Blackwell.

———. 2007. *What Is Genocide?* Cambridge: Polity.

Sundberg, Juanita. 2008. "'Trash-talk' and the Production of Quotidian Geopolitical Boundaries in the USA–Mexico Borderlands." *Social & Cultural Geography* 9, no. 8: 871–890. https://doi.org/10.1080/14649360802441424.

Sundberg, Juanita, and Bonnie Kaserman. 2007. "Cactus Carvings and Desert Defecations: Embodying Representations of Border Crossings in Protected Areas on the Mexico–US Border." *Environment and Planning D: Society and Space* 25: 727–744. https://doi.org/10.1068/d75j.
Thomas, William. 1995. *Scorched Earth: The Military's Assault on the Environment*. Philadelphia: New Society.
Till, Karen E. 2005. *The New Berlin*. Minneapolis: University of Minnesota Press.
———. 2008. "Artistic and Activist Memory-work: Approaching Place-based Practice." *Memory Studies* 1, no. 1: 95–109. https://doi.org/10.1177/1750698007083893.
———. 2011. "Resilient Politics and Memory-work in Wounded Cities: Rethinking the City Through the District Six in Cape Town, South Africa." In *Collaborative Resilience*, ed. Bruce E. Goldstein, 283–307. Cambridge, MA: MIT Press.
———. 2012. "Wounded Cities: Memory-work and Place-based Ethics of Care." *Political Geography* 31: 2–14. https://doi.org/10.1016/j.polgeo.2011.10.008.
van der Tuin, Iris. 2015. *Generational Feminism: New Materialist Introduction to a Generative Approach*. Lenham: Lexington Books.
Winning, Anne. 1990. "Homesickness." *Phenomenology & Pedagogy* 8: 245–258. https://doi.org/10.29173/pandp15139.

3
GEOGRAPHICAL WARFARE IN PALESTINE

Lethal Geographies, Slow Violences

In his 1976 book, *La géographie, ça sert, d'abord, à faire la guerre*,[1] Yves Lacoste formulates a controversial claim that geography—typically seen as a method of describing space which considers both its human and physical characteristics—must be understood as a major tool of social organization and control, as well as of warfare. Geographical reasoning, Lacoste notes, has "a strategic role to play" (2012, xi) in the organization of the world at different scales. If we want to appreciate the strictly political character of geographical investigations, they need to be paired with a historical narrative which makes possible the consideration of "a strategic situation" and the preparation of "either a political or military operation" (2012, iii). Given the history of colonial takeovers, it is necessary to pay attention to the principal role of geographers in this violent enterprise. As Lacoste indicates, "All colonial conquests were first geographical undertakings not only through the drawing of maps of the topography for reconnaissance purposes but also of the territorial and historical disputes between different ethnic groups" (2012, iv). So even though—in line with the dominant realist understandings of scientific objectivity—geography may appear to be an innocent method of mapping space, in fact it intersects with ideologies and politics, serving as a potent instrument in the hands of the powerful.[2] As I argue in this chapter, the topography-based Israeli land policies in Palestine can serve as an illustrative example of Lacoste's contested views on how spatial data come to be weaponized in a state-orchestrated military effort.

Geography, according to Lacoste, combines different ways of looking at the world. Its strategy includes "a range of tools that helps the consideration of the complexities of terrestrial space at different levels of spatial analysis and in interaction, from local to national and to the planetary and back," and focuses on "specific cartographic configurations and intersections of several spatial sets of differing sizes" (Lacoste 2012, xiv). These sets refer to, for instance, hydrographic and geological data, climatic phenomena, ecological entities, populations, economic and social structures, political organisms spatially defined by borders, religious, and linguistic sets (Lacoste 2012, xiv). Lacoste also encourages us to think of geography in both human and physical dimensions at the same time; it is not enough to consider territory (its surface area, topography, resources) in isolation from the people who inhabit and make use of that land or the configuration of authorities extending over it (Lacoste 2012, xiv). As such, in order to truly understand *the content* of geography, as well as its significance for warfare, it is necessary to take account of the different ways in which it intersects with other fields of knowledge; it is also of utmost importance to realize the political reverberations of geographical inquiry and their salience for strategic geopolitical thinking, generating meaningful consequences. Thus, in such an understanding, "geography does not amount to a mere tool for knowing about the world; it is an instrument for action" (Gilbert 1989, 222). This action can take diverse forms, unfold at different speeds, and produce singular contributions to policy-making processes.

When geographically mapped, territory emerges as a complex material-semiotic entity, a combination of "world" and "word" (Kirby 1997, 2006, 2008, 2010, 2011) materializing from a conglomerate of the natural forms and forces and the cultural meanings attributed to them, as well as techniques and tools which enable the mapping process. It functions as a principal element of politics—after all, states are unthinkable in other than territorial and ideological terms, where a certain space, marked by historically shaped borders, participates in the processes of forging political communities as well as in confronting other political organisms. Such an understanding of the procedures of mapping space, or of turning space into a territory, reveals how maps may serve as potent instruments of power. As Lacoste explains, a map should be conceived as being "designed and motivated by practical (political and military) concerns"; it assists in the politically informed processes of dominating and controlling space. To map "means to formally define space along the lines set within a particular epistemological experience; it actually transposes a little-known piece of concrete reality into an abstraction which serves the practical interests of the State machine" (2008a [1973], 620). Although Lacoste primarily means this in terms of the power of representing space, when approached from a new materialist point of view, the process of mapping space emerges as a complex entanglement of its various multidimensional materialities and their socio-cultural understandings.

In the context of the issues explored in this book, the potency of mapping the territory is recognized by Edward Said, who notes—when offering a critique of the Oslo Accords, which in the early 1990s were drafted to quell the violent Israeli-Palestinian war—that one of the problems of the Palestinians was that they have long been "mapless"; "They had no detailed maps of their own at Oslo; nor, unbelievably, were there any individuals on the negotiating team familiar enough with the geography of the Occupied Territories to contest decisions or to provide alternative plans" (2000, n.p.). This, for Said, can partly explain the unusual territorial arrangements decided upon in Oslo (to the detriment of the Palestinians), which separate different parts of Area A (under complete Palestinian control) from each other, surrounding them with territories classified as Area B (shared control), and Area C (Israeli control), as well as by delineating special areas H1 and H2 (for the divided city of Hebron) (Figure 3.1). This spatial organization of the contested territory dissects Palestinian land into what Said calls "besieged spots on the map" (2000, n.p.), hampering any efforts at establishing an independent, coherent territorial entity with a consistent political authority extending over it. This outcome clearly demonstrates the political importance of the processes of mapping space, even though cartography is not the only plane on which geographical practice clearly links with the structures of power; how the topographical and demographic characteristics of specific space can be strategically used, or mobilized, in a military effort remains equally important. As Lacoste reminds us, the "use" of geographical knowledge for the purpose of warfare includes the

> destruction of vegetation, the transformation of the physical characteristics of the soil, the deliberate precipitation of new erosional processes, the rupture of hydrological systems in order to change the level of the table water (so as to dry up wells and rice paddies), and also a radical change in the distribution of population (2008a [1973], 621; see also Lacoste 1972, 1973, 1976a, 1976b, 1984, 2008b).

Such developments cannot be seen as "unintended consequences of the massive scale of lethal means available for technological and industrial warfare; they are the result of a deliberate and minutely articulated strategy, the elements of which are scientifically coordinated in time and space" (Lacoste 2008a [1973], 622). This clearly demonstrates that geographical discourse, as well as mapping and measuring technologies used within this field of knowledge, must be perceived as concerned with issues of power, while the different more-than-human agencies of space—or materialities of terrain, as Elden proposes (2021)—should be carefully considered in any analysis of political processes. In that sense, geographical knowledge, as Lacoste claims, actively participates in the execution of "geographical warfare" and, as such, it should be cautiously scrutinized, even denounced, as contributing to the serious destruction (of people, land, environment, community, etc.). Its effects, for Lacoste, "are difficult, if at all possible, to repair" (2008a [1973], 623).

According to such a conceptual framing, urbicide should be seen as one of the forms of geographical warfare, as political violence consisting of the deliberate destruction—either fast or slow—of the built environment requires

GEOGRAPHICAL WARFARE IN PALESTINE

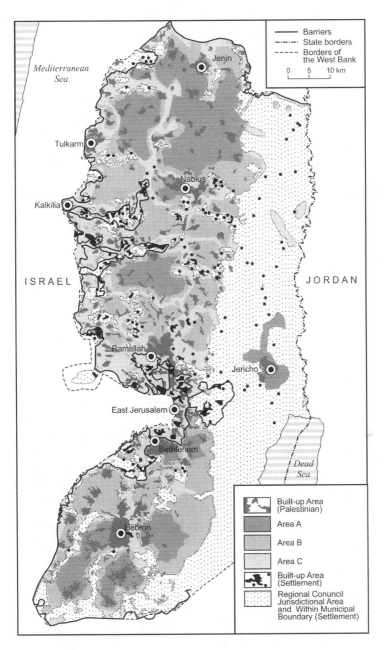

Figure 3.1 Administrative division of the West Bank (Oslo II Accord) and the Jewish settlements in the area. Compiled based on datasets made available by United Nations Office for the Coordination of Humanitarian Affairs, B'Tselem, and PeaceNow.

a powerful fluency in mastering multifaceted geographical information. The latter includes the eloquence and slickness involved in analyzing interactions between physical data and human factors, each determined by the other. Hence, as the case study of Palestine clearly reveals, it is necessary to acknowledge the strategic role of demographers, statisticians, geographers, architects, and planners in state efforts to deepen control over occupied (or annexed) spaces (see Weizman 2004). One of the central tasks within the project of colonization of Palestine has been to obliterate geographical conditions that are indispensable for the lives of people inhabiting these territories—the Palestinian-Arabs. Their presence on the "promised land" seems to have been purposefully ignored by both the Zionist leaders and the international community. The subsequent regular (although relatively slow) colonization of these territories could not have been accomplished without the accompanying systematic investment in cartographical planning, deliberate destruction—or partial reconfiguration—of the existing built environment, and carefully designed construction of new infrastructures. Given the complexity of this process, as both Weizman (2002, 2004, 2007) and Graham (2004a) argue, it is necessary to realize the multidimensional character of urbicidal violence perpetrated in the Occupied Territories and in the Israeli heartland, which simultaneously consists of both *destruction* and *construction* of particular infrastructures. This points to a "generative" nature of urbicidal policy, which works for the purpose of producing specific forms of Israeli territoriality in the concerned regions. This strategy has been made possible due to the persuasiveness of discursive narratives aimed at demonizing the Arab "others" and describing their cities and homes as places where terrorist activity allegedly breeds, especially—although not exclusively—in the aftermath of the 9/11 attacks. Underpinned by the state-induced rhetoric strategy of criminalization of the urban areas populated by the Palestinian-Arabs, the meticulously planned policy consists of the annexation of their land, the destruction of their houses and olive groves, and the severe limitation of grazing spaces or dry agriculture facilities (a substantial source of income for Palestinian-Arab rural communities), as well as gradual ethnic cleansing of selected geographical areas. An equally important (and similarly destructive) dimension relates to the construction of Jewish settlements (including industrial ones) on carefully chosen spots both in the Occupied Territories and in Israel proper; the development of a complex network of Israeli-only bypass roads in the West Bank connecting the settlements with each other and with the Israeli heartland; the erection of a dividing wall between Israel proper and the Occupied Territories (which has an important additional role in cutting off Palestinian urban spaces from each other and constraining their natural, spontaneous development); the construction of ethnically segregated townships in the Naqab/Negev region with unequal access to basic infrastructures and facilities; and the implementation of a meticulously designed system of permanent and ad hoc checkpoints which severely limit Palestinians' mobility within the Occupied Territories and between them and the Israeli mainland. All of these factors translate into the growing impoverishment of the Palestinian-Arab population (in its whole diversity), seriously restricting its fundamental rights. There is a broad range of policies in place that together make up a system of state-controlled oppression in which various more-than-human agencies are subtly mobilized and tacitly operationalized to further constrain the life of Palestinian-Arabs. In the following pages I will investigate the ways in which the more-than-human forces are recruited, or activated, by Israeli politicians, strategists, and planners for the purpose of implementing efficient urbicidal policies in Palestine, through two case studies in which slow-motion strategies are used to produce the forms of ethno-territoriality desired by the Israeli state. In this context, it is useful to refer to Nigel Thrift's formulation that violence should be seen as "an expanding series of practices in which objects—many of them of a sophisticated kind—have a more than incidental place and that, increasingly, violence works to an agenda driven by the requirements of these objects" (2007, 277). Through a closer glimpse at the *practices* of geographical warfare, and how they tend to operate in the broader material-semiotic contexts of the enduring Israeli colonial project in Palestine, my intention in this chapter is to pay attention to the multipart composition of the acts of slow political violence and to examine how it mobilizes, or is co-constituted by, both human and more-than-human agents and forces.

In his brief analysis of the 2003 Middle East peace initiative, which was intended to end the escalation of violence connected to the so-called Al-Aqsa Intifada, Weizman (2004) notes that the "roadmap" clearly recognizes the political salience of the role of architects and planners in generating this conflict. While stating that the Palestinian authority should invest in efforts to prevent attacks (including suicidal ones) carried out by armed organizations against Israeli civilians and dismantle their infrastructures, it also recommends that Israel should stop establishing new settlements in the Occupied Territories and disassemble those erected in breach of Israeli law. In fact, by setting up such conditions, the agreement openly equates the activities of each side as contributing in comparable ways to the conflict (Weizman 2004, 172). Such a framing of the peace initiative seems to suggest that the construction efforts in which Israel has been investing financially, militarily, demographically, and emotionally since 1967 should be considered a form of warfare targeted against Palestinian communities populating the territories of the West Bank and Gaza, and a continuation of a strategy of systematic colonization regularly implemented since the withdrawal of the British from this territory. Certainly, the year 1967 must be seen as an important caesura, signaling a substantial redefinition of the Israeli (or Zionist) colonial project. Even though, after the swift victory in the Six-Day War, Israel's political elites were clearly aware of the fact that they would probably have to return the now-Occupied Territories of the West Bank to Jordan, they nevertheless launched a slow-motion policy of gradual land seizure, initially represented as a temporary project undertaken for military (or security) purposes. The implementation of this plan eventually resulted in the creation of the rather unconventional geography of the Occupied Territories, hampering the future establishment of a separate Palestinian state spanning a politically well-defined and jurisdictionally coherent space. This policy was undertaken not only via strictly military means. Rather, as Weizman explains, "In this process the transformation of the territories occupied by Israel since 1967 became a parallel conflict carried out with pencil lines on the drafting tables of military and civilian planners and architects" (2004, 172). Importantly, as he further indicates, "It developed as an 'urban war' in which urbanity provided not only the arena of war but also its very weapons and ammunition. Just like a gun or a tank, mundane building matters have been used by the Israeli state to apply its strategic and political agenda" (2004, 172; see also Weizman 2007; Lein and Weizman 2002; Segal and Weizman 2003).

Even though "a gun" or "a tank" should also be seen as a more-than-human agent operating in complex material-discursive contexts and generating similarly complex consequences, mobilizing aspects such as the architectural planning of mundane family houses, industrial and infrastructural developments, the topographical characteristics of the terrain, construction patterns and techniques, or natural resources (such as water) for the purpose of conducting war appears to be a less obvious warfare strategy. In such a context, these factors emerge as important political agents in the multifaceted Israeli project of colonizing Palestine. As Rafi Segal and Eyal Weizman argue in their groundbreaking work, *Civilian Occupation* (2003),[3] through its carefully undertaken processes of planning and building in the West Bank, Israel is effectively implementing a political agenda by means of well-designed spatial manipulations. Worth noting is the fact that similar undertakings have been characteristic of the process of building territoriality in the Israeli heartland since 1948 (Leshem 2016; Jabareen 2015). This stratagem involves the meticulous exploitation of a set of connections, or entanglements, among national narratives, law, (history of) conflict, and geography. It also makes use of carefully devised linkages between geographical representations and ideological performance. These complex entwinements, and their agential enactments, need to be carefully investigated for the purpose of offering a nuanced understanding of the processes accompanying the Israeli colonial presence in Palestine. In such an account, the environment and landscape (the indispensable elements of a particular territory) can no longer be conceived as brute, inert, or fixed backdrops of conflict but rather should be seen, as Lacoste suggested, as "an active, operational constituent of war" (Bowd and Clayton 2013, 640). New materialism seems to offer adequate conceptual tools to expose these deadly connections. Denouncing their lethal assemblage-like operations, this perspective substantially adds to the extant scholarship exploring Israeli policies in Palestine. The academic dialogue between these explorations and the theoretical developments emerging around Nixon's concept of slow violence (2009, 2011) can contribute to the shedding of new light on the analyzed phenomena further revealing state-sponsored efforts at reconfiguring the more-than-human geographies of both the Occupied Territories and the Israeli mainland.

In the following sections, I will look at two examples of slow urbicidal policies undertaken by the Israeli authorities in Palestine. The cases, or stories, under discussion relate to different phases of the Israeli colonization of the territory of the former British Mandate of Palestine and to geographical areas with very different political statuses; even though these processes have been ongoing since the late 1940s, their intensity has been sinusoidal. It is not possible within such a short book to cover these complex "policies" in great detail, and such an attempt is not an aim of this chapter. Rather, my analysis will focus on the entanglement of the human and more-than-human dimensions of these enduring initiatives, looking into the complex character of political violence and the diversity of practices involved in slow urbicide in Palestine. My attempt at theorizing the more-than-human agencies involved in the violent developments in the two selected areas stems from the conviction that such a conceptualization—still missing from extant studies of such processes wrapped around the aforementioned notions of "verticality" (Graham 2004b, 2016; Graham and Hewitt 2012; Weizman 2002, 2007; Segal and Weizman 2003) and "volume" (Elden 2013, 2017, 2021)—can substantially reconfigure our thinking about the role of space/spatiality in international and security politics. Partly abandoning the technocratic and disengaged gaze present in such analyses (Adey 2013; Harker 2011), I am more interested in the *how* question of urbicide in Palestine, exposing the material-semiotic character of these developments and looking into the complex consequences they generate for the topographical and "topological" (Harker 2011, 2014) organization of urban communities. My focus is also on the relational nature of violence targeting the indigenous populations in the regions under consideration, as well as on the shifting temporalities of the violent policies launched by the Israeli state within the scope of its colonial enterprise. I will relate the exploration of these processes to the two core concepts around which my narrative is built: "the right to the city" and "ethno-territoriality."

Geographical warfare, as these examples are intended to demonstrate, has been systematically used by the Israeli authorities in their well-planned settlement project. The forces of nature, as much as the various instances of natural-cultural, human-nonhuman, or material-semiotic entanglements, have been instrumentalized in this political endeavor. In paying attention to the specific mobilizations of different materialities, my intention is to expose the slow—seemingly innocent—operations of political violence in the region. As my case studies demonstrate, even though in Lacoste's original formulation of the term "geographical warfare" the landscape was mostly viewed as a kind of enemy to be destroyed as part of the military effort, in the case of the conflictual relations between the Israeli state and the Palestinian-Arabs the term now stands for a strategic use of landscape and/or natural forces as tools for political violence. In this sense, the agencies of landscape/climate/topography are clearly acknowledged and subsequently entangled with human-induced processes (e.g., pollution, toxicity, urbanization) as well as the semiotic structures and ideology-infused ideas that have populated the arena of the Israeli politics in Palestine since the very inception of the Israeli state. This demonstrates the crucial agencies, or determinations, generated by space in, as Thrift underlines, "setting up and breeding certain forms of violence" (2007, 274). In that sense, geographical space, with its diverse natural-cultural attributes and characteristics, cannot be approached solely as a context; rather, it "provide[s] a medium and a means and a momentum, as well as a measure" (Thrift 2007, 274).

Case Study 1. Cartographies of Domination in the West Bank

To fully understand the operations of slow urbicide in the West Bank it is necessary to recall at least the most important facts and turning points in the decades-long history of Israeli-Arab, and then Israeli-Palestinian, relations.[4] In 1948, in the aftermath of the Second World War on the one hand and in the context of intense decolonization processes in the Middle East region on the other, Israel—declared as a new independent state in May 1948—took over most of the territory of a historical organism called Mandatory Palestine. Even though, as signaled in the Introduction, the Zionist policy was premised on the appealing slogan "a land without a people for a people without a land,"[5] resonating with the post-war discomfort about the terrifying fate of the Jewish community in Europe, the territory annexed by the Israeli state was by no means unpopulated. In order to take control over the land, Israeli military forces destroyed and depopulated 531 Arab villages (Said 2000; see also Pappé 2006; Hassan and Hanafi 2009), violently relocating a great number of the Arabs originally inhabiting this land. This process initiated one of the biggest and most persistent waves of refugees in the world (Abujidi 2014; Morris 1987). Except for the West Bank (which came under the control of Jordan[6]) and the Gaza Strip (which came under the control of Egypt), the whole territory of the former British Mandate was turned into the newly established independent State of Israel. This fact violated the decisions—even though widely contested by both sides—set up in UN Resolution 181, recommending the creation of two independent states on the territory of Mandatory Palestine and delineating their borders. The newly proclaimed state launched a project of (re)settlement and development of its (still unrecognized) territory with the aim to build a prosperous political organism, able to fully participate in both regional and global politics. This was executed at the cost of people already inhabiting the land, who were brutally dispossessed of their belongings and expelled.[7] The ethnic composition of the territory has been radically reworked according to the narrative of Jewish belonging in the mythical "promised land."

The situation took another turn in 1967 when, as a result of the Six-Day War, Israel extended its military and political control over Gaza and the West Bank, considered since then the Occupied Territories. Even though the UN Security Council Resolutions 242 and 338 stipulate that this land must be given back, these regulations have been consistently ignored by Israel, which was unwilling to return the newly acquired land. Immediately after this acquisition, not only did Israel literally annex the extended territory of East Jerusalem and its suburbs[8] (earlier under Jordanian rule), but also initiated a regular policy of building and expanding Jewish settlements in the West Bank. This process contributed to redefining the land ethnically along the lines of Jewish belonging therein and informally, yet factually, extending Israeli territoriality over it. This project continues to seriously constrain the natural development of the Palestinian communities. The settlement enterprise persistently violates Palestinians' "right to the city," affecting their traditional ways of dwelling that combine human and more-than-human aspects of communal living. These entanglements embrace not only the long-cultivated practices of constructing and organizing housing and how this relates to established agricultural traditions, but also includes routine movements, daily rhythms, seasonal adaptations, and ecosystemic relations often dictated by natural forces and the specificities of the climate, as well as established customs, spatial navigations, family relations, and time management. Israeli infrastructural developments also limit Palestinian-Arabs' possibilities for shaping the urban space according to their communities' needs by imposing discriminatory land regulations and implementing a policy of systematic land seizure for what the former claim to be the public good. The previously mentioned Oslo peace process, instead of solving the conflict, further exacerbated the territorial arrangements already in place, hampering any attempts to establish a sovereign, territory-based Palestinian state. Obviously, this remains in line with the original goals of the Israeli policy. As Orna Ben-Naftali et al. explain, the Israeli regime "sustains an indefinite occupation that amounts to de facto annexation," using the indeterminacy of this system "to legitimize what would otherwise be clearly illegal" (2009, 31). In effect, the international regime of occupation "has been manipulated in a manner that legitimizes the tearing apart of the fabric of Palestinian life while advancing the political agenda of Israeli expansionism" (Ben-Naftali et al. 2009, 32). If approached from the perspective of ethno-territorial logic, the presence of Jews in the West Bank can only be premised on the systematic uprooting of Palestinian ways of dwelling, the erasure of their traditional activities, the dissipation of their dependence on land, and the denial of their political and physical visibility. Such a situation seriously affects the possibilities of Palestinians to exert their most basic rights, constraining their aspirations to self-governance and territorial independence.

The forms of occupation largely differ in the West Bank. While in certain areas (such as Hebron) settlements are not spatially removed from Palestinian urban spaces and should rather be seen as "two overlapping polygons, settlers literally on top of Palestinians" (Smith 2011, 319), in others separation between the communities of Palestinians and those of settlers is well articulated through, for instance, the material-semiotic agencies of the dividing wall (as in Bethlehem or Ramallah). Also, the occupation's intensity differs across the West Bank. The Oslo system describes the juridical reality on the surface of the land, as what is under and above the ground remains in fact under Israel's authority, which translates into what Weizman calls a "politics of verticality" (2002). Conventional two-dimensional maps, typically used for delineating the political borders of a state have, in Weizman's words, "failed to capture its vertical dimensions" (2002, n.p.). This is also because geopolitics, typically a "flat discourse" shaped by legacies of traditional military and political renditions of spatialities, "largely ignores the vertical dimension and tends to look across rather than to cut through the landscape" (2002, n.p.). This, however, does not apply to the convoluted nature of territorial arrangements in the West Bank, in which the vertical politics seems to substantially structure the understandings of territoriality. Nevertheless, in order to capture the dynamics of verticality and how it configures communities in spatial terms, it seems necessary to complexify it with the analysis of the shifting temporalities according to which political power (or violence) operates. The analysis of vertical dimension of politics, paying attention to what is above and below the territory and how these dimensions translate into uneven geographies of oppression *on the surface*, is not sufficient to do justice to the tangled operations of political violence which are often distributed across *both* space and time. Neither is the conceptual shift from "battlefield" (understood as flat) to "battlespace" (conceived of as multidimensional) (Elden 2021; see also Virilio 1993 [1976], 2008 [1975]) enough to elaborate a complete picture of the urbicidal developments in Palestine. The complex character of this form of violence, I argue, can be better grasped if the vertical/volumetric analysis is paired with investigations of the temporal dimension of these political developments. Such a perspective has the potential to shed light on violence's more discreet operations, exposing those circumstances that can easily be "objectified" (as, for instance, "natural") by means of the ideology-infused rhetoric disseminated by the state.

Worth noting is also the fact that the complex cartographical and political organization of space in the West Bank creates "microgeographies of occupation" (Smith 2011) which are very different from each other. The strategies of (slow) destruction of Palestinian urbanity, however, work in similar ways in these zones, although with different frequencies and intensities. Rather than exploring these important divergences, the goal of my analysis is to reveal the tangled operations of the means through which slow urbicide is carried out in the region, as well as to pay attention to its enduring attritional consequences.

Violent Cartographies

Although the building of durable infrastructure in territories under occupation breaches international law, and especially the Fourth Geneva Convention, since 1967 Israel has regularly expanded the construction of settlements in the West Bank. Over time, under slight shifts in political conditions, especially in relation to the Israeli political ruling forces, a series of construction plans has been implemented. The plans of each period reflected the then-current nationalist narratives and visions of the future informed by the politics of the day, offering up-to-date justifications for the need to carry out settlement activity in the regions referred to in the Israeli state's official rhetoric as "Judea and Samaria."[9] These include Alon's plan (1967-1970), Drobless's plan (1977), Dayan's plan (1978-1979), and Sharon's plan (1981).[10] Originally, Alon's plan was meant to remake the borders of Israel by including the Jordanian Valley and the Judea Desert, and justified the establishment of settlements for security reasons. This was perceived as a first step to the annexation of these territories. Within the plan, the Israeli government succeeded in establishing approximately 30 Jewish settlements in the West Bank, making the Israeli presence visible in the region (Lein and Weizman 2002, 12; see also Benvenisti and Khayat 1987). The plans that were drafted after the nationalistically oriented Likud came to power in 1977 further expanded the assumptions of Alon's plan, recommending the policy of establishing Jewish settlements throughout the West Bank, while avoiding those areas that were most densely populated by Palestinians (see Benvenisti and Khayat 1987, 65). This strategy was meant to accentuate Jewish presence in the region, eradicating the Palestinian traces left there, and denying Palestinians their territorial belonging. Before the Oslo negotiations started, there were 120 Jewish settlements established in the West Bank (excluding the East Jerusalem area); directly before the Al-Aqsa Intifada, this number had risen to almost 200 (Lein and Weizman 2002, 18). This number encompasses both the "legal" settlements, organized with the support of the Israeli state, and the outposts established in breach of Israeli law. The intention embodied in the settlement project was to both Judaize the occupied areas and impair the continuity of the Palestinian land, physically diminishing the potential territory of any future Palestinian state (Lein and Weizman 2002, 18).

In 1984, preference was again officially given to the settlement project in the Jordanian Valley; however, the process continued across the whole occupied region. Though coupled with slightly different ideological assumptions and nation-centered narratives, the strategy of making Jewish presence noticeable in the West Bank has, since 1967, remained essentially the same, especially when approached from a topographical and architectural perspective. In brief, the strategy exploits and politicizes the natural agencies of the landscape for the purpose of the Zionist colonial project. Interestingly, the discursive tactics and the material developments have typically mutually co-formed each other. Hence, the mechanisms used by the Israeli government for land acquisition could only work as a result of the material-discursive entanglements of the legal system, ideologically shaped colonial objectives, military rhetoric, and the history of conflict, *as much as* the region's topography and the (im)possibility of agricultural cultivation it offers. This combination enabled the processes of slow urbicidal violence, while keeping them to a great extent beyond the immediate interests of the international community. Through the systematic use of a range of manipulative mechanisms, Israel has managed to declare and register a substantial part of the Occupied Territories as "state land," offering persuasive official justifications for the seizure of Palestinians' private property, thus depriving them of their rights. This has remained fully in line with ethno-territorially defined colonial policy.

Settlement building patterns in the West Bank are shaped by the dynamic entanglements of the topographical features of this geographical region and the availability of ideologically distorted legal mechanisms of land seizure. These mechanisms include the requisition of land for military purposes, the expropriation of land for public needs, the declaration of land as abandoned property, and the appropriation of uncultivated areas (Abu-Lughod 1982; Aloni 2016; Hareuveni 2010; Lein and Weizman 2002; Nijim and Muammar 1984). To enhance this policy, the official strategy was also to facilitate land purchase by Jewish citizens on the free market, while the Israeli High Court also contributed to the system of dispossession, creating "an illusion of legality" (Lein and Weizman 2002, 46). Added to this must be "the privatized mechanism through which settlers help the state expand and solidify its control over ... land" (Aloni 2016, 5), consisting mostly of self-declared appropriation or cultivation of the land to which the original Palestinian owners are regularly denied access. The frequent acts of violent re-appropriation committed by Jewish settlers are typically not penalized by the state, further contributing to the emergence of discriminatory geography in the region, with Palestinians being heavily disadvantaged vis-à-vis the Jews in not only spatial, but also legal terms.

The measures applied to seize control of the land in the West Bank shuffle legislations from different historical periods, including remnants of Ottoman and British Mandate law partly absorbed into the Jordanian legal system or ad hoc orders issued by Israeli military commanders (Lein and Weizman 2002, 48). Many of the decisions to take control of land for military needs (which should by definition be temporary) were justified by the reason that the settlements established on these territories perform important defensive and military functions. The application of this mechanism stopped in 1979, due to two High Court interpretations of cases in which settlements established by the conservative spiritual movement Gush Emunim were ordered to be dismantled, since the argument that settlements served primarily military purposes and thus were only temporary was unacceptable for the movement.[11] As a result, a new mechanism—based on the application of the Ottoman Land Law of 1858, subsequently incorporated into first British and then Jordanian legal regulations—was established as a means of declaring the land to be state property, which, from the Israeli perspective, solved the problem of constructing settlements on seized private lands. This law allowed the state to take control of land that has not been farmed for at least three consecutive years or has been farmed for less than ten years by the same farmer (who has therefore not yet secured the property rights to the land); the state could also control the rocky land situated away from the villages on the basis that it was inappropriate for agricultural use.[12] The original legal formulation was meant to serve the interests of both the inhabitants and the state, ensuring that as much land as possible was cultivated and could therefore be taxed. Nevertheless, the tricky application of this regulation by Israel in fact mocked its original logic. In 1979 the Israeli government conducted a detailed survey of the land in "Judea and Samaria," taking control of all the areas formerly managed by the Jordanian authorities, any land with unclear property titles (unregistered with Ottoman, British, or Jordanian authorities[13]), and all land uncultivated for three consecutive years or cultivated for a period shorter than ten years. Additionally, any property considered "abandoned" was taken over by the state and used according to its will. Given the fact that since 1967 Israel has systematically prevented the return of war refugees to the West Bank, the property rights of this last category of land were transferred to the Israeli government and subsequently passed to new Jewish settlers.

Since most of the land that could be declared state property via the employment of these mechanisms was located on rocky hilltops (and hence, often, uncultivated and/or perceived as strategically situated in military terms), Israel was able to take control of these elevated spots, creating an additional urbanized and industrialized layer of the territory. The settlements were built along three strips running from north to south of the West Bank. The strip that most affects highly urbanized Palestinian areas is the Mountain Strip, which is situated in the vicinity of the six largest Palestinian urban centers: Jenin, Nablus, Ramallah, East Jerusalem, Bethlehem, and Hebron (Figure 3.1). It spreads out in two chains along the routes 60 and 458—the two principal traffic arteries in the West Bank. Other strips mostly negatively affect Palestinian villages, often hindering the villagers' regular access to their land, properties, or other villages and towns. Currently there are 132 Jewish settlements established by the Israeli government in the West Bank (excluding the East Jerusalem area) and 141 illegal Jewish outposts (PeaceNow 2022).[14] They have been additionally expanded through the creation of "special security areas" or "natural reserves" around them, as well as through minor acts of informal re-bordering and appropriation implemented by Jewish settlers by material means such as, for instance, planting trees and erecting barbwire fencing (Joronen 2021). Although represented as serving public interests, in general these terrains are closed to Palestinian entry (Feuerstein 2008), even though Israel applies a policy of varying strictness regarding the issuing of access permits which corresponds to the actual need for Palestinian labor or resources; these terrains, however, remain informally open to the Jewish settlers.[15]

The settlement policy required the creation of an appropriate road infrastructure (B'Tselem 2004, 5). Again, in order to take control of the land necessary for the pavement of roads, Israel used both the strategy of requisition of land for military needs and that of expropriation for public use, with a slight preference for the latter (B'Tselem 2004, 6; see also Abu-Lughod 1982; Nijim and Muammar 1984; Lein and Weizman 2002). Against the principle of public use,[16] however, in most of the cases, Palestinians have been informally denied access to these roads as much as to the areas situated in their direct vicinity. As activists from the B'Tselem organization note, "the roads regime in the West Bank has never been put on paper, neither in military legislation nor in any official decision" and "is based solely on verbal orders given to the security forces," which entails a great "degree of arbitrariness" (B'Tselem 2004, 3). Despite the unregulated status, Palestinians are strongly discouraged (also by frequent acts of violence by settlers) from using this infrastructure and they do not approach or cross the roads, even when it is necessary for them to do so to access and cultivate their properties (see Aloni 2016; Feuerstein 2008; Handel 2009). They are thus forced to use different routes (of significantly lower quality, including the passes below, and bypasses of, the Israeli-only roads), which makes trips to their land much longer and often unpredictable. In cases where bypass routes are unavailable, based on a somewhat arbitrary system of special permits, the legal owners of agricultural land are occasionally granted entry to their fields located within or across the closed areas, yet not frequently enough to secure a decent harvest. This has a negative impact on income and, subsequently, on the quality of Palestinians' living conditions. Furthermore, the Israeli architectural developments impair mobility, further exacerbated by the deployment of Israeli Defence Forces (IDF) checkpoints throughout the Occupied Territories, causing random obstructions in everyday mobility. To this must be added the consequences of constructing the dividing wall, whose trajectory was in many cases dictated by the policy of including several Jewish settlements established in the West Bank within the fenced Israeli-only zone (Figure 3.1). Again, this has severely impeded Palestinians' daily existence and the quality of their urban spaces, now often squeezed between the wall and the strip of constantly expanding Jewish settlements, and cut off from other Palestinian communities, with arbitrary and very limited access granted to non-residents. The town of Qualqilya may serve as one of the most spectacular examples of the Israeli policy of physical containment effectuated by means of the material-semiotic agencies of the dividing wall on the one hand, and the developing Jewish settlements, on the other.

Erected on hilltops (usually very close to, and overlooking, Palestinian urban areas, typically located in the valleys) and connected with each other by a network of Israeli-only bypass roads, the settlements and their accompanying infrastructures serve as physical barriers to spatial expansion of the indigenous built environment. Their material agencies have the effect of limiting spontaneous urban development, at least in certain directions, producing diverse negative consequences. In highly urbanized areas (such as Ramallah or Bethlehem, situated in Area A) these include serious housing problems, the degeneration of the urban tissue through unsuitable—often provisional—construction and overuse, excessive congestion, overcrowding, and reduced access to necessary services and infrastructures. As the boundaries of the territories under Palestinian authority (Area A) in many cases correspond to the limits of urbanized areas (as in Bethlehem or Ramallah) and their lateral expansion has been physically blocked, additional construction is only possible within the already overexploited space, often producing urban spaces with an unaesthetic materiality, visually and physically unfriendly to its inhabitants. In urban areas situated near the Green Line (and thus, since 2002, often next to the dividing wall) or of strategic significance (such as East Jerusalem and nearby villages annexed to Israel in 1967; or divided Hebron, Areas H1 and H2), similar processes cause depopulation, deterioration of the urban tissue, abandonment of properties, and severe poverty—a result of "economic and physical strangulation" (Smith 2011, 324). At the same time, the newly constructed Israeli roads premeditatedly circumvent Palestinian urbanized areas, cutting them off from commercial chains and hindering their integration within broader networks of exchange of goods and services, imposing on them the fate of self-contained and self-sufficient enclaves, to a great extent physically separated from the external world. Restrictions on mobility and isolation from fast routes of transportation translate into the substantial impoverishment of Palestinians, further limiting their possibilities of social and cultural development, thus aggravating—albeit indirectly—the quality and usability of their urbanized sites.

This kind of deliberate policy, which amounts to a subtle form of geographical warfare, besets indigenous urban areas, worsens their material characteristics, pollutes them, and causes their systematic socio-economic "de-development" (Roy 1987). Simultaneously, it invisibilizes the existence of the deteriorating Palestinian urbanity, removing it from the sight of both foreigners and, often, also Israeli citizens commuting in the region.[17] Importantly, given the fact that complex spatial developments impede traditional agricultural routines and turn the usual rural income-generating activities into a significant challenge, most of the West Bank Palestinians currently reside within the urban areas. Cities situated next to the Israeli mainland—such as Ramallah or Bethlehem—remain the most congested areas, attracting a substantial cohort of the newcomers. This is mostly due to the fact that the mobility restrictions in place in the West Bank are experienced less severely in sites geographically close to Israeli territory, which often translates into increased opportunities for employment and physical mobility for those possessing work permits. The condition of these spaces, however, remains far from desirable, owing—inter alia—to the poor quality of local infrastructures and insufficient availability of public services (including, for instance, sanitary and waste management systems). The politically informed Israeli developments in the West Bank greatly contribute to the further degeneration of the Palestinian urban areas, gradually reconfiguring them in both the topographical and topological sense; they continually incumber Palestinian communities' growth and impair their opportunities for spatial self-organization.

Notably, the carrying out of slow urbicidal policies—resulting in the gradual deterioration of urbanity in the West Bank—has been enabled by a complex entanglement of discursive and material factors mobilized for the advancement of the Israeli expansionist project. On the one hand, this project's shape and strategies are premised on the material qualities of the region, recruiting their agencies for political purposes. On the other hand, they are sustained by—and themselves sustain—the rhetoric strategies which praise the infrastructural development and modernizing efforts sponsored by the Israeli state in the region under its protracted occupation. As Weizman notes, "the terrain dictates the nature, intensity and focal points of confrontation" (2002, n.p.), making possible the implementation of a settlement strategy based on visual control, or what Gil Hochberg aptly calls "visual occupation" (2015). Thus, the agencies of the region's natural topography co-shape specific occupational policies, slowly and silently contributing to the increasing fragmentation of Palestinian spatiality, while putting it under the constant surveillance of the settlers. This is partly enabled by the scenery of the region, co-constituting the ideologically shaped apparatus of visual control and operationalizing its disciplinary panoptical qualities. Whereas the interiors of the settlements located on elevated spots and their surrounding areas remain inaccessible to Palestinians, their own villages and towns, situated down in the valleys, are exposed to visual penetration by settlers and IDF soldiers, creating traumatizing mechanisms of permanent optical invigilation. The effects of this new geography, dotted with settlements and cut with road infrastructure, are equally vehement, producing "a physical barrier to stifle Palestinian urban development" and preventing "the natural joining of communities and creation of a continuous Palestinian built-up area" (B'Tselem 2004, 6). Such a spatial reconfiguration disrupts what Harker calls "ordinary topologies," or intensive (rather than solely extensive) relations rooted in "the material, affective and imaginative actions of bodies" (2014, 323)—a dense "time-space" in which much happens (Harker 2014, 325) and which substantially transforms as an effect of premeditated spatial manipulations. These processes involve the loosening of family relations and partial dissolution of the extended sociocultural networks of community ecosystems.

Thus, functioning as instruments of warfare (albeit unconventional), Israeli architectural developments in the West Bank negatively affect the indigenous ways of dwelling, which typically combine human and more-than-human aspects of communal living. These include customary ways of constructing and organizing housing and the relation of this to agricultural traditions and the production associated with livestock, as well as the spatial and temporal routines of movement and travel, seasonal practices, family relations, customs and celebrations, and so on. This strategy of architecture warfare leads to the gradual eradication of certain forms of spatial organization and the successive emergence of territorial arrangements preferred by the Israeli state—a system which obviously works to the advantage of the Jewish settlers and which prioritizes their needs over those of the indigenous Palestinian inhabitants of the region. In the case of the West Bank, as evidenced in this analysis, slow urbicide—in contrast to fast destructive tactics—advances through construction (of Jewish infrastructures), control (through a system of checkpoints, mobility restrictions, and visual surveillance), and physical containment (through the material suppression, or siege, of Palestinian urbanity). Premised on the mastery of topographical data and cartographical techniques, these violent developments gradually generate a new geography in the region, affecting its human and nonhuman components and visually reconfiguring its original settings. The latter process, however, is co-constituted by slow operations of another cohort of more-than-human agents, severely impacting upon the natural conditions of the area.

Environmental Injustice

The new infrastructural developments in the West Bank generate negative consequences for the region's natural environment, mostly to the detriment of the Palestinians. As Jad Isaac and Jane Hilal underline, "there is an organic relationship between environmental degradation in the Occupied Palestinian Territory ... and the political conflict" (2011, 413). The policy of land confiscation for civil settlement, as well as industrial and military purposes, produces substantial disruption for the area, connected to the mismanagement of wastewater (both Israeli and Palestinian), shortages in potable water, intensive desertification, pollution of land, and degeneration and erosion of soil (the last phenomenon also results from overgrazing of the area that remains available to the Palestinian herders). The West Bank suffers severely from water shortages on the one hand, and contamination by untreated wastewater on the other. These problems are tightly interrelated and are further exacerbated by both the everyday functioning of the occupational regime and the topographical organization of settlement projects in the area, developments which heavily shape the hydro-social relations in the region. Waste and topography emerge as important political agents in the colonization of Palestinian bodies and spaces.

There are two shared water sources in the area: the Jordan River (including the Upper Jordan and the streams flowing into it, the Sea of Galilee, the Yarmuk River, and the Lower Jordan River) and the Mountain Aquifer, an extensive system of groundwater basins transecting the border between Israel and the West Bank. Following the Oslo Accords, Israel maintained almost total control over water resources in the region. Palestinians, in breach of international regulations, are banned from access to the Jordan River waters, which have been unilaterally diverted by Israel to the Naqab/Negev desert and other destinations. This, together with the ongoing climate change in the whole Middle East region[18] and the systematic Israeli policy of afforestation accompanied by the strategy of uprooting olive groves for the purpose of building new Israeli infrastructure in the West Bank, has contributed to the severe desertification of the region, endangering its endogenic biodiversity as well as reconfiguring the typical ways the local population makes use of these resources (Agha 2019; Issac and Hilal 2011; Mizyed 2009; Nofal and Barakat 2001). In the face of these processes, as Sophia Stamatopoulou-Robbins underlines, in order to understand the nature of the water problem in the West Bank, it is necessary to focus on the relationship between climate temporalities and political possibilities (2018, 385). As she insists, "Water scarcity in Palestine is not natural; it is political" (2018, 396), and the issue should be situated against the background of the realities of occupation in the region.[19]

The water resources from the Mountain Aquifer are shared by Israel and the West Bank, but around 80% of its waters are earmarked for the use of Israeli citizens inhabiting both Israel's heartland and the settlements (Lein 1998, 2000, 2001). This uneven distribution impedes Palestinians' access to water suitable for drinking, household needs, agriculture, industry, and public uses, forcing people to partly rely on other resources, such as springs, wells, rainfall collection, and purchasing water from tankers. Restrictions on mobility connected to the official policy of ensuring the security of Jewish settlers in the West Bank, along with the policy of refusing to issue permits to drill new wells and create new rainwater cisterns, substantially hamper Palestinians' access to these alternative water resources (Aloni 2016). This has a negative impact on the situation of individuals, as much as the quality of their urban areas, which are practically devoid of green/recreational public spaces (which would require regular watering). The quality of water from alternative resources (except for water tankers)—being uncontrolled by any official authorities—is also poor, which poses a serious threat to the health and well-being of the population that relies on them.

The policy of expanding Israeli presence in the West Bank, and the failure to secure appropriate infrastructure to serve both the settlements and the indigenous population, generates serious environmental problems. According to official estimates, settlements—connected to the Israeli water supply system—generate more than twice the average per capita amount of wastewater produced by Palestinian communities in the West Bank (Hareuveni 2009, 5). At the same time, more than one-third of settlements are unequipped with appropriate wastewater treatment plants. Furthermore, some of the Jewish colonies in the West Bank are in fact industrial zones, where Israel has relocated several polluting businesses, adding even more pressure to the natural environment resulting from the discharge of untreated industrial waste, including severely polluted wastewater. Due to gravity, the sewage generated by Jewish hilltop colonies runs unrefined into nearby wadis, Palestinian agricultural lands, and municipal areas, as well as contaminating nearby streams, springs, and wells, and endangering the quality of the groundwater. Again, the topographical situation of the region acts to the advantage of one side of the conflict and causes damage to the other, polluting crops, devastating landscapes, producing unpleasant smells, and endangering the health and well-being of people and livestock. The system of political control extending over the West Bank effectively obstructs any attempts at improvement of the miserable environmental situation in the region. Added to the pollution produced by the Israeli colonies is the fact that about 95% of Palestinians' wastewater is not treated at all, due to the lack of appropriate infrastructure, ending up in valleys, sewers, and irrigation channels (Hareuveni 2009, 19).

Since Israeli approval is needed in Area C of the West Bank when a new wastewater treatment facility is to be built, this instrument has regularly been used as political leverage, pressuring Palestinians to agree to link the settlements to the planned infrastructural developments, thus in a way recognizing their existence in the West Bank. Clearly, this has been politically unacceptable for the Palestinian Authority. As a result, the process of issuing permits to construct new Palestinian wastewater treatment plants has systematically been intentionally delayed (Hareuveni 2009). By restricting access to treated water, causing serious environmental damage while limiting the possibilities of repair, Israeli policy contributes extensively to the aggravation of the poor sanitary conditions in Palestinian towns and villages, while leaving the population more vulnerable to climate change and desertification. As a result, any attempts to improve the situation, if at all viable, must be adjusted to both environmental change and the political conditions of occupation. Realization of the effects of these two ongoing processes calls for, in Stamatopoulou-Robbins's words, "an epistemological shift from occupation as injustice to occupation as hazard" (2018, 399). Under conditions of continuous political tension, vulnerabilities stemming from exposure to the detrimental effects of certain natural processes unfolding in the region, as well as human-induced harmful developments, are distributed unequally across the members of population inhabiting the area, with Palestinians facing by far the greatest risk.

Additionally, Israel is responsible for severe toxic pollution in the West Bank due to its policy of establishing waste treatment facilities there, delineating so-called "sacrifice zones"—geographic areas condemned to environmental damage—in which to dispose of its hazardous waste.[20] As Aloni details, "Israel transfers to the West Bank various types of waste: sewage sludge, infectious medical waste, used oils, solvents, metals, electronic waste and batteries" (2017, 6). This policy amounts to what Stamatopoulou-Robbins aptly calls a "waste siege," causing a situation in which various kinds of waste function as "unaccounted-for actors, mediating and complicating life at multiple scales" (2020, ix). Obviously, Palestinians also produce their own waste which, for lack of appropriate management facilities, visibly litters urban and suburban areas in the West Bank. Garbage piled and burnt at the edges of inhabited spaces is not an uncommon view in Palestine. Inadequately disposed of waste, as Stamatopoulou-Robbins notes, reenters Palestinians' lives "through their lungs as dioxins carried by the smoke" (2020, ix), generating delayed harm. Thus, not only does mismanagement of waste and sewage negatively impact the quality of the built environment (especially, the functioning of sanitary systems), but also directly injures human bodies forced to reside in waste's direct proximity, exposed to its lethal agencies. Occupational policies of intentional abandonment and neglect further complicate the texture of slow violence perpetuated in the West Bank.

Parallel Geographies

There are important similarities in the ways that slow violence and urbicidal policies of territorial expansion operate. Indeed, as mentioned earlier, in the preface to his book, Nixon explicitly acknowledges that the inspiration for his thinking comes from, among other things, engagement with Edward Said's writing on the Israeli-Palestinian conflict, indicating the conceptual "reproachment between postcolonial and environmental studies" (2011, xi). As the analysis presented in the previous section indicates, the Israeli colonial project makes use of the shifting temporalities of urbicidal violence, causing damage both to Palestinian communities and the natural environment of the region. The meticulously planned Israeli architectural developments in the West Bank contribute to the gradual creation of parallel geographies, where two communities located within the same cartographical contours of a region in fact inhabit two dramatically different legal and material planes. Such arrangements emerged as a result of a series of measures used by the Israeli government to deepen its control over the West Bank, assured by a complex cartographical system consisting of a superimposition of "discontinuous maps over each other" (Weizman 2002, n.p.). This produces a complex spatiality premised on, and further exacerbating, the existing ethnic divisions within both the Israeli state and the territories it controls.

The policy of gradual Zionist colonization of the West Bank, which aims to construct an extended Israeli territoriality in this area, represents a subordination of this territory's resources to primarily political (colonial) ends. This bears a striking resemblance to the processes of the Judaization of the newly established State of Israel, which started as early as 1948 and have continued since then (Leshem 2016). According to Yosef Jabareen's comprehensive analysis (2015), it seems that Israel used a similar mechanism of land acquisition and strategic architectural planning to accentuate the Jewish presence in this land and to erase its Arab identity. This has also resulted in limitation of the natural expansion of Palestinian urbanity in Israel's mainland and reconfiguration of the ethnic, economic, and spatial dynamics of its territory. Since 1967, an analogous legal-territorial-economic-military apparatus has been used in the West Bank to enable the gradual eradication of indigenous Palestinian practices of dwelling, with the aim of dissipating Palestinians' "sense of place" (McKittrick 2011) as well as—in a strictly political manner—the eventual appropriation of this territory and its incorporation within the Israeli state. This testifies to the colonial, rather than occupational, Zionist presence in the region. Along these political lines, the process of intensive development of industrial, residential, and transport infrastructure tightly connects the West Bank with the Israeli heartland, turning two territories with different political statuses into a single organism. This coherence is, however, only apparent, as the system of the Israeli-only bypass roads alienates Israeli settlers from the place in which they dwell on an everyday basis, creating a somewhat prosthetic topography which runs parallel to the original tissue of the region, now cut into isolated and deteriorating enclaves. As Weizman states, such spatial organization "entails re-visioning of existing cartographic techniques" and consists of a certain multiplication of the territory for specific political purposes (2002, n.p.). In fact, it promotes slow urbicide, mobilizing different material-semiotic forces for the purpose of increasing territorial expansion and impairing Palestinian self-governance mechanisms. The spatial manipulation of the West Bank's territoriality amounts to a "violent act of exclusion" (Elden

2007; see also Connolly 1995; Jabareen 2015), which further contributes to the emergence of discriminatory spatiality, perpetuating spatial injustice (Soja 2010). The efficiency of such a policy is enabled by complex, dynamic entanglements of legal systems, ideologically shaped colonial objectives, military rhetoric, a history of conflict, and international politics, *as much as* by the region's topography and the specific opportunities for land use that it offers, as they have been assembled against the indigenous population.

In its urbicidal orientation, the policy of intense, cartographically premeditated settlement in the West Bank, or the creation of competing geographical planes, mobilizes one form of urbanity (Israeli) against another (Palestinian) and is deliberately aimed at the suppression, or physical strangulation, of the latter. This clash is heavily asymmetrical, to the disadvantage of Palestinians, and fosters a policy that prioritizes the security of Israeli citizens, premised on the growing insecurity of indigenous inhabitants. Additionally, as evidenced in the earlier analysis, infrastructural developments also serve as an apparatus for spreading another form of slow violence: producing environmental degradation that further threatens Palestinians' well-being and livelihoods, often forcing them to abandon traditional ways of life. This testifies to the exponential aspect of slow urbicide, "operating as a major threat multiplier" (Nixon 2011, 3). Hence, the Israeli expansionist project, advancing via its slow urbicidal tactics, targets Palestinians directly (through the gradual strangulation, degeneration, and eradication of their urban fabric) and indirectly (through the destruction of factors that have typically co-shaped the existence of Palestinian communities, including the development of their urbanity and local agriculture-based sources of income). The latter strategy, consisting partly in the mobilization of agencies of the local landscape against its indigenous population, steadily eliminates the typical ways of relational co-existence of land and people, developed and cultivated across long periods of time. This amounts to an intentional reversal of the ways in which societies use public space. As Ariel Handel underlines, whereas human movement within space typically resists the structured, rational control imposed by design and planning, in the West Bank "the ruling power itself produces rhizomatic, changing, and fluid space, while the users are the ones to struggle to reintroduce predictable features into their living space" (2009, 182), an attempt which is frequently unsuccessful.

The quest for the right to shape urban life remains uneven, as the familiar spaces of home and the immediate environment—so vital to the thriving of human communities—are turned into political agents inflicting harm. Thus, as a result of Israeli spatial developments in the West Bank, alongside systematic expulsions and forced relocations, Palestinians who reside there are doomed to what Nixon calls "a more radical form of displacement," which refers to the loss of land, resources, or places of belonging—a form of uprooting which does not necessarily entail the physical transfer of people to a different location (2011, 19). This form of displacement is articulated through the geographical/political/discursive reconfiguration of the landscape and its stripping of those original characteristics that enabled habitual forms of relational dwelling. It describes a situation in which the indigenous population finds itself under pressure *from within*, a result of materially rich encounters with the harmful agencies of the immediate surroundings weaponized by Israel in the colonial effort. Deracination of the Palestinians in the West Bank is thus effectuated through a substitution of the vernacular landscape with an official politically informed and formalized setting that "writes the land in a bureaucratic, externalizing, and extraction-driven manner that is often pitilessly instrumental" (Nixon 2011, 17). The shifting temporalities of urbicidal violence, therefore, operate as modalities through which the gradual submission and eradication of Palestinian urban culture in the West Bank is articulated and on which this discriminatory policy heavily relies.

Case Study 2. Regularization in the Naqab/Negev Desert

In their struggle for consolidation of the Jewish presence in, and thus ownership of, the Palestinian land, the Israeli authorities have invested in the assertion of territoriality as a central objective of the spatial policy implemented not only in the Occupied Territories but also within the political contours of Israel proper. This project was launched as early as 1948 (or even earlier, if less formal strategies are considered), and it aimed to methodically design the spatial relations over which the state's authority would subsequently spread. The construction of a nation-centered Israeli territoriality has been premised on several spatial manipulations targeting indigenous[21] forms of inhabitance; the objective—similarly to the case of the Occupied Territories—was to dismantle the traditional practices of collective dwelling and to gradually dissolve these communities' internal bonds. This has been achieved via the application of a complex assemblage of technologies, including cartographical strategies of dividing the land, the implementation of incentive programs dedicated to relocated communities, the reinterpretation and discriminatory application of legal regulations, the construction of a discourse on the (il)legality of certain forms of using space, a premeditated selective promotion of specific hydro-social relations and agrarian projects, and an increasing militarization of space. In this multifaceted context—co-shaped by the dynamic enmeshment of natural features of the region and semiotic structures affecting the dominant understandings of its landscape—space was conceived as "a repertoire of points, lines, and areas that delineated territory and exerted state interests with increasing scientific authority" (Krupar 2015, 92).

Several scholars emphasize that mapping technologies are in fact at the roots of statehood.[22] Thus maps—and the apparatuses involved in the process of their creation—must be seen as active agents, as they participate in the procedures of constructing knowledge and sustaining power (Crampton and Krygier 2006). Due to their agential capacities, maps—as Sébastien Caquard and Claire Dormann note—have been "designed and used for centuries for highly strategic purposes such as planning and executing war, locating valuable resources, collecting taxes, claiming territories, and participating in the creation and recognition of nation-states" (2008, 51). Mastery of cartographical technologies (of surveying, measurement, averaging, printing, distributing, interpreting, etc.) is essential for producing specific visualizations, understandings, and experiences of the space which help to impose a concrete structure onto a given territory (Harley 2001; Pickles 2004; Wood 2010). The work of such instruments, however, does not consist in *representing* the territory, but actively contributes to its very *production*. For these reasons, cartographic strategies tend to be employed by state agents as meaningful tools (King 1996; Corner 2011; Pickles 2004; Strandsbjerg 2008) for the purpose of the production of their territoriality.

As such, even though maps themselves do not provide particular spatial constrains, they must be approached as operating within complex material-semiotic contexts co-constituted by practices and ideas which define the conditions of possibility of both the cartographic tools and their products (Branch 2017). As Jordan Branch explains, "[t]he definition and operationalization of territory as spatial expanses separated by lines depends on the ability to negotiate, measure, and draw those lines, on maps and on the ground" (2017, 137). Certainly, the lines sketched on the maps (isomers, isohyets, isohalines, isotherms, isobars, etc.) are less elusive than those drawn on the ground. Their positioning results from practices of careful monitoring and averaging, emerging as a combination of material facts on the ground and of cultural categories or concepts used for making sense of, and cartographically stabilizing, these dynamic materialities. Hence, the fluency in operationalizing drawing practices contributes to the materialization, or consolidation, of certain predominant ways of thinking, such as, for instance, that "the entire land surface of the globe should be divided among exclusive state claims" (Branch 2017, 137), or that advantage should be taken of every piece of arable land. Looking closely into the entanglement of practices and ideas within the cartographical technologies, K. J. Holsti exposes the fact that mapping *enables* certain forms of territoriality, which are then constituted through various interactions between material artifacts, meaningful ideas, and sociocultural practices (2004, 79). Mapping, therefore, is revealed as a powerful and consequential political tool, and—as such—it should be approached as an instrument of possible intervention in how people relate to, or make use of, the space (or land), or what forms of spatiality they are able to construct. The situation of the Bedouin community in the Naqab/Negev—unfolding in the shadow of the enduring Israeli-Arab conflict—provides an illuminating example of how cartographic strategies, as well as their profoundly material-semiotic effects, can be employed for the purpose of an ethnicity-based urbicidal project.

Technologies of Drawing

The understanding and experience of territory depend upon a series of boundary-drawing technologies which, as Frédéric Vandenberghe (2007) observes, constitute an assemblage of material agents and human relations, illustrating how—in certain conditions—ideas materialize as powerful material forces. Fluent command of cartographical and meteorological tools can enable the transformation of ideas into material realities. As demonstrated by Weizman (2015), the ideology-driven materialization of the aridity line in the Naqab/Negev had detrimental consequences for the quality of life of the Bedouins who had inhabited this area for centuries. According to meteorological definitions, a desert starts at the threshold of 200 mm of annual rainfall. Different aridity indicators are used to identify regions suffering from a deficit of water. The "deficit," however, is understood through an anthropocentric lens as a condition that severely limits the possibilities of human use of the land for agriculture or livestock farming. Such an approach considers these conditions, as well as the potentials they create, from a Eurocentric perspective, ignoring other, less popular methods of cultivating the land (e.g., the different practices of dry agriculture developed by people inhabiting arid areas). The aridity line—as well as its specific understandings and uses—emerges, as Weizman (2015, 8) acknowledges, from a complex interplay of different factors. In a new materialist idiom, it consists of the semiotic entanglement of meteorological data (which itself is a result of specific practices and technologies of monitoring, measurement, and averaging of natural conditions in the area, as well as a material-semiotic effect of scientific classificatory endeavors), a human approach to the land and how it can be exploited (agriculture and diverse farming machineries used for it), and soil conditions and botanical characteristics (both natural and those connected to intensive farming, synthetic agents, modification of the morphology/quality of the cultivated plants or seeds, etc.). In addition, cartographical practice—the act of drawing the desert's edge—is itself a material-semiotic process, as well as a venture rich in material-semiotic consequences. The situation of the Naqab/Negev Bedouins is a striking example of the kind of consequences such a form of geographical warfare can potentially generate.

The term Bedouin (from Arabic *bedû*, or desert dwellers; desert was referred to as *Bâdiya*)[23] is used to describe several populations inhabiting different locations in the Middle East and Africa. It alludes to the specific tribal structure of these communities and their nomadic-pastoral livelihood practices. Since the twentieth century, the latter element has gradually been losing its significance in defining these populations, as they have increasingly been forced into permanent settlements and modern labor markets (Razon 2017) driven by capitalist logic based on the principle of property ownership (Brighenti 2010) rather than seasonal mobility. The semi-nomadic and self-reliant character of the Bedouin communities stands in contrast to the "modern" organization of socio-economic life (Dinero 2010); thus, state authorities invest in eradicating such ways of relating to the land, also through the premeditated employment of tactics of slow urbicidal violence.

In 1946 the number of Naqab/Negev Bedouins was estimated at between 57,000 and 95,000 people (Muhsam 1966, 22; detailed registers are not available). They currently comprise around 3.5% of the population of the State of Israel. In the 1940s most of the Naqab/Negev Bedouins were located in the western part of the country, where the land is more fertile, and led a half-settled life, engaging in pastoralism and dry farming. Although after the 1948 war most of the Bedouins left or were expelled from the territory of the newly established state and took refuge in the West Bank, Gaza, or North Sinai, a significant number concentrated in the Naqab/Negev Desert, where they were placed by the state in an area corresponding to around 10% of this geographical region. In 1953, the number of Bedouins remaining in the Naqab/Negev was estimated at approximately 11,000 people, located to the east and the north of Beersheba where, until 1966, they were subdued under Israeli military rule in a zone known by the name al-Siyāj (*Sayig*, translated as "fence")[24] (Marx 1967, 12; Nasasra 2015; Law-Yone 2003; Lithwick 2003). The residents of the zone needed special permission not only to move outside the restricted area but also to commute within it (Meir 1998; Abu-Saad 2005). The site was located to the south of the geographical line defining the north boundary of the desert. The land of those who fled or were forcibly relocated was confiscated: as a result, during the 1950s, 90% of the desert and 50% of the enclosed area were appropriated by the State of Israel (Falah 1989). Currently, the former inhabitants of these lands are deemed as "illegal intruders" and are regularly harassed by the state agencies when they mobilize to protect their remaining land from further encroachment by the state (Marx and Meir 2005, 53; Rotem 2017), or when they opt for indigenous tradition-based practices of living. The rights of those Bedouins who, after all the land south of Beersheba was declared to be state land in 1950, remained in tenuous possession of land have been systematically undermined by the state. Nevertheless, those who still own land often try to accentuate their presence on it by regular, albeit limited, cultivation or grazing in hope that this will protect them from expropriation. In practice, many such attempts fail.

As Weizman notes, "the zone of dispossession in the Naqab/Negev is coextensive with the meteorological definition of the 'desert'" (2017, 228). In this context, the activity of the State of Israel in the Naqab/Negev should be seen as a carefully calculated effort to make use of geographical instruments to implement a thought-out policy toward the land and the people inhabiting it, or to advance the process of geographical and demographical "regularization" of space. The categorization of the land as desert (or "dead land") facilitated its appropriation by the state. In that sense, the drawing of the desert's edge (and the subsequent realization of the state-sponsored project to "make the desert bloom," so crucial to the Zionist ideology) was an effect of the material-semiotic entanglement of geographical, cartographical, geological, botanical, demographical, agricultural, and military forms of knowledge, as well as technological agents (e.g., aerial visualization, measurements), all profoundly shaped by widespread colonial discourses. This has been instrumentalized in the Zionist enterprise of the Jewish settlement in Palestine, embracing the regularization of its space/spatiality as well as its adaptation to the new economic, social, and cultural needs of the settler population. The processes on the ground and in the air—along with the natural characteristics of the monitored, measured, calculated, classified, and codified geographical zone—have produced a new understanding of the land in question and enabled the development and implementation of a policy that remains in line with the current objectives of the "ethnocratic state" (Yiftachel 2006). The official rhetoric disseminated by the Israeli authorities propels the discursive linking of the identity of the Jews to a certain territory, naturalizing the idea, as Emily McKee indicates, "that Jews' security rests on exclusive territorial control" (2016, 81), therefore the state must invest in ensuring its territoriality is maintained using all possible means. Preoccupied with the principle of Jewish ownership of the land, this policy has targeted the Bedouin community of the Naqab/Negev with systematic property destruction (including self-afflicted but enforced demolitions[25]) and forced urbanization, aimed at eradicating indigenous ways of inhabiting and cultivating the desert, as well as challenging indigenous modes of dwelling, maintenance of communities, and the intensive topological relations which co-constitute them. Apart from investing in ethnicity-based efforts to change the demographic profile of the population located in this extensive region (the Naqab/Negev Desert constitutes over a half of Israel's territory), this policy endeavors to partly reconfigure the local landscape in terms of both its human and its natural characteristics. This constitutes another facet of the project to "regularize" the space, with the aim of better integrating it within the prevailing Zionist—that is, nationalist and progressive—ideology of Jewish "redemption" of the original land and the colonial/ethnicized politics associated therewith. In what follows, I will briefly look at these two aspects of the Israeli policy through the lens of slow urbicidal violence.

The Violence of Urbanization

The program of the "regularization" of space (Rotem 2017), delineating how space can be used by different communities, started in the 1970s and was aimed at transferring the remaining Bedouin population to deliberately designed townships. The idea behind this project was to take even more extended control over the space of the Naqab/Negev by cleansing it of indigenous inhabitants and to further accentuate its formal belonging to the State of Israel by constructing specific, Jewishness-centered forms of territoriality there. The broad program of evictions and resettlement was also designed—at least formally—to serve as a means to integrate the Bedouin population within the national market economy. In fact, however, it worked according to the well-known logic, delineating that physical, active presence on a particular piece of land may signal a right, or even a legal title (as is the case in particular regulations of the 1858 Ottoman Land Law), to ownership of this land. It must be noted that organized efforts at "managing" Bedouin communities in the Middle East have a longer history. The authorities of the British Mandate, and earlier those of the Ottoman Empire, had already invested in reshaping the Bedouin lifestyle, attempting to force the community into at least partial sedentarization (Nasasra 2015). This policy was typical of centralized governments around the world that were focused on closer monitoring and the efficient collection of taxes within state territories (Ginat and Khazanow 1998; Ramos 1998). These efforts dramatically intensified in Palestine after 1948, when the Israeli authorities demanded that each Bedouin must register with one of the identified 19 tribes (whose chiefs were officially appointed by Israel, in many cases without taking into consideration the actual distribution and relations of power within these communities) (Marx 1967). This step was disrespectful toward traditional ways of governing and subsequently contributed to the partial disorganization of the internal life of the communities in question.

The intense program of urbanization launched in the late 1960s further diminished the possibility of cultivating traditional ways of governing Bedouin communities and severely affected the customary modes of relating to the land, both being understood as structuring dimensions of the semi-nomadic communal life. Importantly, the project of urbanization was premised on the careful cartographic documentation of the land (also based on the aerial photography from the period of British rule in Palestine) and implied the systematic zoning of the Naqab/Negev into residential, agricultural, military, and public areas. The regularization of the region's geography, based on the study of the material conditions of the land and their classification—or "classifixation," as van der Tuin proposes (2015)—according to well-established categories, has been used as a tool to declare the uncultivated land as *mawat*[26] (or "dead land") and thus to consider it as state land. This decision was based on a rather twisted interpretation of the 1858 Ottoman Land Law, while the identification of what counts as *mawat* was enabled by a detailed geographical inspection of the region from the air and from the ground, assisted by the agencies of visualization and measurement technologies. Thus, contortions of Ottoman law were entangled with "the facts on the ground" or the natural conditions of the area. The geographical categorization of the Naqab/Negev region as a desert authorized this strategy, allowing for classification of the whole area as too dry for agrarian uses (even though the indigenous people had for decades engaged in dry agriculture). Thus, as a result of the zoning of the land, since the 1970s the Bedouin settlements have been delegalized, left out of official maps, and deemed, as Yiftachel observes, to increasing informality and temporality (2006, 199), a status further aggravated by their very limited—if any—access to even the most basic state services (such as electricity, waste management, or health protection).

In 1965, the first township intended for the Naqab/Negev Bedouins was established next to Beersheba. Tel as-Sabi (Tel Sheva), however, was designed as a conglomeration of buildings with two-room units which were not suitable for the needs of the Bedouin community, which is based upon extensive family relations. The conditions set by the local authorities under which Bedouins could move to the new places were equally discouraging, as the land on which the buildings were erected was to remain the property of the state, while a system of 49-year leases was to be implemented. Additionally, those who wanted to relocate to Tel as-Sabi were asked to sign away all their property claims to land that they had owned in the past. Even though they were lured with certain incentives (Dinero 2010; Yiftachel and Meir 1998), the Bedouins were not willing to move to the newly established town, which remained undeveloped and scarcely populated until 1980. A different approach to planning was subsequently adopted to construct other townships in the area, dedicated exclusively to the Naqab/Negev Bedouins. Rather than offering the finalized buildings, this time the authorities opted for the provision of developed building plots, leaving the final design to the Bedouins themselves (Marx and Meir 2005). Again, the title to construct a house on the plot did not imply any right to own the land, so the offer was only appealing to landless people. Rahat settlement was planned as a collection of hamlets (33 in total) separated by stretches of wasteland (or wadis), each theoretically dedicated to a different descent group. To attract Bedouins, as Marx and Meir (2005, 49) underline, the state agreed to allow a large tract of state land to revert to freehold for non-Jews, which was unprecedented and testified to a huge determination to force the Naqab/Negev Bedouins into the towns.[27] The layout and the location of Rahat, however, did not contribute to consolidating the urban community; nor did it encourage the emergence of urban spatiality. It did not comply with the traditional practices of dwelling worked out for decades by the Bedouin communities, and neither did the architecture of the township attend to the needs of the extended Bedouin families. The settlement remained quite undeveloped in these terms, serving mostly as a huge dormitory for the population working in and around Beersheba.

In 1980 other towns were set up, partly due to the pressure to relocate the Israeli military bases from Sinai to the Naqab/Negev after the signing of the peace treaty with Egypt in 1979. This demanded further expropriation of Bedouin land and property which, in the new political context, had to be settled peacefully in order not to antagonize the Arab world. This led to an agreement according to which the Bedouins had a right to compensation for any lost land (at market value) and were not asked to sign away any property claims. Even though initially designed as more compact, the five new towns—Ar'arat an-Naqab (Ar'ara BaNegev), Kuseife (Kseife), Shaqib al-Salam (Segev Shalom), Hura, and Lakiya (Figure 3.2)—which were established between 1980 and the mid-1990s eventually ended up with a layout similar to that of Rahat (Marx and Meir 2005). This made it harder for the inhabitants to create truly urban communities, especially because the Bedouins themselves were excluded from planning and were not even consulted over development decisions. As a result, the needs of these communities for at least a partial continuation of their established ways of dwelling were not attended to in the planning process. For instance, in 2017 there was only one Bedouin employee out of a total of 13 officials (the remaining 12 all being Jewish) in the Authority for Development and Settlement of the Bedouins in the Negev, a governmental body responsible for the development of the Naqab/Negev Bedouin recognized settlements (Rotem 2017, 24). Thus, even though formally urbanized, the townships did not have any characteristics of urban space, at least as it is understood as resulting from a collective effort of the community inhabiting it; nor did they develop any specific spirit typically associated with the conditions of urbanity (as defined by Lefebvre 1968). The townships have never enjoyed a flourishing growth. The realities of living in neighborhood of unrelated lineages, untypical in Bedouin traditions, hampered any attempts at producing a common and truly shared spatiality. In fact, as McKee (2016, 118) observes, the spatial distribution of Bedouin families, determined by the architecture of the township, has led to a number of confrontations between neighbors:

> Residents trying to continue agropastoral taskscapes in the urban township not designed for them displeased some neighbors with the smell of their goats, or slaughtered animals in their courtyards and let blood run into the streets. These residents were resisting the pressures of de-cultural accommodation that push Bedouin Arabs to relinquish cultural practices and conform to state demands that they become urban, wage-earning subjects. But because many of the planned township spaces did not meet residents' expectations, they "made do" in ways that contributed to the township's disheveled landscapes.
>
> (2016, 118)

GEOGRAPHICAL WARFARE IN PALESTINE

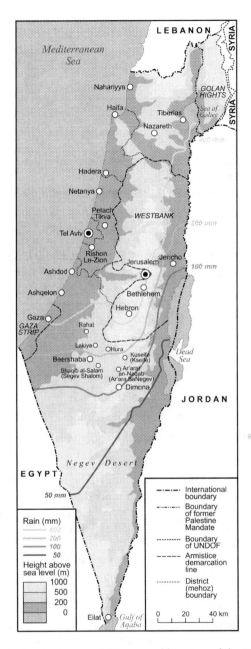

Figure 3.2 Precipitation in the Naqab/Negev and location of the Bedouin townships established by the Israeli government. Partly based on data made available by the Israel Meteorological Service.

Also, even though state agencies have been actively engaged in concentrating Bedouins in the towns, they have invested little in the development of infrastructure and services available to these new urban communities, effectively killing in advance the spirit of urbanity and thus indirectly denying the inhabitants' "right to the city." Deprived of the shared history of collective dwelling, the Bedouin inhabitants of the townships are unable to engage in shared practices of creating a common space for which they can collectively care.

While, since 1999, the State of Israel has officially recognized 11 Bedouin villages, the remaining 35 still await a governmental decision. Their inhabitants are considered a "diaspora" while the structures they erect in the context of current regulations materialize as illegal, as a result of which they suffer frequent demolition. Located mostly within the region formerly delineated as *Sayig*, the villages are not marked on official Israeli maps, as the authorities systematically deny their legitimacy, erasing them from the cartographical and demographical registers. This fact has far-reaching political consequences, as without official addresses, people inhabiting these villages are not allowed to vote in local elections and their councils remain unrecognized; nor are they eligible for state-financed health services and other infrastructural amenities. Delegalized and erased from official maps, the "illegal" villages are further ignored when certain facilities (such as noisy electricity grids or toxic industries[28]) are placed in their direct proximity, causing damage to the livelihoods of the population and inflicting physical harm on the bodies of the inhabitants of these villages. This politically informed practice—a classical example of slow violence—can generate atrocious but delayed effects for the Bedouin communities in question.

The standard of living in Bedouin villages (both recognized and unrecognized) is extremely poor: they lack any planning, construction permits are not issued, there is no adequate infrastructure (including water supply, electricity, sewage and garbage disposal, roads, health services, schooling, and public transportation), and demolitions are carried out regularly by governmental bodies. Israel undertakes demolitions of what are considered "illegal structures" through regular operations by several state-funded units which document land use, open lawsuits, issue demolition orders, and execute the bulldozing. These entities are the National Unit for Building Inspection (established in 1988), the Unit for Enforcement in Open Spaces (also known as the "Green Patrol," established in 1976), the Israeli Land Administration (established in 1960 and responsible for the management of all lands in Israel: state lands, Development Authority lands, and Jewish National Fund lands), and the Yoav Unit (a police unit that assists enforcement bodies in locating and demolishing "undesired" Bedouin structures; established in 2012 under the Prawer-Amidror Plan,[29] it continues to operate despite having being temporarily suspended) (cf. Swirski and Hasson 2006). Demolitions are thus used as a tool of regularization or a form of "correction" of the "misused space." The recent governmental plan (2017-2021) tackling the Naqab/Negev Bedouin community resumes this approach. While it envisions investment in the townships established by the governments and some support for the recognized villages, it assumes that enforcement authorities will pursue a coercive and punitive policy toward the unrecognized villages in the Naqab/Negev. Such vindictive measures affect the population of approximately 70,000 Bedouins who still inhabit "illegal"—thus cartographically "invisibilized"—villages or other areas of the region (while the total of the Naqab/Negev Bedouin populations is currently estimated at over 240,000 people) (Rotem 2017, 7).

Destroying one form of urban life by forcing another form of urban organization, the policy dismantles the traditional ways of living in the Naqab/Negev, producing (often by coercion) specific spatial practices and space uses, which are guided by ethnicity-based assumptions and generate strikingly discriminatory practices. The (forced) urbanization, in fact mobilized as an urbicidal enterprise, serves as a regular weapon against indigenous ways of dwelling grounded in a complex and dynamic entanglement of humans and the land. It is strengthened by a scientifically motivated cartographical project of mapping (and zoning) space, as well as the biased application of legal regulations, contributing to the criminalization of the Bedouin presence in the Naqab/Negev and framing the representatives of this community—despite their status as Israeli citizens—as "illegal" or as "trespassers" on their own land (Kedar 2001, 927). Based on discriminatory principles and a deeply asymmetrical approach, the whole project of forced urbanization has been used to uproot original practices of relating to the land, to enhance control over the population, and also—eventually—to substantially retard its traditional land-based development. In fact, forced urbanization has served as a weapon in the process of the de-Arabization of the Naqab/Negev through gradually eradicating the original forms of urbanity developed and cultivated in the desert, and turning the inhabitants into township dwellers incapable of reconstructing the traditional lifestyle or forms of mobilization associated with it (including those aimed at countering the authority of a ruler). This violent policy of regularization has also produced a whole range of spatial injustices, all a consequence of the ethnicity-based and territory-oriented politics of "making the desert bloom."

Landscape Politics

In its endeavors to assert concrete forms of territoriality over the land, the ethnocratic state designed a meticulous plan of how to make use of the *mawat*. The "dead land" doctrine has thus been instrumentalized to legitimize the extensive dispossessions but also, as Kedar et al. argue (2018), to enable denial that dispossessions have in fact taken place. This is important, given that the notion of indigenousness, and the aspirations of the

Naqab/Negev Bedouins to be considered as an indigenous community, has conflicted with the Zionist idea of a modern nation-state. Both land and its resources are the most important factors for indigenous people, as they remain intricately entangled with their territories in the process of sustaining their culture and specific modes of dwelling. These resources, however, are equally important for nation-states and their political (often violent) involvement in the process of upholding their territoriality, understood as a factual authority extending over a particular territory. Such deep attachment to the land transpires in the Zionist construction of "Eretz Yisrael," which translates as "the Land of Israel"; even though the official name of the political organism is the "State of Israel," its location is in the particular land. Given the fact that nations tend to be discursively represented as rooted in concrete geographical areas, the policy of inventing these roots has been put in place in order to consolidate the Jewish belonging in Palestine, as well as to geographically define the discourse on Jewish territorialism. One of the strategies to accentuate the Jewishness of the Naqab/Negev was the policy of assigning Hebrew biblical names to these places, linking the modern settlement project to ancient Jewish genealogies (Masalha 2007). This task was accomplished by the Committee for the Designation of Place-Names in the Negev Region appointed for this purpose. This symbolic appropriation of land—through (re)naming places on maps while simultaneously erasing the original Arab designations from them—was an important dimension of a far-reaching Israeli policy of colonizing the region, both symbolically and factually.

The construction and sustenance of the Israeli nation-state required both the cleansing of the land of the undesired semi-nomadic indigenous population and the conquest of the desert. Such a framing has fitted well within the Zionist narrative of "making the desert bloom," an imaginary construction nourished by archaeological evidence of the existence of flourishing ancient cities in the Naqab/Negev. As McKee underlines, one of the central discourses for Zionism was the rhetorical positioning of agriculture as redemption, "both of individual laborers and of neglected land" (2016, 30). Physical labor has for long been conceived of as valuable for this process (Sternhell 1998; Zakim 2006). The "dead land" of the desert was, in such a context, seen as a frontier for Jewish colonization—a conquest which was perceived as a progressive march from dark backwardness to enlightened modernization. Framed as a symbol of desolation and emptiness, the Naqab/Negev was perceived as an enemy to be conquered (Zerubavel 2008). In practical terms, given the ongoing process of constructing Israeli territoriality, the realization of these goals called for the implementation of specific ethnopolitics constructing the indigenous Arab inhabitants of the region as primitive, inefficient, or even inexistent; in contrast, the Jewish settlers were depicted as modern, knowledgeable, and progressive (cf. Dinero 2010). Such a plan also required a denial of the fact that the land ideologically represented as empty and serene had in fact long been inhabited and cultivated by Bedouin Arabs.

The conquest of the desert was not only perceived in terms of territorial expansion; it also related to the need for substantial infrastructure building and climate engineering, as has also been typical for other colonial enterprises.[30] The Naqab/Negev region is not hospitable for settlers. It is host to demanding topographical and hydrological conditions. It reaches altitudes of 1,000 m above sea level in the southern highlands and falls below sea level in the northern Arava Valley. Annual rainfall averages at 100-150 mm per year in the arid north and 80-100 mm per year in the hyper-arid central and southern parts. The natural vegetation is zonal, matching the precipitation gradients and soil conditions (which include sand, dunes, loess, alluvium, and limestone). As Petra Vaiglova et al. point out, in such an arid climate, vegetation is primarily concentrated in the wadis during the wet season. The wadis channel rainfall northwest toward the Mediterranean Sea or northeast toward the Dead Sea. The total rainfall and runoff water amounts to an average of 200-300 mm per year in the wadis, while the loess soil above the dams preserves moisture during the dry season (2020, 2). The natural conditions are therefore quite fragile and unsuitable for conventional agricultural techniques. Hence, the Naqab/Negev has been considered a frontier land since the very inception of the Israeli state, and a region where Jewish settlement and development have been understood as crucial aspects of state policy (Yiftachel 2006, 193) as much as a spiritual quest.

The Jewish ownership of these territories has been accentuated by the politics of the "regularization" of the landscape. Consequently, Jewish presence on this land manifests, among other things, in intensive and extensive plans of afforestation, artificial irrigation, and technologically enhanced agriculture. As Shaul Ephraim Cohen (1993) points out, "the politics of planting" has typically been used in the Israeli-Arab conflict as a tool to display a physical presence in the contested territories and to accentuate the belonging of this land to a specific ethnic group. Such a strategy, as Cohen notes (following Baruch Kimmerling [1977]), is compatible with the list of elements mobilized "in the struggle to control territory: sovereignty, ownership, and presence" (1993, 2). Thus, the process of constructing territoriality—which in the case of Israel is often termed as the policy of "creating facts"—engages the agencies of the area's materialities: its natural atmospheric conditions, specific plant species, cultivation techniques, hydrologic characteristics, and so on. Interestingly, the practice of planting prevents "encroachment" or "land alienation" and can be used for boundary building (Cohen 1993, 3). Tree planting has for long been symbolically weighty for Judaism and was further equipped with major significance in the aftermath of the Holocaust, standing for the revival of the Jewish nation (Zerubavel 1996). Additionally, it also plays a role, as Pappé (2006) suggests, in hiding the remnants of former Arab villages "cleansed" since 1948, as the process of building the homeland for a nation requires a thorough reconfiguration of the history of both the region and the nation(s) in question. Such projects are therefore multidimensional, assembling the complex agencies of non-human actors (plants, land, climate, air) with religious, historical, social, economic, and political phenomena. Thus, in the context of ethnocentric politics, the belief that desertification can be prevented by imposing limitations on grazing (traditionally practiced by indigenous populations), along with a policy of extensive afforestation, has been mobilized against the Naqab/Negev Bedouin community. As a result, their lands have been confiscated and forests planted on their former settlements, and their traditional reliance on livestock has been severely limited by legal regulations.

In the highly ideological process of colonizing the threshold of the desert, and of marking the Jewish presence on the territory, the Jewish National Fund has for decades carried out a rigorous program of planting.[31] This was accompanied with the strategy of disseminating an environment-sensitive discourse on the need to restore overused and devastated land, while rhetorically subscribing—in a rather manipulative manner—to global campaigns for the need to "green" the land and counter the negative effects of climate change.[32] The biggest afforestation project in the Naqab/Negev is Yatir Forest,[33] which consists of over 4 million trees; smaller projects include Lahav and Beeri forests. Currently, there are two different afforestation programs in Israel, extending over significant areas of the Naqab/Negev: one is a dense planting of Aleppo pine (these kinds of forest also serve as living memorials to the victims of the Holocaust) and the other is a low-density planting of exotic drought-tolerant deciduous species (a strategy known as "savannization"). While the former requires generous irrigation (which causes salinization of soil and—paradoxically—so-called heat island effects as darker areas absorb more solar radiation), the latter is considered to exacerbate the degradation of natural conditions in the region. It involves the removal of endemic vegetation, as well as landscaping to create terraces to capture surface runoff which, as a result, does not end up in the wadis, the main areas for Bedouin agricultural cultivation. Moreover, the survival of the forest depends on irrigation infrastructure. New saplings do not grow without irrigation, while dry years produce massive losses of mature trees. The forests do not renew in the natural cycle and require constant human intervention. Ironically, the state-sponsored program designed to battle desertification ended up producing greater water shortages; the negative consequences of this are experienced most severely by the most fragile Palestinian-Arab communities.

The process of pushing the aridity line southward was accompanied by a strategy of Judaization of the territory, manifesting in the creation of new settlements built on state land and accessible only to Jews. As early as the 1950s and 1960s, seven development towns were established (Arad, Dimona, Mitzpe-Ramon, Netivot, Ofaqim, Sderot, and Yeroham), while the existing towns of Beersheba and Eilat grew substantially (Portnov and Erell 1998). Other settlement projects quickly followed. The policy of encouraging the Jewish citizens of Israel to move to urban sites established in the desert intensified in 1970 with incentives such as government loans, provision of public housing, and tax exemptions. Due to extensive agricultural use of virtually all land located in the north and northwest of the Naqab/Negev region—enabled by artificial irrigation from wetter regions (mostly Jordanian Valley), mechanized cultivation, extensive use of new seed types, synthetic fertilizers, and pesticides—those practicing traditional and more sustainable forms of land use were pushed to drier areas, which are typically more susceptible to degradation. Thus, the vast program of rehabilitating the desert lands, or "regularization" of the naturally dry landscape, remains at the expense of degradation elsewhere, mostly in neighboring areas from which water has been systematically diverted. The effects of these environmental transformations—induced by the entanglements of human and nonhuman agents and forces—are most severely experienced by the most vulnerable sections of Israeli society.

Intensive afforestation, agrarization, urbanization, industrialization, and militarization—all employed in the service of the "regularization" of the Naqab/Negev space, and all preceded by a carefully undertaken politics of cartographical planning—have generated several spatial problems. The Naqab/Negev Bedouin communities, since being made more exposed through relocation and space management, continue to be substantially unprivileged in comparison with other (Jewish) inhabitants of the region. The politics of the distribution of space rests on ethnicity-based principles, according to which the representatives of the dominant group (that is, the Jews) are placed above the minoritarian communities in the socio-political hierarchy. This affects both the quantity and the quality of space placed at the disposal of different ethnic groups. The policy is openly discriminatory—while the lands of the Bedouins are systematically confiscated, within the project "Loner Farms" (*havot bodedim*) the state opens programs granting several Jewish families land in the Naqab/Negev for intensive cultivation. As a result of such state interventions, spatial injustices emerge. Whereas Bedouins currently comprise more than a third of the population of the Naqab/Negev, only 12.5% of the officially recognized settlements are designated for this community (see Rotem 2017); out of 136 settlements in the region, only around 15% are recognized Bedouin communities. Similar disproportions apply to the patterns of land administration in the Naqab/Negev. For instance, while the populations of townships designed for Bedouins constitute around 16% of the people inhabiting the whole Beersheba subdistrict, their jurisdiction covers only 0.5% of this area (Abu-Saad and Creamer 2012, 36). Additionally, the traditional Bedouin techniques of low-intensity cultivation and grazing have been severely limited, significantly affecting indigenous lifestyles, which typically rely on situated forms of human-land relationality. The Bedouin communities are now squeezed between the northern desert edge (spotted with Jewish-only settlements and covered with vast green areas) and the hyper-arid terrains in the south (which the processes of desertification systematically push northward) (Figure 3.2).

The indigenous communities are presented with the difficult choice of either moving to the low-quality, impoverished townships or remaining invisible in the delegalized villages erased from the official maps and deficient in even the most basic infrastructure. Neither of these alternatives is attractive; both have been systematically used to dismantle the Bedouin community or to forcibly "modernize" it. While the illegal villages offer disastrous living conditions, permanent insecurity, systematic harassment by state-sponsored demolitions, extremely poor infrastructure, insufficient services, limited possibilities for land cultivation or grazing, and exclusion from official registers and cartographies, the unfriendly structure of the townships conflicts with and disrupts Bedouins' traditional organization of sociality, culture, and economy. The budgets of these urban zones are the lowest in the entire country (Swirski and Hasson 2006, 51), while overall infrastructural conditions remain miserable. The inhabitants of these areas are to a large extent economically dependent on the state, while traditional tribal Bedouin governance structures have been discontinued, partly because it has been popular to claim that the Bedouins are incapable of governing themselves (Swirski and Hasson 2006; Yiftachel 2006). The townships do not resemble well-functioning urban centers and do not offer a space for cultivating the spirit of urbanity. As such, they limit the possibilities for effective self-organization, as well as for demonstrating the community's resistance toward official state policies. In the Israeli "ethnocracy" (Yiftachel 2006), in which ethnicity is the primary criterion for the distribution of rights, citizen status is not premised on nondiscriminatory values, relying instead on a differential model (Ben-Porat and Turner 2011; Rabinowitz and Abu Baker 2005). It therefore seems that the process of reorganizing, or "regularizing," the space along the lines of the state's aspirations has intentionally produced a situation in which the Bedouins' citizenship rights, as much as their "right to the city"—typically associated with the right to counter state policies and to construct urban sociality according to the inhabitants wishes and needs—have been rendered completely meaningless. Both human and nonhuman agencies and forces have been mobilized in the state's efforts to mark its presence and construct ethno-territorial authority over the vast space of the Naqab/Negev desert.

Notes

1 The title translates into English as "The Purpose of Geography is Primarily to Make War." The book was originally published in 1976; for the purpose of the

present study I engaged with its 2016 edition, supplemented with an extended commentary by the author.
2 Yves Lacoste was, in the 1970s, a member of the stimulating intellectual community of Université de Vincennes in Paris, where such prominent poststructuralists as Michel Foucault and Gilles Deleuze worked at that time. This should explain, at least partly, the infusion of Lacoste's ideas with the ways of thinking typical for this influential and internally diverse philosophical school.
3 The material the book contains was originally prepared for an exhibition during the World Congress of Architecture in Berlin. Commissioned by the Israel Association of United Architects, the book—meant to serve as a catalog for the exhibition—was eventually banned by the same organization, as it was seen as too explicit (and perhaps also mendacious) with regard to the oppressive politics of planning within the West Bank. The project was later published via a cooperation between Babel (a Tel Aviv-based publisher) and Verso. The context that surrounded the (non)publication of the book, however, clearly revealed the politics behind the state-encouraged Israeli policies of architecture and planning, illustratively discussed by Segal and Weizman.
4 A detailed account of Israeli-Palestinian relations is beyond the scope of this book. It is, however, necessary to situate my analysis in the context of certain important geopolitical processes which made possible the cartographic developments discussed in this chapter.
5 This formulation is attributed to one of the early Zionist settlers, Israel Zangwill, who used this expression for the purpose of delineating the political objectives of the Eastern European Zionist movement.
6 Transjordania, at that time.
7 The atrocities accompanying the process of establishing the Israeli state at the turn of 1948 have been investigated by Pappé (2006).
8 Even though they were de facto annexed, the territories of East Jerusalem and its suburbs should still be considered occupied in light of international regulations. As Ben-Naftali et al. explain, the illegality of this act "was affirmed by both [the] Security Council and the General Assembly, with the consequence that under international law, the area is still considered occupied" (2009, 40). As the same authors explain, even if the occupation of a territory is occasioned by a legal use of force (e.g., war in self-defense, a narrative officially assumed by the Israeli state in reference to the 1967 war), it cannot confer legal title (2009, 40).
9 For a comprehensive discussion of the Israeli settlement enterprise in the West Bank, see Zertal and Eldar (2007).
10 Sharon's Plan was not officially adopted by the government, but it offered principles for the operation of the Ministry of Agriculture, which was in charge of managing the land.
11 The official explanation provided by Gush Emunim was that their settlements in the West Bank were meant to be *permanent* establishments, which seriously undermined the official argument that the land had been intended to *temporarily* serve military purposes. In consequence, the strategy of military requisition of land ended, even though the appropriated land has never been returned to the original owners. Israel returned to this policy in 1994, after signing the Oslo I Accord. This time, the confiscated land was used to build a network of Israeli bypass roads in the West Bank.
12 For a discussion of strategies of land seizure in the West Bank, see Chapter 3 of Lein and Weizman (2002). Other sources tackling this issue include Shehade (1993, 1997), Matar (1997), Hareuveni (2010), Shalev (2012), and Hareuveni and Etkes (2021).

13 As Handel (2009) explains, in 1968, Israel froze the process of land registration in the West Bank, justifying this decision by the need to avoid causing harm to those who left the area during war, as they would not have been able to prevent their land being registered in someone else's name. Also, due to the wish "to avoid tax payments and the existence of traditional communal agricultural practices, more than 70% of West Bank lands were not registered in any way before the order was given" (Handel 2009, 197), which facilitated the process of land confiscation in the region.

14 PeaceNow gathers detailed data on infrastructural developments in the West Bank. Up-to-date information can be accessed at the organization's official website: https://peacenow.org.il/en/settlements-watch/settlements-data/population.

15 In 2008, there were 12 "special security areas" established around Jewish settlements in the West Bank and there were plans to expand this policy. Even though the lands that were turned into security zones were formally owned by Palestinians, their access to them is seriously limited by physical barriers (fences) as well as the military orders. The owners need to prove their property rights and pressure the administration to set a schedule according to which they can access their property (for purposes of cultivation, for instance). The settlers also use "piratical closing of land" without governmental authorization, practically cutting off the Palestinian owners from their property and using violence to keep them away. In most of the cases, such illegal actions meet with no reaction from the occupying authorities (B'Tselem 2004; Feuerstein 2008).

16 Even though international law does not allow for land seizure in occupied areas, it nevertheless makes exceptions in cases where the land is temporarily confiscated for military reasons, or if it remains in accordance with the local law and is meant to serve the needs, or improve the living conditions, of the local population.

17 Interestingly, according to the legal regulations currently in place in the State of Israel, the holders of Israeli passports are not allowed to enter Area A territories, thus they have no opportunity to directly interact with Palestinian urban communities.

18 For discussion of the impact of climate change in the Occupied Territories, see Messerschmid (2012), Mason et al. (2011), and Mason et al. (2012).

19 For a detailed exploration of water politics in Israel/Palestine, see Alatout (2008) and Zeitoun (2008).

20 Detailed information about such zones has not been made available to the public by the Israeli government (Aloni 2017, 5).

21 The issue of "indigeneity," or of what kind of communities should be defined as indigenous, is complicated. The idea of indigenous rights refers, by definition, to the rights of a community (rather than individual rights of its members). International law does not mention such rights, as it remains conservative in its understanding of a state's integrity; it also refers to a state as a social contract between the citizens and the sovereign. However, due to a surge in claims for the recognition of indigenous rights raised by many groups around the world, in 2007, the Declaration on the Rights of Indigenous Peoples was approved by the UN General Assembly with the support of more than 140 nations. Four nations voted against it (the United States, Canada, Australia, and New Zealand) but eventually withdrew their opposition. Israel did not participate in the voting. The declaration, however, did not include any precise definition of indigenous people, as it was not possible to agree on that matter; the category remains fluid and to a great extent relies on context-bound operationalizations. In the case of Israel and the claims to indigenousness raised by Palestinian-Arabs (including the Naqab/Negev Bedouin community), there is a dispute over who counts as "more indigenous" in the context of the long and convoluted history of the

region, marked by multidirectional migrations and shifts in power among different ethnic communities. Obviously, the issue is highly politicized and it is often a matter of political choice to use the term "indigenous" in reference to specific groups (of Jewish or of Arab origin). However, since I perceive the twentieth- and twenty-first-century expansion of Jewish presence in Palestine in terms of a colonial project (in line with the claims of Oren Yiftachel [2012]), both in relation to the inhabitants of the Occupied Territories and to those of Israel's heartland, I use the term "indigenous" in reference to the various Palestinian-Arab populations inhabiting both the territories that have remained, since 1967, under the Israeli occupation and those of Israel proper. For a detailed discussion of the problem of indigenousness in international law, see Lerner (2003), Anaya (2004), Thornberry (1991), Wiessner (1999), Abu-Saad and Champagne (2006), and Champagne and Abu-Saad (2003). For a discussion of the Naqab/Negev Bedouins' indigenousness, see Stavenhagen and Amara (2012), Martinez-Cobo (1986), and Amara et al. (2012).

22 See Briggs (1999), Branch (2014, 2017), Neocleous (2003), Steinberg (2005), Strandsbjerg (2008), Krupar (2015), and Caquard and Dormann (2008). For counter-mapping, see Peluso (1995), Perkins (2004), Firth (204), Johnson et al. (2006), Pinder (2007), and Wood (2006).

23 Before 1948, the Naqab/Negev Bedouin population was better known as the Arabs of Beersheba (*arab as-saba*). The members of this group preferred the term *arab* rather than *bedû*, while the term *fellahîn* was used by them to denote the group of Arab farmers. The term *bedû*, on the other hand, was popular among farmers to refer to the nomadic inhabitants of the desert. For details, see Parizot (2001).

24 This happened despite the fact that most of the Naqab/Negev Bedouins obtained Israeli citizenship in 1954, formally becoming a part of the Muslim Arab group in Israel.

25 Many people decide to demolish their properties or structures after the relevant order is issued by the Israel Land Authority, as they want to avoid the trauma of the unexpected demolitions inflicted on them by others (that is, the officials accompanied by the police and bulldozers), or because they want to save their belongings or construction materials, which would inevitably be lost if the troops in charge of the demolition arrived unexpectedly.

26 Crucial to understanding any move to declare a particular land as *mawat* is the difference between the *mawat* and *miri* land, as articulated in the 1858 Ottoman Land Code (articles 78 and 105). *Mawat* is a land inappropriate for cultivation, or a "dead land," uninhabited and not possessed by any individual. As Amara and Miller explain, "[l]and was determined as *mawat* based on three possible measurements: (1) the point at which a loud voice from the nearest village, town, or inhabited place could no longer be heard; (2) half an hour's walk from the nearest inhabited place; or (3) 1.5 miles away from the inhabited place" (2012, 82). However, the same regulations state that if anyone revived *mawat* and cultivated it for ten years without dispute, that person would acquire a titled deed to the land, even though it was still formally owned by the state. Such land was than categorized as *miri*. The fact that—for fear of taxation on the one hand, and because their ownership rights were not threatened by the ruler on the other (Kedar 2001; Swirski 2008)—the Naqab/Negev Bedouins did not register the land they used with the authorities in 1921 (under the ordinance that everyone wishing to cultivate *mawat* had to obtain state permission and thus register with the state) worked to their disadvantage under Israeli rule. The state authorities refused to consider their land as *miri* or as inhabited, as they had an interest in declaring as much land as possible as *mawat*, so that it could—by definition—be categorized as state land.

27 For elaboration of this issue in the context of operation of the Jewish National Fund (JNF, or the Keren Keyemet L'Yisrael), see also Lehn and Davis (1988) or Katz (2016). The JNF was established in 1901 to acquire land in Palestine for Jewish settlement. Under David Ben-Gurion's government, JNF was turned into a semigovernmental organization to which over a million dunams of land was transferred. This process was legalized retroactively when appropriate laws had been passed (Forman and Kedar 2004). JNF is the largest agricultural landowner in Israel and acts to the benefit of the Jewish population.

28 For a more comprehensive discussion of toxicity in the Naqab/Negev, consult Almi (2003) and Tal (2002).

29 The five-year Prawer-Amidror Plan was approved in 2011 and, in its declared attempt to increase the economic development of the Naqab/Negev Bedouin community, it assumed a relocation of the populations living in unrecognized settlements to the recognized townships. The plan was protested against and eventually halted in 2013. Unofficial implementation of its objectives—in the form of enforced demolitions—has continued.

30 For the analysis of colonial policies of building infrastructure and landscape engineering, see, for instance, Lines (1991) and Scott (1998).

31 It is estimated that the JNF has, to date, planted over 250 million trees in Israel (Pearce 2019).

32 Similar strategies have been used in other colonial contexts, framed as a policy of "green imperialism" (Grove 1995). For analysis of Middle East region from this perspective, see Davis and Burke (2011).

33 The Yatir Forest spreads along the border between the West Bank and the Israeli mainland.

Bibliography

Abu-Lughod, Janet. 1982. "Israeli Settlements in Occupied Arab Lands: Conquest to Colony." *Journal of Palestine Studies* 11: 16–54. https://doi.org/10.2307/2536268.

Abu-Saad, Ismael. 2005. "Forced Sedentarisation, Land Rights and Indigenous Resistance: The Palestinian Bedouin in the Negev." In *Catastrophe Remembered: Palestine, Israel and the Internal Refugees: Essays in Memory of Edward W. Said (1935–2003)*, edited by Nur Masalha, 113–139. London: Zed Books.

Abu-Saad, Ismael, and Cosette Creamer. 2012. "Socio-Political Upheaval and Current Conditions of the Naqab Bedouin Arabs." In *Indigenous (In)justice. Human Rights Law and Bedouin Arabs in the Naqab/Negev*, edited by Ahmad Amara, Ismael Abu-Saad, and Oren Yiftachel, 19–66. Cambridge, MA: Harvard University Press.

Abu-Saad, Ismael, and Duanne Champagne, eds. 2006. *Indigenous Education and Empowerment: International Perspectives*. Walnut Creek, CA: AltaMira Press.

Abujidi, Nurham. 2014. *Urbicide in Palestine. Space of Oppression and Resilience*. Kindle edition. New York and London: Routledge.

Adey, Peter. 2013. "Securing the Volume/Volumen: Comments on Stuart Elden's Plenary Paper 'Secure the Volume.'" *Political Geography* 34: 52–54. https://doi.org/10.1016/j.polgeo.2013.01.003.

Agha, Zena. 2019. "Climate Change, the Occupation, and a Vulnerable Palestine." *Al-Shabaka*. The Palestinian Policy Network. 26 March 2019. Available at: https://al-shabaka.org/briefs/climate-change-the-occupation-and-a-vulnerable-palestine/. Accessed 27 June 2021.

Alatout, Samer. 2008. "States of Scarcity: Water, Space, and Identity Politics in Israel, 1948–59." *Environment and Planning D: Society and Space* 26: 959–982. https://doi.org/10.1068/d1106.

Almi, Orly. 2003. *No Man's Land: Health in the Unrecognized Villages in the Negev*. Tel Aviv: Physicians for Human Rights and the Regional Council of Unrecognized Villages of the Negev.

Aloni, Adam. 2016. *Expel and Exploit. The Israeli Practice of Taking over Rural Palestinian Land*. Jerusalem: B'Tselem.

———. 2017. *Made in Israel: Exploiting Palestinian Land for Treatment of Israeli Waste*. Jerusalem: B'Tselem.

Amara, Ahmad, and Zinaida Miller. 2012. "Unsettling Settlements: Law, Land, and Planning in the Naqab." In *Indigenous (In)justice. Human Rights Law and Bedouin Arabs in the Naqab/Negev*, edited by Ahmad Amara, Ismael Abu-Saad, and Oren Yiftachel, 68–125. Cambridge, MA: Harvard University Press.

Amara, Ahmad, Ismael Abu-Saad, and Oren Yiftachel, eds. 2012. *Indigenous (In)justice. Human Rights Law and Bedouin Arabs in the Naqab/Negev*. Cambridge, MA: Harvard University Press.

Anaya, James S. 2004. *Indigenous Peoples in International Law*. Oxford and London: Oxford University Press.

B'Tselem. 2004. *Forbidden Roads. Israel's Discriminatory Road Regime in the West Bank*. Jerusalem: B'Tselem.

Ben-Naftali, Orna, Aeyal M. Gross, and Keren Michaeli. 2009. "The Illegality of the Occupation Regime: The Fabric of Law in the Occupied Palestinian Territory." In *The Power of Inclusive Exclusion. Anatomy of Israeli Rule in the Occupied Palestinian Territories*, edited by Adi Phir, Michal Givoni, and Sari Hanafi, 31–88. New York: Zone Books.

Ben-Porat, Guy, and Bryan S. Turner. 2011. *The Contradictions of Israeli Citizenship: Land, Religion and State*. New York: Routledge.

Benvenisti, Meron, and Shlomo Khayat. 1987. *The West Bank and Gaza Atlas. West Bank Data Project*. Jerusalem: The Jerusalem Post.

Bowd, Gavin P., and Daniel W. Clayton. 2013. "Geographical Warfare in the Tropics: Yves Lacoste and the Vietnam War." *Annals of the Association of American Geographers* 103, no. 3: 627–646. https://doi.org/10.1080/00045608.2011.653729.

Branch, Jordan. 2014. *The Cartographic State: Maps, Territory, and the Origins of Sovereignty*. Cambridge: Cambridge University Press.

———. 2017. "Territory as an Institution: Spatial Ideas, Practices and Technologies." *Territory, Politics, Governance* 5, no. 2: 131–144. https://doi.org/10.1080/21622671.2016.1265464.

Briggs, Michael. 1999. "Putting the State on the Map: Cartography, Territory, and European State Formation." *Comparative Studies in Society and History* 41, no. 2: 374–405. https://doi.org/10.1017/S0010417599002121.

Brighenti, Andrea M. 2010. "Lines, Barred Lines. Movement, Territory and the Law." *International Journal of Law in Context* 6, no. 3: 217–227. https://doi.org/10.1017/S1744552310000121.

Caquard, Sébastien, and Claire Dormann. 2008. "Humorous Maps: Explorations of an Alternative Cartography." *Cartography and Geographic Information Science* 35, no. 1: 51–64. https://doi.org/10.1559/152304008783475670.

Champagne, Duane, and Ismael Abu-Saad, eds. 2003. *The Future of Indigenous Peoples: Strategies for Survival and Development.* Los Angeles: UCLA and American Indian Studies Center.

Cohen, Shaul Ephraim. 1993. *The Politics of Planting.* Chicago: The University of Chicago Press.

Connolly, William E. 1995. *The Ethos of Pluralization.* Minneapolis: University of Minnesota Press.

Corner, James. 2011. "The Agency of Mapping: Speculation, Critique and Invention." In *The Map Reader. Theories of Mapping Practice and Cartographic Representation,* edited by Martin Dodge, Rob Kitchin, and Chris Perkins, 89–101. London and New York: Wiley & Sons.

Crampton, Jeremy W., and John Krygier. 2006. "An Introduction to Critical Cartography." *ACME: An International E-Journal for Critical Geographies* 4, no. 1: 11–33.

Davis, Diana, and Edmund Burke, eds. 2011. *Environmental Imaginaries of the Middle East and North Africa.* Athens, OH: Ohio University Press.

Dinero, Steven C. 2010. *Settling for Less: The Planned Resettlement of Israel's Negev Bedouin.* New York: Berghahn Books.

Elden, Stuart. 2007. "Terror and Territory." *Antipode* 39, no. 5: 821–845. https://doi.org/10.1111/j.1467-8330.2007.00554.x.

———. 2013. "Secure the Volume: Vertical Geopolitics and the Depth of Power." *Political Geography* 34: 35–51. https://doi.org/10.1016/j.polgeo.2012.12.009.

———. 2017. "Legal Terrain: The Political Materiality of Territory." *London Review of International Law* 5, no. 2: 199–224. https://doi.org/10.1093/lril/lrx008.

———. 2021. "Terrain, Politics, History." *Dialogues in Human Geography* 11, no. 2: 170–189. https://doi.org/10.1177/2043820620951353.

Falah, Ghazi. 1989. "Israeli State Policy towards Bedouin Sedentarization in the Negev." *Journal of Palestinian Studies* 18, no. 2: 71–91. https://doi.org/10.2307/2537634.

Feuerstein, Ofir. 2008. *Access Denied. Israeli Measures to Deny Palestinians Access to Land Around Settlements.* Jerusalem: B'Tselem.

Firth, Rhiannon. 2014. "Critical Cartography as Anarchist Pedagogy? Ideas for Praxis Inspired by the 56a Infoshop Map Archive." *Interface: A Journal For and About Social Movements* 6, no. 1: 156–184.

Forman, Geremy, and Alexandre Kedar. 2004. "From Arab Land to 'Israel Lands': The Legal Dispossession of the Palestinians Displaced by Israel in the Wake of 1948." *Environment and Planning D: Society and Space* 22: 809–830. https://doi.org/10.1068/d402.

Gilbert, Anne. 1989. "The New Regional Geography in English and French-Speaking Countries." *Progress in Human Geography* 4: 208–228. https://doi.org/10.1177/030913258801200203.

Ginat, Joseph, and Anatoly M. Khazanov. 1998. *Changing Nomads in a Changing World.* Brighton: Sussex Academic Press.

Graham, Stephen. 2004a. *Cities, Wars and Terrorism: Towards an Urban Geopolitics.* Malden: Blackwell Publishing.

———. 2004b. "Postmortem City: Towards an Urban Geopolitics." *City* 8, no. 2: 165–196. https://doi.org/10.1080/1360481042000242148.

———. 2016. *Vertical: The City from Satellites to Bunkers.* London: Verso.

Graham, Stephen, and Lucy Hewitt. 2012. "Getting Off the Ground: On the Politics of Urban Verticality." *Progress in Human Geography* 37, no. 1: 72–92. https://doi.org/10.1177/0309132512443147.

Grove, Richard H. 1995. *Green Imperialism: Colonial Expansion, Tropical Island Edens, and the Origins of Environmentalism, 1600–1860.* Cambridge: Cambridge University Press.

Handel, Ariel. 2009. "Where, Where to, and When in the Occupied Territories: An Introduction to Geography of Disaster." In *The Power of Inclusive Exclusion. Anatomy of Israeli Rule in the Occupied Palestinian Territories*, edited by Adi Phir, Michal Givoni, and Sari Hanafi, 179–222. New York: Zone Books.

Hareuveni, Eyal. 2009. *Foul Play. Neglect of Wastewater Treatment in the West Bank.* Jerusalem: B'Tselem.

———. 2010. *By Hook and by Crook. Israeli Settlement Policy in the West Bank.* Jerusalem: B'Tselem.

Hareuveni, Eyal, and Dror Etkes. 2021. *This is Ours—And This, Too. Israel's Settlement Policy in the West Bank.* Jerusalem: B'Tselem.

Harker, Chris. 2011. "The Only Way is Up? Ordinary Topologies of Ramallah." *International Journal of Urban and Regional Research* 38: 318–335. https://doi.org/10.1111/1468-2427.12094.

———. 2014. "Geopolitics and Family in Palestine." *Geoforum* 42: 306–315. https://doi.org/10.1016/j.geoforum.2010.06.007.

Harley, J. B. 2001. *The New Nature of Maps: Essays in the History of Cartography.* Baltimore: Johns Hopkins University Press.

Hassan, Sheik I., and Sari Hanafi. 2009. "(In)security and Reconstruction in Post Conflict Nahr al Barid Refugee Camp." *Journal of Palestine Studies* XL, no. 1: 27–48. https://doi.org/10.1525/jps.2010.xl.1.027.

Hochberg, Gil Z. 2015. *Visual Occupations. Violence and Visibility in a Conflict Zone.* Durham: Duke University Press.

Holsti, K.J. 2004. *Taming the Sovereigns: Institutional Change in International Politics.* Cambridge: Cambridge University Press.

Isaac, Jad, and Jane Hilal. 2011. "Palestinian Landscape and the Israeli-Palestinian Conflict." *International Journal of Environmental Studies* 68, no. 4: 413–429. https://doi.org/10.1080/00207233.2011.582700.

Jabareen, Yosef. 2015. "Territoriality of Negation: Co-production of 'Creative Destruction' in Israel." *Geoforum* 66: 11–25. https://doi.org/10.1016/j.geoforum.2015.09.003.

Johnson, Jay T., Renée Pualani Louis, and Albertus Hadi Pramono. 2006. "Facing the Future: Encouraging Critical Cartographic Literacies in Indigenous Communities." *ACME: An International E-Journal for Critical Geographies* 4, no. 1: 80–98.

Joronen, Mikko. 2021. "Unspectacular Spaces of Slow Wounding in Palestine." *Transactions of the Institute of British Geographers* 46, no. 4: 995–1007. https://doi.org/10.1111/tran.12473.

Katz, Yossi. 2016. *The Land Shall Not Be Sold in Perpetuity: The Jewish National Fund and the History of State Ownership of Land in Israel.* Oldenburg: De Gruyter.

Kedar, Alexandre. 2001. "The Legal Transformation of Ethnic Geography: Israeli Law and the Palestinian Landholders 1948–1967." *Journal of International Law and Politics* 33: 923–1000.

Kedar, Alexandre, Ahmad Amara, and Oren Yiftachel. 2018. *Emptied Lands. A Legal Geography of Bedouin Rights in the Negev*. Stanford: Stanford University Press.

Kimmerling, Baruch. 1977. "Sovereignty, Ownership, and 'Presence' in the Jewish-Arab Territorial Conflict: The Case of Bir'in and Ikrit." *Comparative Political Studies* 10, no. 2: 155–176. https://doi.org/10.1177/001041407701000201.

King, Geoff. 1996. *Mapping Reality: An Exploration of Cultural Cartographies*. New York: St. Martin's Press.

Kirby, Vicki. 1997. *Telling Flesh: The Substance of the Corporeal*. New York and London: Routledge.

———. 2006. *Judith Butler: Live Theory*. London and New York: Continuum.

———. 2008. "Natural Convers(at)ions: Or, What if Culture Was Really Nature All Along?" In *Material Feminisms*, edited by Stacy Alaimo and Susan Hekman, 214–236. Bloomington: Indiana University Press.

———. 2010. "Original Science: Nature Deconstructing Itself." *Derrida Today* 3, no. 2: 201–220. https://doi.org/10.3366/drt.2010.0204.

———. 2011. *Quantum Anthropologies: Life at Large*. Durham and London: Duke University Press.

Krupar, Shiloh. 2015. "Map Power and Map Methodologies for Social Justice." *Georgetown Journal of International Affairs* 16, no. 2: 91–101.

Lacoste, Yves. 1972."Bombing the Dikes: A Geographer's On-the-site Analysis." *The Nation* 9, no. October: 298–301.

———. 1973. "Ecocide." *Security Dialogue* 4, no. 1: 35–36.

———. 1976a. "Enquête sur le bombardement des digues du fleuve Rouge (Vietnam, été 1972)." *Hérodote* 1: 87–117.

———. 1976b. *La géographie, ça sert, d'abord, à faire la guerre*. Paris: Maspero.

———. 1984. "Geography and Foreign Policy." *SAIS Review* 4, no. 2: 213–227. https://doi.org/10.1353/sais.1984.0024.

———. 2008a [1973]. "An Illustration of Geographical Warfare: Bombing the Dikes on the Red River, North Vietnam." In *Critical Geographies: A Collection of Readings*, edited by Harald Bauder and Salevatore Engel-Di Mauro, 620–636. Kelowna: Prexis (e)Press.

———. 2008b. "La géographie, la géopolitique et le raisonnement géographique." *Hérodote* 130, no. 3: 17–42. https://doi.org/10.3917/her.130.0017.

———. 2012. "Geography, Geopolitics, and Geographical Reasoning." *Hérodote* 146–147, no. 3–4: i–xxx.

Law-Yone, Hubert. 2003. "From Sedentarization to Urbanization: State Policy towards Bedouin Society in Israel." In *The Future of Indigenous Peoples: Strategies for Survival and Development*, edited by Duane Champagne and Ismael Abu-Saad, 175–182. Los Angeles: University of California Press.

Lefebvre, Henri. 1968. *Le droit à la ville*. Paris: Anthropos.

Lehn, Walter, and Uri Davis. 1988. *The Jewish National Fund*. London: Kegan Paul International.

Lein, Yehezkel. 1998. *Disputed Waters. Israel's Responsibility for the Water Shortage in the Occupied Territories*. Jerusalem: B'Tselem.

———. 2000. *Thirsty for a Solution. The Water Crisis in the Occupied Territories and its Resolution in the Final-Status Agreement*. Jerusalem: B'Tselem.

———. 2001. *Not Even a Drop. The Water Crisis in Palestinian Villages Without a Water Network*. Jerusalem: B'Tselem.

Lein, Yehezkel, and Eyal Weizman. 2002. *Land Grab*. Jerusalem: B'Tselem.
Lerner, Natan. 2003. *Group Rights and Discrimination in International Law*. The Hague: Martinus Nijhoff Publishers and Kluwer Law International.
Leshem, Noam. 2016. *Life after Ruin*. Cambridge: Cambridge University Press.
Lines, William J. 1991. *Taming the Great South Land: A History of the Conquest of Nature in Australia*. Berkeley: University of California Press.
Lithwick, Harvey. 2003. "Urbanization Policy for Indigenous Peoples: A Case Study of Israel's Negev Bedouin." In *The Future of Indigenous Peoples: Strategies for Survival and Development*, edited by Duane Champagne and Ismael Abu-Saad, 184–203. Los Angeles: University of California Press.
Martinez-Cobo, José. 1986. "Study of the Problem of Discrimination Against Indigenous Populations." In *Sub-Commission on the Prevention of Discrimination and the Protection of Minorities*, U.N. Doc. E/CN.4/Sub.2/1986/7/Add.4.
Marx, Emanuel. 1967. *The Bedouin of the Negev*. Manchester: Manchester University Press.
Marx, Emanuel, and Avinoam Meir. 2005. "Land, Town and Planning: The Negev Bedouin and the State of Israel." *Geography Research Forum* 25: 43–61.
Masalha, Nur. 2007. *The Bible and Zionism: Invented Traditions, Archaeology and Post-Colonialism in Palestine-Israel*. London: Zed Books.
Mason, Michael, Mark Zeitoun, and Rebhy El Sheikh. 2011. "Conflict and Social Vulnerability to Climate Change: Lessons from Gaza." *Climate and Development* 3: 285–297. https://doi.org/10.1080/17565529.2011.618386.
Mason, Michael, Mark Zeitoun, and Ziad Mimi. 2012. "Compounding Vulnerability: Impacts of Climate Change on Palestinians in Gaza and the West Bank." *Journal of Palestine Studies* 41: 38–53. https://doi.org/10.1525/jps.2012.XLI.3.38.
Matar, Ibrahim. 1997. "The Quiet War: Land Expropriation in the Occupied Territories." *Palestine-Israel Journal of Politics, Economics and Culture* 4, no. 2: n.p.
McKee, Emily. 2016. *Dwelling in Conflict. Negev Landscapes and the Boundaries of Belonging*. Stanford: Stanford University Press.
McKittrick, Katherine. 2011. "On Plantations, Prisons, and a Black Sense of Place." *Social & Cultural Geography* 12, no. 8: 947–963. https://doi.org/10.1080/14649365.2011.624280.
Meir, Avinoam. 1998. *As Nomadism Ends: The Israeli Bedouin of the Negev*. Boulder: Westview Press.
Messerschmid, Clemens. 2012. "Nothing New in the Middle East: Reality and Discourses of Climate Change in the Israeli-Palestinian Conflict." In *Climate Change, Human Security and Violent Conflict, Hexagon Series on Human and Environmental Security and Peace*, edited by Jürgen Scheffran, Michael Brzoska, Hans Günter Brauch, Peter Michael Link, and Janpeter Schilling, 423–453. Berlin: Springer-Verlag.
Mizyed, Numan. 2009. "Impacts of Climate Change on Water Resources Availability and Agricultural Water Demand in the West Bank." *Water Resources Management* 23, no. 10: 2015–2029. https://doi.org/10.1007/s11269-008-9367-0.
Morris, Benny. 1987. *The Birth of the Palestinian Refugee Problem 1947–1949*. Cambridge: Cambridge University Press.
Muhsam, Helmut V. 1966. *Bedouins of the Negev*. Jerusalem: Jerusalem Academic Press.

Nasasra, Mansour. 2015. "Bedouin Tribes in the Middle East and the Naqab. Changing Dynamics and the New State." In *The Naqab Bedouin and Colonialism: New Perspectives*, edited by Mansour Nasasra, Sophie Richter-Devroe, Sarab Abu-Rabia-Queder, and Richard Ratcliffe, 35–56. New York and London: Routledge.

Neocleous, Mark. 2003. "Off the Map: On Violence and Cartography." *European Journal of Social Theory* 6, no. 4: 409–425. https://doi.org/10.1177/13684310030064003.

Nijim, Basheer K., and Bishara Muammar. 1984. *Toward the De-Arabization of Palestine/Israel, 1945–1977*. Dubuque: Kendall/Hunt Pub.

Nixon, Rob. 2009. "Neoliberalism, Slow Violence, and the Environmental Picaresque." *MFS Modern Fiction Studies* 55, no. 3: 443–467. https://doi.org/10.1353/mfs.0.1631.

———. 2011. *Slow Violence and the Environmentalism of the Poor*. Cambridge, MA: Harvard University Press.

Nofal, Issam, and Tahseen Barakat. 2001. "Desertification in the West Bank and Gaza Strip." In *Combating Desertification with Plants*, edited by Dov Pasternak and Arnold Schlissel, 369–374. Boston: Springer.

Pappé, Ilan. 2006. *The Ethnic Cleansing of Palestine*. Oxford: Oneworld Publications.

Parizot, Cédric. 2001. "Gaza, Beersheba, Dhahriyya: Another Approach to the Negev Bedouins in the Israeli-Palestinian Space." *Bulletin du Centre de recherche français à Jérusalem* 9: 98–110.

PeaceNow 2021. "Population." Available at: https://peacenow.org.il/en/settlements-watch/settlements-data/population. Accessed 28 March 2022.

Pearce, Fred. 2019. "In Israel, Questions Are Raised about a Forest that Rises from the Desert." *Yale Environment 360*. Available at: https://e360.yale.edu/features/in-israel-questions-are-raised-about-a-forest-that-rises-from-the-desert. Accessed 22 October 2021.

Peluso, Nancy Lee. 1995. "Whose Woods Are These? Counter-mapping Forest Territories in Kalimantan, Indonesia." *Antipode* 27, no. 4: 383–406. https://doi.org/10.1111/j.1467-8330.1995.tb00286.x.

Perkins, Chris. 2004. "Cartography – Cultures of Mapping: Power in Practice." *Progress in Human Geography* 28, no. 3: 381–391. https://doi.org/10.1191/0309132504ph504pr.

Pickles, John. 2004. *A History of Spaces: Cartographic Reason, Mapping and the Geo-coded World*. London and New York: Routledge.

Pinder, David. 2007. "Cartographies Unbound." *Cultural Geographies* 14, no. 3: 453–462. https://doi.org/10.1177/1474474007080782.

Portnov, Boris A., and Evyatar Erell. 1998. "Development Peculiarities of Peripheral Desert Settlements: The Case of Israel." *International Journal of Urban and Regional Research* 22, no. 2: 216–232. https://doi.org/10.1111/1468-2427.00136.

Rabinowitz, Dan, and Khawla Abu Baker. 2005. *Coffins on Our Shoulders: The Experience of the Palestinian Citizens of Israel*. Berkeley: University of California Press.

Ramos, Alcida Rita. 1998. *Indigenism: Ethnic Politics in Brazil*. Madison: University of Wisconsin Press.

Razon, Na'amah. 2017. "Seeing and Unseeing Like a State: House Demolitions, Healthcare, and the Politics of Invisibility in Southern Israel." *Anthropological Quarterly* 90, no. 1: 55–82. https://doi.org/10.1353/anq.2017.0002.

Rotem, Michal. 2017. "'Negotiation' Under Fire. House Demolitions as a Central Tool of Dispossession and Concentration of the Bedouin Community in the Negev/Naqab." Negev Coexistence Forum for Civil Equality.

Roy, Sara. 1987. "The Gaza Strip: A Case of Economic De-development." *Journal of Palestine Studies* 17, no. 1: 56–88. https://doi.org/10.2307/2536651.

Said, Edward. 2000. "Palestinians Under Siege." *London Review of Books* 22, no. 24: n.p. Available at: https://www.lrb.co.uk/the-paper/v22/n24/edward-said/palestinians-under-siege. Accessed 12 July 2021.

Scott, James C. 1998. *Seeing Like a State: How Certain Schemes to Improve the Human Condition Have Failed.* New Haven: Yale University Press.

Segal, Rafi, and Eyal Weizman. 2003. *Civilian Occupation.* London: Verso.

Shalev, Nir. 2012. *Under the Guise of Legality. Israel's Declarations of State Land in the West Bank.* Jerusalem: B'Tselem.

Shehade, Raja. 1993. *The Law of the Land—Settlement and Land Issues Under Israeli Military Occupation.* Jerusalem: PASSIA.

———. 1997. "Land and Occupation: A Legal Review." *Palestine-Israel Journal of Politics, Economics and Culture* 4, no. 2: n.p.

Smith, Ron J., 2011. "Graduated Incarceration: The Israeli Occupation in Subaltern Geopolitical Perspective." *Geoforum* 42: 316–328. https://doi.org/10.1016/j.geoforum.2011.02.005.

Soja, Edward W. 2010. *Seeking Spatial Justice.* Minneapolis: Minnesota University Press.

Stamatopoulou-Robbins, Sophia. 2018. "An Uncertain Climate in Risky Times: How Occupation Became Like the Rain in Post-Oslo Palestine." *International Journal of Middle East Studies* 50: 383–404. https://doi.org/10.1017/S0020743818000818.

———. 2020. *Waste Siege.* Stanford: Stanford University Press.

Stavenhagen, Rodolfo, and Ahmad Amara. 2012. "International Law of Indigenous Peoples and the Naqab Bedouin Arabs." In *Indigenous (In)justice. Human Rights Law and Bedouin Arabs in the Naqab/Negev*, edited by Ahmad Amara, Ismael Abu-Saad, and Oren Yiftachel, 158–192. Cambridge, MA: Harvard University Press.

Steinberg, Philip E. 2005. "Insularity, Sovereignty, and Statehood: The Representation of Islands on Portolan Charts and the Construction of the Territorial State." *Geografiska Annaler* 87: 253–265. https://doi.org/10.1111/j.0435-3684.2005.00197.x.

Sternhell, Zeev. 1998. *The Founding Myths of Israel: Nationalism, Socialism, and the Making of the Jewish State.* Princeton: Princeton University Press.

Strandsbjerg, Jeppe. 2008. "The Cartographic Production of Territorial Space: Mapping and State Formation in Early Modern Denmark." *Geopolitics* 13, no. 2: 335–358. https://doi.org/10.1080/14650040801991639.

Swirski, Shlomo. 2008. "Transparent Citizens: Israel Government Policy toward the Negev Bedouins." *HAGAR Studies in Culture, Polity and Identities* 8, no. 2: 25–45.

Swirski, Shlomo, and Yael Hasson. 2006. *Invisible Citizens: Israel Government Policy toward the Negev Bedouin.* Tel Aviv: Adva Center.

Tal, Alon. 2002. *Pollution in a Promised Land: An Environmental History of Israel.* Berkeley: University of California Press.

Thornberry, Patrick. 1991. *International Law and the Rights of Minorities.* Oxford: Clarendon Press.

Thrift, Nigel. 2007. "Immaculate Warfare? The Spatial Politics of Extreme Violence." In *Violent Geographies. Fear, Terror, and Political Violence*, edited by Derek Gregory and Allan Pred, 273–294. New York and London: Routledge.

Vaiglova, Petra, Gideon Hartman, Nimrod Marom, Avner Ayalon, Miryam Bar-Matthews, Tami Zilberman, Gal Yasur, Michael Buckley, Rachel Bernstein, Yotam Tepper, Lior Weissbrod, Tali Erickson-Gini, and Guy Bar-Oz. 2020. "Climate Stability and Societal Decline on the Margins of the Byzantine Empire in the Negev Desert." *Scientific Reports* 10, no. 1: 1512. https://doi.org/10.1038/s41598-020-58360-5.

van der Tuin, Iris. 2015. *Generational Feminism: New Materialist Introduction to a Generative Approach*. Lanham: Lexington Books.

Vandenberghe, Frédéric. 2007. "Régis Debray and Mediation Studies, or How Does an Idea Become a Material Force?" *Thesis Eleven* 89: 23–42. https://doi.org/10.1177/0725513607076130.

Virilio, Paul. 1993 [1976]. *L'insécurité du territoire*. Paris: Galilée.

———. 2008 [1975]. *Bunker Archaeology*. Princeton: Princeton University Press.

Weizmam, Eyal. 2002. "Introduction to The Politics of Verticality." *Open Democracy*. Available at: https://www.opendemocracy.net/ecology-politicsverticality/article_801.jsp. Accessed 17 March 2018.

———. 2004. "Strategic Points, Flexible Lines, Tense Surfaces and Political Volumes: Ariel Sharon and the Geometry of Occupation." In *Cities, War and Terrorism: Towards an Urban Geopolitics*, edited by Stephen Graham, 172–191. Oxford: Blackwell Publishing.

———. 2007. *Hollow Land: Israel's Architecture of Occupation*. New York: Verso.

———. 2015. *The Conflict Shoreline*. New York: Steidl.

———. 2017. *Forensic Architecture. Violence at the Threshold of Detectability*. New York: Zone Books.

Wiessner, Siegfried. 1999. "Rights and Status of Indigenous Peoples: A Global Comparative and International Legal Analysis." *Harvard Human Rights Journal* 12: 57–128.

Wood, Denis. 2006. "Map Art." *Cartographic Perspectives* 53: 5–14. https://doi.org/10.14714/CP53.358.

———. 2010. "Counter-mapping and the Death of Cartography." In *Rethinking the Power of Maps*, 111–155. New York: Guilford Press.

Yiftachel, Oren. 2006. *Ethnocracy: Land and Identity Politics in Israel/Palestine*. Philadelphia: University of Pennsylvania Press.

———. 2012. "Naqab/Negev Bedouins and the (Internal) Colonial Paradigm." In *Indigenous (In)justice. Human Rights Law and Bedouin Arabs in the Naqab/Negev*, edited by Ahmad Amara, Ismael Abu-Saad, and Oren Yiftachel, 289–318. Cambridge, MA: Harvard University Press.

Yiftachel, Oren, and Avinoam Meir. 1998. *Ethnic Frontiers and Peripheries: Landscapes of Development and Inequality in Israel*. Boulder: Westview Press.

Zakim, Eric. 2006. *To Build and Be Built: Landscape, Literature, and the Construction of Zionist Identity*. Philadelphia: University of Pennsylvania Press.

Zeitoun, Mark. 2008. *Power and Water in the Middle East: The Hidden Politics of the Palestinian-Israeli Water Conflict*. New York: I.B. Tauris.

Zertal, Idith, and Akiva Eldar. 2007. *Lords of the Land. The War over Israel's Settlements in the Occupied Territories 1967–2007*. New York: Nation Books.

Zerubavel, Yael. 1996. "The Forest as a National Icon: Literature, Politics, and the Archaeology of Memory." *Israel Studies* 1, no. 1: 60–99. https://doi.org/10.1353/is.2005.0045.

———. 2008. "Desert and Settlement: Space Metaphors and Symbolic Landscapes in the Yishuv and Early Israeli Culture." In *Jewish Topographies: Visions of Space, Traditions of Place*, edited by Julia Brauch, Anna Lipphardt, and Alexandra Nocke, 201–222. Burlington: Ashgate.

CONCLUSIONS

In contrast to the spectacular, attention-drawing occurrences of political violence, which yield massive destruction and enormous losses in an instant, slow urbicide tends to remain tacit and hidden, operating discreetly in the background and accumulating its atrocious effects over extended periods of time. Although produced at a slower pace, the consequences of such a form of violence are, nevertheless, equally vehement, resulting in radical forms of displacement, unrecoverable damage, and enduring trauma. New materialist analysis, focusing on the dynamic entanglements of material phenomena and socio-political forces, enables a more insightful examination of these less discernible vicious mechanisms, revealing the shifting temporalities of political violence as well as its pernicious long-term effects. The slowness of urbicidal tactics—and their reliance on carefully identified material processes, such as the reconfiguration and modernization of infrastructure, environmental transformations, the development of new forms of urbanity, and new techniques of land use—can potentially advance very dangerous ways of thinking, postulating the "objectification" of these processes (as, for instance, "natural" or "inevitable"), and thus isolating them from the socio-political contexts from which they emerge. Such a strategy may effectively obscure the violent dimension of certain political decisions and obfuscate the implication of state in them; it can also contribute to denying their methodical nature, ignoring their detrimental effects and disregarding any claims for social justice formulated by the affected communities.

On the one hand, the common strategy employed by Israel for the purpose of discursively framing its settlement project in Palestine in specific ways has relied on the rhetoric of modernization and development (both constructed as entirely positive phenomena). On the other hand, it has underlined the need to effectively counter the effects of climate change (ironically so, given that many of the state's interventions, such as "greening the desert," have in fact led to increased environmental degradation and depletion of water resources in other parts of the country). A detailed examination of the more-than-human dimension of political developments, or how *the political* tends to rely on the premeditated recruitment of material agencies and forces, contributes to creating a more complete picture, and a more nuanced understanding, of contemporary acts of political violence, exposing their intricate material-semiotic character and highlighting their deliberately induced consequences. It also demonstrates how these destructive assemblages operate within the broader ideological, colonial, symbolic, financial, and material global circuits and how they are mobilized for the advancement of specific political agendas. New materialist ways of thinking thus expose how what is understood as *the political* embraces a number of forces and phenomena, both natural and cultural, virtual and actual, material and semiotic, and so on, exposing the increasing politicization of everyday practices, natural agencies, and human-induced processes, and their mobilization for the accomplishment of the goals laid down by the state. Such semiotic technologies substantially help in justifying the policy of undertaking specific infrastructural developments on the territory controlled by Israel, effectively limiting the possibilities of open contestation of—and organized resistance toward—state-imposed policies. By means of objectifying certain (even though partly human-induced) processes as "natural," the state gives itself the right to intervene, including in violent ways, with an aim of ensuring its broadly defined security and survival.

The new materialist approach can assist us in the process of unmasking these complex entanglements and manipulative instrumentalizations, while paying careful attention to the dispersed agential materialities assembled with sophisticated semiotic technologies for the purpose of the Israeli project of colonial expansion. It also exposes how an assault on the landscape, or reconfiguration of the land's characteristics, simultaneously constitutes an assault on human communities (cf. McKittrick 2011), whose lives are always already co-determined by these more-than-human factors and circumstances. In the conditions of occupation or ethnocratic discriminatory politics, adaptation to the environmental changes poses an important challenge for the affected populations, which is a question still poorly explored in the extant scholarship. So, while scholars have demonstrated increasing interest in climate transformations as possible causes of conflict across the world in general and in the Middle East in particular (Barnett and Adger 2007; Weizman 2015, 2017), research on how people living in conditions of protracted conflict, or under occupation, frame these conflicts as they simultaneously struggle to adapt to the effects of climate change remains undeveloped (Stamatopoulou-Robbins 2018). Analyses drawing solely on concepts of "verticality" (Weizman 2002, 2007; Graham 2004a, 2004b, 2010, 2016; Graham and Hewitt 2013) or "volume" (Crampton 2010; Elden 2009, 2010, 2013, 2017, 2021; Billé 2018, 2019, 2020; Hawkins 2019) are not fully capable of acknowledging the shifting dynamics of the voluminous space, often leaving its complex more-than-human agencies unaccounted for. As Bruce Braun underlines, critical efforts must be undertaken if we want to be able to "continually distinguish between nature's innovative force and the mechanisms that seek to capture this force in the service of capital and state" (2015, 1). New materialism may provide us with conceptual tools to approach these compound material-semiotic phenomena and to expose the mechanisms which are used to politicize new agents (such as waste, topography, or water resources) for the purpose of slow warfare. While this kind of philosophically informed approach calls for a nuanced and multiscale analysis, such explorations must always remain situated in particular cultural and geopolitical circumstances. Relating to the issues discussed in this book—that is, the intentional destruction of the built environment and its surroundings—this perspective clearly indicates that when landscape/cityscape is destroyed, so is the community which dwells in it, and the thus produced damage is difficult—if indeed possible—to repair.

As discussed in this book, the Israeli enterprise of accentuating the Jewish presence in "the promised land" recruits several material-semiotic technologies adjusted to the current needs of the ongoing colonial project. It is worth noting—following Shaul Ephraim Cohen—that the policy of establishing the state's presence in Palestine, which manifests in the construction of Jewish settlements both in the West Bank and within the Israeli mainland, as well as eradication of their indigenous counterparts, would not serve as a successful method of colonization without all the accompanying strategies of asserting territoriality. Settlements occupy a relatively small amount of land and require both investment and continuous occupation (Cohen 1993, 2). Therefore, to truly display ownership of the contested land, other, less obvious, technologies—such as the politics of planting, climate engineering, and infrastructural development—must be employed for the purpose of implementing this meticulously engineered colonial project. The "slowness" of such enterprises may be misleading, removing them from the immediate scope of interests of the broader public while obscuring their premeditated character. Hence, the elucidation of the complex unfolding of state-inflicted atrocities aspires to reveal and counter the strategy of invisibilizing violence, thus partially undermining the manipulative policies of denial or negation. This seems to be a necessary step on the way to consolidating organized resistance, as well as doing justice to the difficult situation of those who are continually discriminated against or ignored in the process, and whose familiar surroundings are turned into politicized agents inflicting harm. Such a perspective sheds light on how the singular lives—co-constituted by the landscapes in which people dwell and the "taskscapes" (Ingold 2000) in which they engage on an everyday basis—*matter* politically and must be accounted for in broader analyses of what is considered *the political*.

Slow urbicide may operate in the background of Israeli-Palestinian conflictual relations, but its after-effects continue to substantially structure the daily lives of the affected communities. As already alluded to in the introduction to this book, Thom Davies (2019), employing Rob Nixon's concept (2009, 2011) in his investigations, critically reflects on the general invisibility of slow violence, drawing attention to the fact that those who are targeted with such violence are very well aware of its implicit, silent processes and experience them bodily on a daily basis. This is also true for indigenous Palestinian-Arabs—those inhabiting the Occupied Territories and those located on the Israeli mainland. Exposed to the chronic operations of slow urbicide, they clearly see and feel their material and psychological effects, a result of the constant condition of being under siege (Smith 2011). Added to these must be the traumatizing consequences of dispossession, degeneration of the urban tissue, state-inflicted demolition, gradual impoverishment and de-development, and lack of access to basic resources and services, as well as the effects of the constant invigilation by an ideologically-materially formed surveillance apparatus which intervenes aggressively in the everyday functioning of indigenous Palestinian communities. These circumstances increase the conditions of fragility, fueling further precaritization of particular groups of people (cf. Butler 2006, 2010; Harker 2012; Harris and Nowicki 2018; Joronen and Griffiths 2019; Lewis et al. 2015; Joronen and Rose 2020), creating socio-political landscapes in which vulnerability is not distributed evenly among the people inhabiting the same area or territory.

Given the systemic nature of the political violence targeting the Palestinian-Arabs and their land, it seems necessary—following Henrik Vigh's point of view (2006, 2008)—to turn to consider crisis *as context* of living of many indigenous populations in Palestine rather than solely approaching individual crises *in the context*. As Vigh explains,

> Crisis is normally conceived of as an isolated period of time in which our lives are shattered. It defines the loss of balance and the inability to control the exterior forces influencing our possibilities and choices. The phenomenon is seen as a temporary disorder, a momentary malformation in the flow of things. Yet, for a great many people around the world crisis is endemic rather than episodic and cannot be delineated as an aberrant moment of chaos or a period of decisive change. For the structurally violated, socially marginalised and poor, the world is not characterised by balance, peace or prosperity but by the ever-present possibility of conflict, poverty and disorder.
>
> (2008, 5)

The continuous and chronic nature of the asymmetrical war in Palestine has not yet been adequately covered in the literature within the academic fields of international relations theory and political science, with authors tending to treat the situation more in terms of an (international) crisis, positioned as a sudden rupture of social routines and habits, rather than a permanent condition. In such a context, my analysis constitutes an attempt at partly reorienting these ways of thinking by looking at the deliberately induced environmental problems and spatial manipulations in the region—all of them leading to a serious reconfiguration of usual intensive and extensive "ordinary topologies" (Harker 2011)—as an important context shaping the living conditions of the Palestinian-Arabs in the West Bank and the Bedouin communities in the Naqab/Negev.

Urbicidal violence, to use Emma Laurie and Ian Shaw's expression offered in a different context, "burns in the background of daily life … it is an existential climate by which localized subjects and worlds condense into being" (2018, 10). Such conditions might possibly lead to the development of a "chronic" (Pain 2019) form of "collective spatial trauma" (Pain 2019, 2020)—a psychological effect of enduring violence against spatiality, which gradually reconfigures traditional life routines and practices of dwelling. Working in silence and across a long period of time, such violence is, as Rachel Pain notes, "characterised by the appearance of normality" (2019, 388), a part of the daily struggle for the reconstruction of predictable spatiality. As Veena Das underlines, in such circumstances conflict and violence can become so embedded in the fabric of social life that they gradually become indistinguishable from it (2006, 80), which forces people to construct their everyday practices in the unfriendly, fragmented worlds with little opportunities for their productive reconfiguration. Slowly, violence descents into the ordinary (Das 2006), structuring the lives of those inhibiting the crisis and forcing its gradual routinization. As Pain elaborates, "With chronic trauma, we are never post-violence, but both violence and trauma wind on as material, embedded, everyday realities" (2019, 390). Instead of moving though a critical situation, people find themselves caught in a prolonged condition of crisis. The persistency of a traumatizing environment corresponds to violence's slow operations spread over a long period of time. Importantly, with no closure of violence, there is no opportunity for healing and repair. In the context of the unconventional urbicidal policies employed both in the West Bank and in Israel proper, it is thus reasonable to suggest—following the conceptual developments offered by Karen Till (2012), Rob Shields (2012), and Rachel Pain (2019)—that the after-effects of chronic trauma could manifest at the urban or community scale, producing a traumatized and vulnerable spatiality mobilized to gradually work *against* the indigenous population. This form of violence can thus be characterized by its peculiar "latency," a notion that refers to its shifting temporalities, "involving periods of apparent dormancy punctuated with times of more visible violence" (Cahill and Pain 2019). Such a conceptual elaboration enables an approach to urbicidal policy as a constant, ever-present process, which creates conditions of chronic exposure to both violence and to its pernicious after-effects.

This triggers the emergence of what Shields calls "communities in shock" (2012, 15), struggling—often unsuccessfully—to counter the politics of spatial oppression methodically inflicted upon them by the "ethnocratic" (Yiftachel 2006) state.

In Palestine, in both cases discussed in this book, slow urbicidal tactics are deliberately employed by the Israeli authorities in an asymmetrically organized project of asserting the state's territoriality over "the promised land" of Palestine. This strategy consists in mobilizing one form of urbanity against another. At first glance, both the settlement enterprise in the West Bank and the state's efforts to "regularize" space through enforced urbanization in the Naqab/Negev may appear as "urbanizing" rather than urbicidal. As such, their violent nature remains hidden behind the ideas of modernization, development, or enhancement of space management. On a rhetoric level, such actions are motivated by the principle of the "common good," while their negative consequences tend to be framed as "collateral damage." The intentional dimension of these material-semiotic processes, or the vehement force of *destruction by construction*, is concealed within the official (Zionist) dogma, infused with the rhetoric of progress, infrastructural advancement, and economic growth. These complex efforts produce uneven geographies of displacement and exclusion, where urbanity becomes both the target and the weapon of destruction. But if we consider urbanity as a specific arrangement of space—embracing humans, material objects, territories, symbolic associations, routine navigations and uses, and so on—then it emerges as a crucial site for community-building processes, a laboratory of collective social activity. Such an understanding exposes the human implication in matter, and vice versa—it reveals how, in their daily functioning, humans are impinged upon by material agencies and forces (Coole 2013). Urban space may serve as an illuminating example of these entangled relationalities. Given such a construal of the concept of urbanity, the new materialist perspective allows us to realize that the physical structure, or materiality of the city/camp/village/neighborhood, not only reflects or serves as a vehicle for social and cultural meanings but it can also actively shape, solidify, affect, and condition social practices and discursive associations. In that sense, identities and physical spaces merge with each other into a dynamically operating material-semiotic assemblage. A new materialist approach facilitates understanding of how this complex entanglement structures, and is structured by, everyday practices and actions, and why—serving as a microcosm of spatially rooted communities as well as a site for their activities, which potentially contest the power of centralized authority—it becomes a possible target of deliberate state-sponsored violence.

The denial of "the right to the city" (Lefebvre 1968)—via demolition of spatiality, understood as a collection of mutually co-formative relations between the social and spatial dimensions of community life (Soja 2010, 4)—may thus be conceived of as a state strategy of suppressing grassroots resistance. As James Scott observes, in its violent assertion of territoriality, the modern state, by definition, attempts to simplify its classic function of "prevention of rebellion" (1998, 3). Moreover, the state's efforts toward standardizing the spatiality—or transforming "what was a social hieroglyph into a legible and administratively more convenient format"—enlarge the state's capacity for more thorough reengineering (Scott 1998, 11) of its territory (or land, and how people make use of it). In such a context, if the pursuit of "the right to the city" is understood both as fighting for the right to shape the urban space in a way that attends to the needs of the inhabitants and as a continuous struggle for reappropriation of the space encroached upon by the state, then the deliberate state-sponsored decomposition of urban spatiality—through physical demolition, intentional neglect, or premeditated de-development—results in the production of geographies whose oppressive structures are difficult to contest.

Deliberate violence against urbanity should therefore be seen as an element of the state's endeavors to take control over space, which is especially vital in such colonial enterprises as the Zionist settlement project in Palestine. These actions rest on, and emerge from, the dynamic assemblages of ideological narratives and material rearrangements. Such processes, as elaborated upon in this short book, have been extensively practiced in Israel and the Occupied Territories, typically causing the estrangement of the indigenous population from their traditional landscape, turning them into trespassers, and criminalizing their customary routines and habits related to their reliance on their land and its vernacular characteristics. As a result of substantial spatial reconfigurations, the affected communities, whose "right to the city" becomes virtually emptied of content, are unable to maximize what Mark Purcell understands as the use value of their space (2002, 103). Rather than engaging in a collective production of spatiality that would attend to the needs of its inhabitants, they remain subordinated to cartographically orchestrated geographies of exclusion, resulting in alienation from their traditional habitat, while their customary reliance on the land and the conventional modes of dwelling associated therewith are gradually deracinated. Slow urbicide contributes extensively to the advancement of these discriminatory processes, deepening spatial injustices.

Considering the concealed operations of destructive tactics, the detailed examination of (slow) urbicide appears to be important and timely, as narratives on the devastation or erasure of urban spaces generate knowledge about a crucial moment in the life of a community, namely its destruction. Given that the history of war is usually written by the victorious party, the documentation of urbicide offers an important counter-narrative that reveals alternative perspectives on history and how it is coped with and remembered. It draws attention to the experience of the devastated communities, revealing stories that are frequently silenced in hegemonic memorial accounts. The salience of exploring the experience of urbicide consists in the focus on a "dark spot of the community's history"—a historical moment, which is typically not well documented, as scholars tend to rather examine reconstruction, renewal, urban planning, and design. This corresponds to the more general construction of Western culture—as Ryan Bishop and Gregory Clancey (2003) argue, the omission of the catastrophic moments in the history of urban communities is a legacy of the Enlightenment; modern urban social science tends to avoid this topic, as the annihilation of urban places conflicts with notions of progress, order, and modernization, which has long worked against any analysis of urban space as a scene of catastrophic death. Such a strategy typically contributes to the erasure of the experiences of affected communities, relegating them to the background of official historical narratives. The slowness of urbicidal violence seems to further aggravate this effect. Thus, also for these reasons, accounting for the shifting temporalities of urbicidal violence in Palestine remains important, as it reveals the complex operations of tangled destructive policies, leading to the gradual material uprooting and psychological exhaustion of the indigenous populations. It also enables a countering of the tendency to bracket the periods and causalities of violence to times of escalation, thus drawing attention to what typically remains out of sight for the wider public and politics.

As George Yancy and Judith Butler warn, when it is "unseen," violence becomes "naturalized" (2015), and the fact that we are no longer able to notice its insipid, covert operations may make us partly complicit in it. It is therefore necessary to expose how harm is repeatedly dispersed in spatial and temporal ways, which makes it often invisible and unaccounted for; it is of utmost importance to disclose the hidden forces through which systematic violence is operationalized and how this process frequently recruits both human (including ideological) and more-than-human (including natural, physical, and topographical) agencies and capabilities. The tacit, slow, and invisible workings of urbicidal policies in Palestine partly acquire their damaging capacities through their silence, which enables denial. The lack of adequate narratives to capture these "unspectacular" violent processes (Nixon 2011) contributes significantly to their operational efficiency. In such a context, exposition of the shifting temporalities of the urbicidal policies employed in Palestine potentially allows us to draw attention to their delayed after-effects, as well as helps us to understand the complex material-semiotic dynamics of the Israeli colonial project in Palestine. In this context, if the dismantling of original spatialities, leading to the gradual eradication of resistance to the ethnocratically organized state, is at the heart of urbicidal practices in Palestine, then efforts aimed at documenting and elucidating the mechanisms of these violent developments should strive to confront the denial of violence. This remains important, as negation—or covert objectification of the continuous unfolding of vehement forces—creates conditions for violence to be silently perpetuated.

Bibliography

Barnett, Jon, and Neil Adger. 2007. "Climate Change, Human Security and Violent Conflict." *Political Geography* 26: 639–655. https://doi.org/10.1016/j.polgeo.2007.03.003.

Billé, Franck, ed. 2018. "Speaking Volumes. Cultural Anthropology." Available at: https://culanth.org/fieldsights/series/speaking-volumes. Accessed 7 March 2022.

———, ed. 2019. "Volumetric Sovereignty. Society and Space." Available at: http://societyandspace.org/2019/03/04/volumetric-sovereignty-part-1-cartography-vsvolumes/. Accessed 7 March 2022.

———, ed. 2020. *Voluminous States: Sovereignty, Materiality, and the Territorial Imagination*. Durham: Duke University Press.

Bishop, Ryan, and Gregory Clancey. 2003. "The City as Target, or Perpetuation and Death." In *Postcolonial Urbanism*, edited by Ryan Bishop, John Phillips, and Wei Wei Yeo, 63–86. New York: Routledge.

Braun, Bruce. 2015. "New Materialisms and Neoliberal Natures." *Antipode* 47, no. 1: 1–14. https://doi.org/10.1111/anti.12121.

Butler, Judith. 2006. *Precarious Life: The Powers of Mourning and Violence*. London: Verso.

———. 2010. *Frames of War. When Is Life Grievable?* London: Verso.

Cahill, Caitlin, and Rachel Pain. 2019. "Representing Slow Violence and Resistance: On Hiding and Seeing." *ACME: An International Journal for Critical Geographies* 18, no. 5: 1054–1065.

Cohen, Shaul Ephraim. 1993. *The Politics of Planting*. Chicago: The University of Chicago Press.

Coole, Diana. 2013. "Agentic Capacities and Capacious Historical Materialism: Thinking with New Materialisms in the Political Science." *Millennium: Journal of International Studies* 41, no. 3: 451–469. https://doi.org/10.1177/0305829813481006.

Crampton, Jeremy W. 2010. "Cartographic Calculations of Territory." *Progress in Human Geography* 35, no. 1: 92–103. https://doi.org/10.1177/0309132509358474.

Das, Veena. 2006. *Life and Words: Violence and the Descent into the Ordinary*. Berkeley: University of California Press.

Davies, Thom. 2019. "Slow Violence and Toxic Geographies: 'Out of Sight' to Whom?" *Environment and Planninc C: Politics and Space. Theme Issue: Spatial Politics of Slow Violence and Resistance* (online first): 1–19. https://doi/org/10.1177/2399654419841063.

Elden, Stuart. 2009. *Terror and Territory: The Spatial Extent of Sovereignty*. Minneapolis: University of Minnesota Press.

———. 2010. "Land, Terrain, Territory." *Progress in Human Geography* 34, no. 6: 799–817. https://doi.org/10.1177/0309132510362603.

———. 2013. "Secure the Volume: Vertical Geopolitics and the Depth of Power." *Political Geography* 34: 35–51. https://doi.org/10.1016/j.polgeo.2012.12.009.

———. 2017. "Legal Terrain: The Political Materiality of Territory." *London Review of International Law* 5, no. 2: 199–224. https://doi.org/10.1093/lril/lrx008.

———. 2021. "Terrain, Politics, History." *Dialogues in Human Geography* 11, no. 2: 170–189. https://doi.org/10.1177/2043820620951353.
Graham, Stephen. 2004a. *Cities, Wars and Terrorism: Towards an Urban Geopolitics*. Malden: Blackwell Publishing.
———. 2004b. "Postmortem City: Towards an Urban Geopolitics." *City* 8, no. 2: 165–196. https://doi.org/10.1080/1360481042000242148.
———. 2010. *Cities Under Siege: The New Military Urbanism*. New York: Verso.
———. 2016. *Vertical: The City from Satellites to Bunkers*. London: Verso.
Graham, Stephen, and Lucy Hewitt. 2012. "Getting Off the Ground: On the Politics of Urban Verticality." *Progress in Human Geography* 37, no. 1: 72–92. https://doi.org/10.1177/0309132512443147.
Harker, Chris. 2011. "The Only Way is Up? Ordinary Topologies of Ramallah." *International Journal of Urban and Regional Research* 38: 318–335. https://doi.org/10.1111/1468-2427.12094.
———. 2012. "Precariousness, Precarity, and Family: Notes from Palestine." *Environment and Planning A: Economy and Space* 44: 849–865.
Harris, Ella, and Mel Nowicki. 2018. "Cultural Geographies of Precarity." *Cultural Geographies* 25: 387–391. https://doi.org/10.1177/1474474018762812.
Hawkins, Harriet. 2019. "(W)holes: Volume, Horizon, Surface: Three Intimate Geologies." *Emotion, Space and Society* 32: 1–9. https://doi.org/10.1016/j.emospa.2019.100583.
Ingold, Tim. 2000. *The Perception of the Environment: Essays on Livelihood Dwelling and Skill*. London: Routledge.
Joronen, Mikko, and Mark Griffiths. 2019. "The Affective Politics of Precarity: Home Demolitions in Occupied Palestine." *Environment and Planning D: Society and Space* 37: 561–576. https://doi.org/10.1177/0263775818824341.
Joronen, Mikko, and Mitch Rose. 2020. "Vulnerability and Its Politics: Precarity and the Woundedness of Power." *Progress in Human Geography* 45, no. 6: 1402–1418. https://doi.org/10.1177/0309132520973444.
Laurie, Emma W., and Ian G. Shaw. 2018. "Violent Conditions: The Injustices of Being." *Political Geography* 65: 8–16. https://doi.org/10.1016/j.polgeo.2018.03.005.
Lefebvre, Henri. 1968. *Le droit à la ville*. Paris: Anthropos.
Lewis, Hannah, Peter Dwyer, and Stuart Hodkinson. 2015. "Hyper-precarious Lives: Migrants, Work and Forced Labour in the Global North." *Progress in Human Geography* 39, no. 5: 580–600. https://doi.org/10.1177/0309132514548303.
McKittrick, Katherine. 2011. "On Plantations, Prisons, and a Black Sense of Place." *Social & Cultural Geography* 12, no. 8: 947–963. https://doi.org/10.1080/14649365.2011.624280.
Nixon, Rob. 2009. "Neoliberalism, Slow Violence, and the Environmental Picaresque." *MFS Modern Fiction Studies* 55, no. 3: 443–467. https://doi.org/10.1353/mfs.0.1631.
———. 2011. *Slow Violence and the Environmentalism of the Poor*. Cambridge, MA: Harvard University Press.
Pain, Rachel. 2019. "Chronic Urban Trauma: The Slow Violence of Housing Dispossession." *Urban Studies* 56, no. 2: 385–400. https://doi.org/10.1177/0042098018795796.

———. 2020. "Geotrauma: Violence, Place and Reposession." *Progress in Human Geography* 0, no. 0: 1–18. Online first. https://doi.org/10.1177/0309132520943676.

Purcell, Mark. 2002. "Excavating Lefebvre: The Right to the City and Its Urban Politics of the Inhabitant." *Geo-Journal* 58, no. 2&3: 99–108. https://doi.org/10.1023/B:GEJO.0000010829.62237.8F.

Scott, James C. 1998. *Seeing Like a State: How Certain Schemes to Improve the Human Condition Have Failed*. New Haven: Yale University Press.

Shields, Rob. 2012. "Urban Trauma: Comment on Karen Till's 'Wounded Cities.'" *Political Geography* 31: 15–16. https://doi.org/10.1016/j.polgeo.2011.10.012.

Smith, Ron J. 2011. "Graduated Incarceration: The Israeli Occupation in Subaltern Geopolitical Perspective." *Geoforum* 42: 316–328. https://doi.org/10.1016/j.geoforum.2011.02.005.

Soja, Edward W. 2010. *Seeking Spatial Justice*. Minneapolis: Minnesota University Press.

Stamatopoulou-Robbins, Sophia. 2018. "An Uncertain Climate in Risky Times: How Occupation Became Like the Rain in Post-Oslo Palestine." *International Journal of Middle East Studies* 50: 383–404. https://doi.org/10.1017/S0020743818000818.

Till, Karen E. 2012. "Wounded Cities: Memory-work and Place-based Ethics of Care." *Political Geography* 31: 2–14. https://doi.org/10.1016/j.polgeo.2011.10.008.

Vigh, Henrik. 2006. *Navigating Terrains of War: Youth and Soldiering in Guinea-Bissau*. Oxford: Berghahn.

———. 2008. "Crisis and Chronicity: Anthropological Perspectives on Continuous Conflict and Decline." *Ethnos* 73, no. 1: 5–24. https://doi.org/10.1080/00141840801927509.

Weizmam, Eyal. 2002. "Introduction to The Politics of Verticality." *Open Democracy*. Available at: https://www.opendemocracy.net/ecology-politicsverticality/article_801.jsp. Accessed 17 March 2018.

———. 2007. *Hollow Land: Israel's Architecture of Occupation*. New York: Verso.

———. 2015. *The Conflict Shoreline*. New York: Steidl.

———. 2017. *Forensic Architecture. Violence at the Threshold of Detectability*. New York: Zone Books.

Yancy, George, and Judith Butler. 2015. "What's Wrong With 'All Lives Matter'?" *New York Times*, 12 January 2015.

Yiftachel, Oren. 2006. *Ethnocracy: Land and Identity Politics in Israel/Palestine*. Philadelphia: University of Pennsylvania Press.

INDEX

Abujidi, Nurhan 1
acts of warfare 58
Adams, Nicholas 2
Adey, Peter 9
agency 20, 38; human-centered concept 39; more-than-human forms 41, 64; pluralization of 48
agential realism 34
agentic capacities 38, 40
Al-Aqsa Intifada 89, 95
Aleppo pine 120
Aloni, Adam 104
Alon's plan 95
alterity approach 78n5
Amara, Ahmad 125n26
anthropocentric philosophical landscape 3
Arabs of Beersheba (*arab as-saba*) 125n23
Arab Spring 1
aridity line 109, 120

Barad, Karen 34–36, 39, 42, 49, 50n8, 50n11
Barkawi, Tarak 32
Bedouin 109
Bedouin community 108, 122; situation of Naqab/Negev 109–111, 113, 117, 121
bedû 125n23
Ben-Naftali, Orna 93, 123n8
Bennett, Jane 39; theorizations of vibrancy of things 78n5
Berman, Marshall 2, 60, 78n2
Bishop, Ryan 143
boundary-drawing practices 42
Braidotti, Rosi 34

Branch, Jordan 13, 108
Braun, Bruce 37, 138
Brighenti, Andrea 13
Brighton, Shane 31, 32
B'Tselem organization 98
buildings, destruction of 2, 3, 62; interpretative themes 62–63
Butler, Chris 12, 17
Butler, Judith 143

Calais Jungle 51n27
Campbell, Elaine 48
Caquard, Sébastien 108
cartographical technologies 108
cartographical thinking 68
chronic urban trauma 9
civil ecology 72
Clancey, Gregory 143
classifixation 66, 112
Clausewitz, Carl von 31
Cohen, Shaul Ephraim 119, 138
collateral damage 62, 141
collective spatial trauma 140
Colman, Felicity 38, 40
colonialism 6, 12
conservative spiritual movement 97
contemporary materialist approach 62
contemporary warfare 51n19
conventional two-dimensional maps 94
Coole, Diana 23, 35–40; new materialist thinking 50n16
Coward, Martin 1, 3, 20, 62–65, 75, 78n4, 78n5, 79n9
crisis 139
critical security studies 32
critical war studies 32

INDEX

Das, Veena 140
Davies, Thom 8, 11, 139
dead land doctrine 117, 125n26
Declaration on the Rights of Indigenous Peoples 124n21
"de-development" 100
Defensive Shield 1, 7
DeLanda, Manuel 34, 35
Deleuze, Gilles 50n7, 123n2
discourse, inclusive notion of 50n9
discourse analysis 35, 50n9
discourse theory 34, 63
dispositif, notion of 41
Dittmer, Jason 4
domicide 70
Dormann, Claire 108
Dowler, Lorraine 47
drawing technologies 109–111

Eastern European Zionism movement 123n5
Eckardt, Wolf von 2
Elden, Stuart 13, 14, 46, 47, 86
environmental injustice 101–104
epistemicide 79n10
Eretz Yisrael ("the Land of Israel") 118
ethico-onto-epistemological 4, 19, 42, 50n8
ethics of mattering 49
ethnocracy 16, 122
ethnocratic discriminatory politics 137
ethno-nationalism 6; conflicts 2, 20, 60
ethno-territoriality 14–16, 89
ethno-territorial politics 3
ethno-territorial projects 76

fast urbicide 10
fellahîn 125n23
feminist new materialism 4
flat discourse 46, 94
Ford, Richard 13
forest, survival of 120
Foucault, Michel 41, 123n2; genealogical approach 66
Fourth Geneva Convention 95
French-British policy 51n27
Frost, Samantha 37
Fullilove, Mindy 73, 74, 79n15

Gaza Strip 92
geographical reasoning 84
geographical warfare 11, 86, 91, 92

geography of (in)justice 18
Graham, Stephen 2, 46, 88
greenery management 7
green imperialism 126n32
Green Patrol 116
Gush Emunim 97, 123n11

Hanafi, Sari 6, 72, 73
Handel, Ariel 106, 124n13
Haraway, Donna 4, 34, 67, 69
Harker, Chris 9, 101
Hewitt, Kenneth 71, 72, 78n3
Hilal, Jane 101
Hochberg, Gil 100
Holmqvist, Caroline 51n21
Holsti, K. J. 108
home 21, 69, 71; intentional destruction of 70
human-centered concept of agency 39
humanism-infused theorizations 65
human-material assemblages 51n21

IDF *see* Israeli Defence Forces
illegal intruders 110
"imagined communities" of nationhood 13
indigeneity, issue of 124n21
indigenous 125n21
indigenous rights, idea of 124n21
international relations theory 19, 20, 35, 38, 72, 49n1
Iraqi urban spaces 61
Isaac, Jad 101
Israel Association of United Architects 123n3
Israeli Defense Forces (IDF) 98
Israeli ethno-territorial project 6
Israeli High Court 96
Israeli Land Administration 116
Israeli policy, in Palestine 14, 61, 103
Israeli political ruling forces 95
Israel Land Authority 125n25

Jabareen, Yosef 105
Jenks, Chris 36
Jewish National Fund (JNF) 120, 126n27, 126n29
Johnson, Nora 70
Jordanian legal system 96–97
Jordanian Valley 96
Jordan River 102
"Judea and Samaria" 95, 97; seize control of land in 96

INDEX

Kaldor, Mary 33
Kedar, Alexandre 117
Keohane, Robert O. 19, 35

Lacoste, Yves 84–86, 90, 123n2; geographical warfare 92
land alienation 119
landscape: agencies of 92; geographical/political/discursive reconfiguration of 107; spatiotemporal materializations of 65; regularization of 119
landscape politics 117–122
Laurie, Emma 140
Lefebvre, Henri 12, 14; "the right to the city" 16–19
linguistic turn 34
"Loner Farms" (*havot bodedim*) 121
Lowenthal, David 70

Mack, Arien 70
Mandatory Palestine 92
mapping space 84–86
mapping urbicidal violence: new materialist understanding 62–67; urbanity as target 58–62
Mariupol (Ukraine) 61
Marx, Emanuel 113
masculinity concept 50n15
material architecture, violent demolition of 59
material-discursive 4, 51n21; practices 41
material evidence 43
material-semiotic processes: inclusions and exclusions of 42; intentional dimension of 141
material turn 40
mawat 112, 117, 125n26
Mbembe, Achille 12, 77
McKee, Emily 111, 114, 118
McKittrick, Katherine 2, 5, 76, 77
Meir, Avinoam 113
Merleau-Ponty, Maurice 39
Middle East peace initiative 2003 89
Miller, Zinaida 125n26
Milliken 50n9
Ministry of Agriculture 123n10
miri 125n26
Moore, Adam 15
"more-than-human" concept 50n6; agencies of space 86; dimension of political developments 137; dimension of urbicidal violence 77

Mountain Aquifer 102
Mountain Strip 97

Nakba (or catastrophe) 7
Naksa 7
Nancy, Jean-Luc 78n5
Naqab desert (Palestinian-Arab population) 23n7
Naqab/Negev Bedouins 109, 110, 113, 114, 117, 121, 125nn23–24, 125n26
National Unit for Building Inspection 116
nation-centered Israeli territory, construction of 107
natureculture 50n5
necropolitics 77
Negev desert (Jewish population) 23n7
new materialism 38, 45, 48, 90, 138; agency of 37–40; political violence 40–49; war as practice 31–33
new materialist investigations 43
new materialist philosophy 39, 67
new materialist theorizing 37
new materialist thinking 37, 41, 48, 50n16
The New Western Way of War (Shaw) 31
Nicolić, Mirko 42
Nixon, Rob 8–10, 91, 104, 106, 139

Occupied Territories 1, 2, 7, 9, 14, 18, 23n2, 86, 88, 89, 107, 139; as state land 96; unconventional geography of 90
Operation Desert Storm 61
Ophir, Adi 18
Oppermann, Serpil 39
Oslo Accords 85, 102
Oslo peace process 93
Oslo system 94
Ottoman Land Law of 1858 97, 112

Pain, Rachel 9, 140
Palestinian urban centers 97
Pappé, Ilan 16, 119, 123n7
parallel geographies 104–107
PeaceNow 124n14
place annihilation concept 71
planting, politics of 7, 119
political-ethical intervention 49
political theory 3, 31
political violence 41; acts of 41; experiential content of 42; networked

INDEX

practices of 59; relational ontology 42; spatially located material acts 44
politics of space 12–14, 18
Porteous, J. Douglas 70, 71
post-anthropocentrism 64
post-humancentric logic 64
Prawer-Amidror Plan 116, 126n29
"promised land" 14, 88, 93, 138, 141
Purcell, Mark 19, 142

Qualqilya, town of 99

rebellion, prevention of 142
reflectivism 19, 35
regularization of space 111
Riedlmayer, Andreas 2
"the right to the city" 14, 16–19, 23n6, 141, 142
roadmap 89
Rogers, A.P.V. 62
"root shock" 73, 74

Sack, Robert 13
sacrifice zones 104
Said, Edward 8, 85, 86, 104
Sassen, Saskia 13
Sauzet, Sofie 39
savannization 120
Sayig 116
Scott, James 142
Segal, Rafi 90, 123n3
settlement policy 98
shadow war 43
Sharon's Plan 123n10
Sharp, Jo 47
Shaw, Ian 8, 140
Shaw, Martin 31, 79n7
Shields, Rob 140, 141
al-Siyāj 110
slow-motion warfare strategies 76
slow urbicidal policies 91; cartographies of domination in West Bank 92–95; regularization in Naqab/Negev Desert 107–109
slow urbicidal violence 6, 11, 14; ethno-territoriality 14–16; "the right to the city" 14, 16–19
slow violence 8–10
slow wounding 76
Smith, John 36
Smith, Sandra E. 70, 71
social constructivism 34, 36, 63

socio-cultural-material landscape 3
Soja, Edward W. 8, 18, 20
sovereignty 12
space 20, 48; politics of 12–14, 18; regularization of 111
spacetimemattering 42, 46, 66
spaciocidal strategy 73
spacio-cide concept 72
spaciocide's target 72, 73
spatial justice 18
spatial relations 12
spatio-temporal contexts 19, 42
Stamatopoulou-Robbins, Sophia 102, 104
State of Israel 105, 110, 112, 116, 118
state power 12
Strachan, Hew 31
survival of architecture and urban life 2

Tel as-Sabi 113
territoriality, nature of 4, 13, 14
territory, concept of 12, 13
Thiele, Kathrin 42, 49
"thing-power," agential materiality of 39
"third debate" 35, 38
threat, discursive construction of 43
Till, Karen 9, 74–76, 140
tree planting 119
Tuin, Iris van der 66, 68, 79n11, 112

UN General Assembly 124n21
Unit for Enforcement in Open Spaces 116
UN Security Council Resolutions 93
"unspectacular" violent process 143
urbanization 8; violence of 111–117
urban space 17, 141; demolition of 21, 59, 68
urbicidal policy 88, 140
urbicidal tactics, slowness of 136, 141
urbicidal violence 3, 59, 62, 140; cartographic approach 68; mapping *see* mapping urbicidal violence; more-than-human dimension of 8; multidimensional character of 88; in post-Cold War politics 64; temporalities of 8
urbicide 2, 3, 5, 59, 60, 64; contemporary materialist approach 62; documentation of 142

INDEX

Vaiglova, Petra 119
Vandenberghe, Frédéric 109
verticality 9, 46; politics of 94
Vibrant Matter (Bennett) 39
Vigh, Henrik 139
violent cartographies 95–101
visual occupation 100
volume concept 9

"war on terror" 1
Weizman, Eyal 5, 7, 51n28, 88–90, 94, 100, 105, 109, 110, 123n3
West Bank 102; Israeli developments in 100, 101, 105; new infrastructural developments in 101; settlement building patterns in 96; traffic arteries 97; Zionist colonization of 105
Western anthropocentric philosophy 32
Whatmore, Sarah 37
Winning, Anne 71
World Congress of Architecture, Berlin 123n3

Yancy, George 143
Yatir Forest 120, 126n33
Yiftachel, Oren 16, 125n21
Yoav Unit 116

Zionist colonial project 14–15, 96
Zionist settlement project 142